DRESS IN AMERICAN CULTURE

Dress in American Culture

Edited by

Patricia A. Cunningham
and
Susan Voso Lab

Bowling Green State University Popular Press
Bowling Green, OH 43403

Copy editing by Jack Vivrett

Copyright © 1993 by Bowling Green State University Popular Press

Library of Congress Catalogue Card No.: 93-70441

ISBN: 0-87972-578-8 Clothbound
       0-87972-579-6 Paperback

Cover design by Laura Darnell Dumm

Dedication

To the people in our lives who never failed to challenge us...

Richard Alan Cunningham,
William Edward Cunningham,
Danielle Elizabeth Lab and
Steven Paul Lab

...and we love them for it!

Contents

Dress in American Culture

Patricia A. Cunningham
Susan Voso Lab

Introduction

The casual reader of this book of essays may be surprised to learn that it has little to do with different styles of clothing or the vagaries of fashion. Rather, the central focus is on the relationship of dress to the unique American experience. That is, we are concerned with such phenomena as the changes which occurred in clothing behavior when immigrants arrived in this country. The aim of the book is to prompt readers to reconsider the place of dress in the interpretation of American culture and life. We examine how Americans accommodated, adapted and manipulated their clothing to reflect their new identities, fill expected and unexpected needs, and express political ideology.

In this book we also consider how Americans have been challenged by the human landscape, physical environment and social institutions to alter their clothing behavior. We are not trying to determine what is distinctively American about our dress. Rather, we demonstrate that the clothing behavior of Americans in adapting to these new situations was part of their unique experience, and that it was linked to their cultural values, attitudes and ideals. Clothing is viewed as a mediating factor in the American experience.

The "Americans" of American culture considered in this book include native Americans and immigrants. The immigrant groups encompass those who chose to emigrate, the first settlers and later ethnic groups from Europe, as well as those who had no choice, the African Americans.

The essays address the subject of dress in American Culture from many perspectives. Above all they reveal the politics, or power of dress, especially in its function as a symbol of American ideals. While several essays deal with American dress as symbol, others examine changes in clothing behavior through a variety of experiences: meeting physical and social challenges and risks in a vast and unfamiliar land, dealing with conflict and concession, taking

1

2 Dress in American Culture

on new identities, and accommodating lives to new roles and altered social positions.

In "From Mocassins to Frock Coats" Linda Welters answers the question "What happened to native American dress between first contact with Europeans and the present?" Welters focuses on the acculturation of native Americans who inhabit southern Massachusetts, Rhode Island and eastern Connecticut. Drawing on a wide variety of documents and archeological textiles Welters observes the disdain of each group for the other's manner of dress. She chronicles the influence of Christian missionaries on altering the dress worn by native Americans, and the ultimate need for them to dress in Euro-American styles in order to survive the hegemony of the dominant white culture. Welters likewise details the renewed interest in native American culture in the 1880s, 1920s, and later in the 1960s and 1970s. She concludes with observations on current expressions of ethnic pride demonstrated through a growing interest in wearing articles of native American clothing. Native dress has become not only a sign of ethnic identity, but also a symbol of the native American struggle to regain the heritage and rights (and land) long witheld from them.

The clothing of early settlers in the Northwest Territory is the subject of Caroline Shine's essay "Dress of Ohio Pioneers." Shine compares fashionable dress of the day to the clothing worn by the first settlers in what is now Ohio. She notes the adjustments in dress made by these settlers as they adapted to the hardships of pioneer life. The men, Shine observes, very quickly substituted their waistcoats, coats and breeches for the typical hunting shirt, leggings, and pantaloons of the woodsman, and moccasins of the native American. The hunting shirt offered not only protection, but a certain cachet and a new identity as well, for during the revolutionary era the woodman's shirt became a symbol of the heroic frontier warrior. Although men substituted fashion with ruggedness, Shine notes the speed with which tailors and tradespeople moved into the territory after initial settlement, and thus how quickly the settlers returned to their fashionable ways.

In her essay, "Nineteenth-Century African-American Dress," Barbara Starke contributes to our understanding of Africans who were thrust into a strange new land where the struggle to survive touched all their basic needs including dress. Africans had their cultural identity stripped away and a new identity forced upon them, shown outwardly through the use of apparel. After the initial adjustments to new physical and psychological environments, dress played an important role in how African-Americans perceived themselves and how they viewed others.

Starke points out that slave clothing styles, when, where and by whom they could be worn, was determined solely by the master. This, she observes, eliminated individuality and choice. Meager yearly clothing allotments meant poor bodily protection and embarrassment over appearance. Starke notes that African-Americans were forced to produce their own cloth in order to survive. However, after freedom, ethnic identity slowly re-emerged and today African-Americans show their pride and dignity by wearing elements of African dress.

In "The American Cowboy: Development of the Mythic Image," Laurel Wilson examines early and evolving ethnic similarities and differences in Spanish versus Northern Plains or Anglo-cowboy dress. She shows us how cowboys adapted their dress to changing landscapes, seasons/climates, and work requirements. Wilson points to initial negative attitudes toward cowboys, Spanish immigrants and native Americans by their eastern neighbors.

To promote western expansion and show that uncharted harsh western lands could be tamed, the image of the cowboy and the land had to change. The cowboy was promoted politically through the use of a rugged, yet romantic and heroic image. The heroic symbol was perpetuated by cowboys themselves. When being photographed they shed their simple working wardrobes for outfits identified as that belonging to "real" cowboys.

Patricia Williams, in "From Folk to Fashion: Dress Adaptations of Norwegian Immigrant Women in the Midwest," points out that the immigrants' rapid change from traditional costume to American fashion indicated their desire to become Americans. Williams reveals that new arrivals clothed in ethnic dress were given little regard, making assimilation into American society difficult. Women were advised to leave their colorful Norwegian dress behind and to purchase proper American-made clothing.

Rural midwest isolation, economic factors and a Lutheran religious movement restricted early clothing primarily to utilitarian styles. A nostalgic revival for traditional colorful Norwegian weddings, however, brought back some of the festive articles of dress. Although Yankee fashions were still strongly advised for women desiring American domestic positions, Norwegian details were added to their best dresses. Ethnic pride in the 1920s reintroduced national Norwegian dress through Norwegian-American organizations and folk festivals.

In "Dressing the Colonial Past: Nineteenth Century New Englanders Look Back," Beverly Gordon examines meanings underlying nostalgia. She reveals the extent to which Americans in the nineteenth century chose colonial dress to both denote and recreate the American past at various fundraising events. For

4 Dress in American Culture

social, church and sanitary fairs women designed booths as vignettes of historic events and dressed up in costumes associated with famous Americans. These historical scenes were viewed as educational. However, more than merely romantic historicism, Gordon observes that these historical recreations allowed nineteenth-century Americans to measure their own achievements. She notes that by placing high value on the largely white Anglo-Saxon protestant heritage by using their dress as a symbol of worthy Americans, these exclusionary events denigrated the worth of more recent immigrants in America.

Patricia Campbell Warner, in "The Gym Suit: Freedom at Last," reminds us that, no matter how distasteful our memories are of those awful looking gymsuits, they provide us with a barometer which measures the roles and responsibilities of women in history. Changes in the form and efficiency of the gymsuit mirror the rise in the number of professional women in higher education and in the number of women's colleges and universities which promoted formal physical training. The development of the gymsuit reflected the transformation of American women from fragile, fainting females to mentally and physically vigorous individuals who were capable team players.

Gymsuit developments also reflected dress reform concepts of non-restricted, simple, hygienic dress. The reforms made in women's exercise dress dealt with the form and function of clothing, including appropriate undergarments, leg coverings, and laundering needs, which reinforced the garments' hygienic appeal. The popular interest in exercise, gymnastics and sports promoted the use of specialized garments whose slow evolution was held in check by societal rules of propriety and etiquette.

"Simplicity of Dress: a Symbol of American Ideals" by Patricia Cunningham focuses on the evolution of dress symbols to denote American ideals, especially the concepts of democracy and liberty. Cunningham notes the pervasiveness of the idea of simplicity in dress to suggest American virtues, and the connection between the classical world and republicanism, a linkage which allowed artists to draw on simply clothed classical figures to symbolize a "virtuous" America in their works. Cunningham discusses the ability of the colonists to produce textiles and the related political function of wearing "simple homespun" during the revolutionary era. She also reveals the concern of American diplomats for expressing the correct sentiment to their European counterparts, and the resulting polemics regarding the perceived need to dress in the "simple clothes of an American citizen" for formal events in the courts of Europe.

Susan Voso Lab examines the effects of conflict on dress in the essay

" 'War'Drobe and World War I." The collective reaction of the country under the stress of world war prompted quick, decisive reforms in dress. Frugal, simple designs mirrored the war's impact on resources and the economy. Garment styles, fabric choices and new silhouettes reflected sentiments of "doing without" or buying "only what was necessary."

Cultural practices and ideals in dress gave way to changes in industry, trade, technology, and the role of women in America. Women's roles and responsibilities were redefined and increased because of labor shortages and rising war needs. Earnest and energetic women proved successful in their new, formerly all-male, occupations. Dress changed to accommodate women's work requirements which in turn reinforced the concept of functional design in apparel.

Clothing, then, can be viewed as a record of the struggles, changes, and adjustments experienced by various people in the process of becoming Americans. Through an understanding of the ways in which we have used clothing as a mediating factor in accommodating, responding and interacting, not only with each other but with the cultural landscape and physical environment, we may gain greater understanding of the various "Americans" who have created American culture.

From Moccasins to Frock Coats and Back Again: Ethnic Identity and Native American Dress in Southern New England

Linda Welters

The sartorial history of southern New England's Indians provides an excellent opportunity for the study of ethnicity in American dress. In the American Northeast during the Contact Period, Indian tribes can be considered one ethnic group and the European newcomers the other.[1] Recent work with archaeological textiles from seventeenth and eighteenth century southern New England Indian cemeteries (Welters, Ordoñez, and Tarleton) has raised many questions regarding dress and ethnic identity in New England's native American communities. What happened to the dress of native Americans in Massachusetts, Rhode Island, and Connecticut between those first initial contacts and the current climate of cultural diversity? How did the expression of ethnicity through dress reflect the attitudes of one group toward the other and among the groups themselves? In what ways did each group adopt and adapt the material culture of the other group in regard to appearance?

In an effort to answer these questions, in this paper I explore the interactions regarding dress between Europeans and the indigenous tribes of southern New England to determine the role that appearance played in proclaiming ethnic identity. Indeed, I propose that among New England's Indian populations, the expression of ethnic identity through dress operated on three levels: 1) as a status marker within each tribe; 2) as a cultural signal between tribes; and 3) as an ethnic marker between the Indian community and the ultimately dominant Anglo-American culture.

The tribes included in this investigation are the Mashpee Wampanoags of Cape Cod, the Narragansetts of Rhode Island, and the Mashantucket Pequots of southeastern Connecticut.[2] Drawing on archaeological textiles, pictorial imagery (woodcuts, paintings, photographs), ethnohistorical accounts, and other documentary and artifactual evidence, this paper covers the period from the

6

Indians' first contacts with Europeans in southern New England to the present day. Discussion in the text is divided chronologically into four parts: 1) Contact Period, 2) King Philip's War to the American War of Independence, 3) New Republic through the Victorian Era, and 4) Revival in the Twentieth Century. A historical overview of the three tribes provides background for the chronological analysis that follows.

Historical Background

In the seventeenth century the Wampanoags, Narragansetts, and Pequots inhabited adjacent lands along the coast of southern New England (Fig. 1). All three tribes spoke the Algonquian language, but with a different dialect. Massachusett was the dialect spoken by tribes living on the coast and islands of Massachusetts. Narragansett was the dialect of the Narragansett tribe, while Mohegan-Pequot was spoken by the Connecticut Indians east of the Connecticut River (Goddard 72).

Mashpee Wampanoags. The Wampanoags of Mashpee originally belonged to the Pokanoket tribe which inhabited villages in northern Rhode Island, southeastern Massachusetts, Cape Cod, Martha's Vineyard, and Nantucket. The epidemic of 1617-19 decimated the Indian population around Plymouth but did not affect those on the Cape or the islands. Under the leadership of Massasoit, the weakened Wampanoags near Plymouth welcomed the Pilgrims as allies (Salwen 171). Richard Bourne, a farmer from Sandwich, began preaching to the Indians at neighboring Mashpee in 1658, eventually establishing Mashpee as an "Indian praying town" (Hutchins 35-36). In 1675-76, the Wampanoag chief Metacom, the son of Massasoit, launched an ill-fated uprising against the colonists from his home in Mount Hope (now Bristol), Rhode Island, in a last attempt to halt European settlement. Metacom was called "King Philip" by the English. The Cape Cod Indians did not take part in King Philip's War, thus escaping slaughter at the hands of the English (Salwen 172).

In 1660, a 50-square-mile reservation was assigned to the Cape Cod Indians. It was incorporated as the District of Mashpee in 1763. The Indians were self-governing until 1788, when a five-member board of white overseers was instituted by the state. After decades of self-interested management by the guardians, the Mashpee Indians returned to self-government in 1834. The reservation was disbanded in 1869 which meant private ownership of land and citizenship for the Indians (Conkey, Boissevain, and Goddard 179-81).

The Indians lived a relatively isolated life in Mashpee until the early twentieth century at which time they underwent a cultural revitalization and united with other Indians to form the Wampanoag nation (Campisi, *Mashpee*

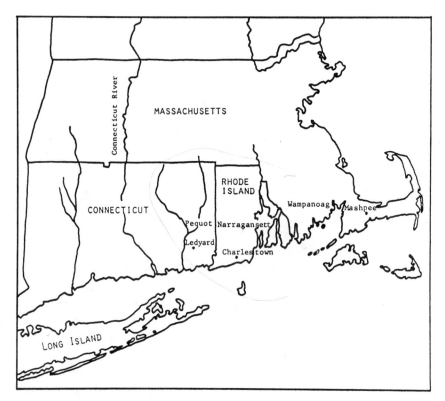

Fig. 1. *Map of southern New England.*

130). The Mashpee Wampanoags fought a legal battle from 1976 to 1979 for federal recognition of tribal status. Their application was denied due to the mixed ancestry of the tribe. Mashpee's Indians had welcomed other ethnic groups to their community over the years which resulted in intermarriage, especially between blacks and Indians (Hutchins 7).

Narragansetts. At the time of English settlement, the Narragansett Indians occupied almost all of Rhode Island and were the most powerful and populous New England tribe. They were distinguished by their skill in trading and their manufacture of shell currency (Simmons 190-91). Both the Dutch and the English traded with the Narragansetts in the 1620s. Roger Williams traded with them after he moved to Rhode Island in 1636 (Williams 163). Sometimes the Narragansetts retraded goods with Indians further inland (Simmons 193).

In 1637, the Narragansetts aided the English in the raid on the Pequots at Mystic, Connecticut. They joined Metacom's uprising late in 1675 and suffered heavy casualties in the Great Swamp fight. The war continued into the next summer and the survivors burned many houses before the war ended. After the war, some Narragansetts went to live with the Niantics on the border of southern Rhode Island and Connecticut while others left New England entirely (Salwen 172).

Sixty-four square miles at Charlestown were allotted to the Narragansetts as a reservation in 1709. Thereafter followed a long history of land encroachment by colonial settlers. To help the Indians manage their affairs, Rhode Island appointed overseers in 1717, a treasurer in 1792, and a commissioner in 1839 (Conkey, Boissevain, and Goddard 181). In 1879 the state detribalized the Narragansetts which resulted in their gaining rights as U.S. citizens. They incorporated themselves in the Indian Reorganization Act of 1934 (Simmons 196). Today the Narragansetts are a federally recognized tribe.

The Narragansetts have experienced strong tribal identity throughout their history. Few converted to Christianity until the Great Awakening of the eighteenth century. Although no longer a reservation, Narragansett-owned property at Charlestown includes a stone meeting house built in 1859 where tribal leaders continue to hold their annual meeting every year in August (Simmons 195-96).

Mashantucket Pequots. In the early seventeenth century, the Pequots held dominion over much of eastern Connecticut, including the Mohegans. Soon after European settlement, a struggle began for control over the Connecticut River and its lucrative trade to New England's interior. This early antagonism between the Indians and the Dutch and English resulted in the Pequot War of

1637. The English massacred hundreds of Pequots at their village in Mystic (Salwen 173).

The survivors scattered throughout New England. One of the bands, under the leadership of Robin Cassacinamon, was known as the Western, or Mashantucket, Pequots. In 1667 a 2000-acre reservation was established for them at Long Pond, in Groton (presently Ledyard), Connecticut. Like the Narragansetts and Mashpees, continual encroachment on Mashantucket Pequot lands by white colonists left them with greatly reduced holdings by the mid-eighteenth century. The population dwindled over the next century, leaving the tribe vulnerable to yet another major land loss when the state of Connecticut auctioned off all but 204 acres in 1855 (McBride, "Historical Archaeology" 104-07).

During the 250 years after the Pequot War, the Mashantucket Pequots practiced subsistence agriculture, found employment as indentured servants or whalers, and manufactured traditional baskets for sale. Some families left the region with the Brothertown Indian movement in the late eighteenth century. By the twentieth century, only a few families were living on the reservation. Two strong Pequot women, Elizabeth Plouffe and Martha Ellal, fought for state services to the Indians. Their actions helped to raise awareness of the Indians' plight and to promote the tribe's identity (Campisi, "Emergence" 138). In 1983 the Mashantucket Pequots received federal recognition of tribal status and were awarded a sum of money to buy back land lost in the 1855 sale. Today families live on the reservation and the tribe is becoming self-sufficient.

Contact Period: 1524-1675

Tribes along the eastern seaboard had contact with Europeans as early as the 1490s according to the historical record (Brasser 79). Throughout the sixteenth century, European explorers, fishermen, and traders offered a wide range of goods, including cloth and ready-made clothing, in exchange for furs and provisions. After successful English settlement of New England in 1620, and Dutch settlement of New Amsterdam, these interactions intensified.

The first recorded interaction between Indians and Europeans in southern New England was in 1524 when the explorer Verrazano sailed into Narragansett Bay. He found the Indians of the area (either Wampanoag or Narragansett) to be the most "beautiful" and "civil" of any he encountered on his voyage. He described both men and women as being naked except for a "stag skin, skillfully worked like damask with various embroideries" (Wroth 138). The men went bare-headed and tied their hair back with various bands, while the women arranged and ornamented their hair in a variety of ways, including braids. Sometimes they painted their faces various colors. Both sexes wore ornaments around their necks and on their ears.

The Indians were equally curious about the style of the Europeans' clothes and the gifts being offered. Much to the Europeans' surprise, the Indians "did not appreciate cloth of silk and gold, nor even of any other kind, nor did they care to have them." The things "they prized the most were little bells, blue crystals, and other trinkets to put in the ear or around the neck." Sheet copper was valued more than gold; the Indians thought gold was "the most worthless of all" (Wroth 138). This early account informs us that the objects of material culture most valued by Europeans, such as precious metals and fine cloth, were of no value to native Americans in the sixteenth century.

The next accounts of interactions between Indians and Europeans did not appear until the seventeenth century when Gosnold (1602) and Champlain (1605) visited the region. After English settlement, the number of accounts dramatically increased, giving us fairly good written descriptions of the Indians' appearance, the European reaction to the appearance of native Americans, and even the Indian response to English fashion as seen through English eyes. These accounts were written by explorers, travelers, traders, colonial settlers, and missionaries. Rather than being restricted to specific tribe, comments on dress and appearance of southern New England's Indians were often drawn from the Indians the writer had encountered.

According to Daniel Gookin, Superintendent of the Indians of the Massachusetts Bay Colony from 1656 to 1687, the traditional clothing of the southern New England Indians "was of the same matter as Adam's was, viz. skins of beasts, as deer, moose, beaver, otters, rackoons, foxes, and other wild creatures. Also some had mantles of the feathers of birds, quilled artificially...." (Gookin 152). English observers, like the traveler Josselyn, noted that "under their belly they wear a square piece of leather and the like upon their posteriors, both fastened to a string tyed about them to hide their secrets" (Lindholt 92). For footwear, the Indians wore "shoes likewise of their own making, cut out of moose's hide" (Wood 84). Sometimes "leather drawers" were worn for warmth or protection (Wood 84). In form these were actually leggings, "like a stirrop stockinge" "fastened above at their belt" rather than a bifurcated garment (Morton 29). Often a tobacco bag was hung from the neck or suspended from the waist, which was "to them in stead of an English pocket" (Williams 121).

Seventeenth-century accounts uniformly report a "desire after many kind[s] of ornaments" (Wood 85). These ornaments included "bracelets, necklaces, and head bands, of several sorts of beads" (Gookin 152); "pendants in their ears, as forms of birds, beasts, and fishes, carved out of bone, shells, and stones" (Wood 85); and "white and blew Beads of their own making" (Lindholdt 93). The latter beads, called wampum, were made from the white and purple shells of clams, and either strung on Indian hemp cordage for bracelets and necklaces or made into multi-strand assemblages. In addition to being "put about their loins" (Wood 85), wampum belts were used as currency. Wampum was "accounted their chief treasure" (Gookin 152) and the wearing of it was reserved for the important members of the tribe. Josselyn stated that wampum was used "to adorn the persons of their *Sagamours* and principal men and young women, as Belts, Girdles, Tablets, Borders for their women's hair, Bracelets, Necklaces, and links to hang in their ears" (Lindholdt 101). According to archaeological evidence, Algonquian Indians of southern New England also placed wampum on their dead before burial. Fragments of wampum headbands have been found in seventeenth-century Mashantucket Pequot and Narragansett graves.

The Europeans carefully observed the manner in which Indians groomed themselves. Body painting, tattooing, and hair dressing regularly received comment. The early explorers, especially, reported examples of face painting. Champlain noted that the "Island Cape" Indians "paint the face red, black and yellow" (73), whereas Brereton wrote in his account of Gosnold's voyage that "their eie-browes" were "painted white" (4). Roger Williams observed that among the Narragansetts, "the women paint their faces with all sorts of colours" (165). Wood's *New England's Prospect* contains very thorough descriptions of tattooing and cosmetic practices. He explained that "many of the better sort" had "portraitures of beasts" on their cheeks which were not painted on but incised in a process where the skin was raised by a small sharp instrument and injected with a substance that made the desired forms permanent (85). Wood also noted that southern New England's Indians annointed their bodies with fish oil and animal fat which in the summer was "the best antidote to keep their skin from blistering" and "their best armor against the mosquitoes," and in the winter protected "their bodies against the nipping winter's cold" (83).

Hair dressing fascinated the Europeans. Verrazano observed that "the hair is long and black, and they take great pains to decorate it" (Wroth 138). Wood said the Indians' natural black hair was improved by "oiling, dyeing, and daily dressing" (83). He described a variety of hair arrangements ranging from long, "loose, disheveled" styles to others "tied up hard and short like a horse tail" to fantastic cuts where the hair was "long on one side, the other being cut short like a screw" (83). Hair was sometimes bound with a "fillet" (Wood 83) or decorated with "feathers of fowls, in fashion of a crownet" (Brereton 11).

Indian attention to and admiration of elaborate hairstyles did not extend to beards, however. According to Champlain, the men "have scarcely any beard, and tear it out as fast as it grows" (73).

Hairstyles and headgear in the sixteenth and seventeenth centuries apparently could denote age, occupation, and marital status within the Indian community. Young boys were not allowed to wear their hair long until age sixteen (Wood 83). Soldiers and young men sported unique styles (Wood 83). Morton noted that young unmarried women wore a "redd cap made of leather in form like to our flat caps" for a period of twelve months to indicate their availability for marriage (Morton 30). According to Verrazano, certain hair arrangements among women seemed to indicate that "these women are older and have been joined in wedlock" (Wroth 138). Such subtleties of hair arrangements and headgear probably were not immediately apparent to the Europeans since the new settlers recorded few observations concerning their exact social meanings.

The Europeans' observations should be viewed in the context of their own culture. The explorers and colonists came from cultures entrenched in a highly-developed fashion system. This system was a legacy of the Renaissance, when fine cloth began to be cut into increasingly elaborate pieces which were then fitted to the body. Changing fashions were based on style innovations emanating from the courts of Europe. Clothing generally covered up the body for modesty, although fashion was at least partially responsible for popularizing eccentricities like codpieces and ruffs. In European eyes, the clothes held in highest esteem were well-tailored, made from technologically sophisticated fabrics, and trimmed with precious materials such as Italian or Flemish lace, or gold edgings. Animal skins were desirable only if reworked into fashionable forms (i.e., beaver hats, muffs, or fur-lined cloaks). Otherwise, the wearing of skins was associated with barbarians, as it had been in classical antiquity.

Apparel was a mark of one's status in the European cultural system. In the ordered universe of the English Puritan, expression of status through clothing was regulated by law. Seventeenth-century sumptuary laws of the Massachusetts Bay and Connecticut colonies incorporated Puritan values by prohibiting extravagance in dress and restricting the wearing of certain prestigious articles of clothing to those of specific rank. Although these sumptuary laws were difficult to enforce, ideally they served to regulate the communication of position, economic achievement, and social standing within the community.

To the Europeans, the appearance of southern New England's Indians brought mixed reactions. On the one hand open admiration for some aspects of native American appearance was expressed. Several accounts read like Josselyn's which comments favorably on the Indians' physical stature: "As for their persons they are tall and handsome timber'd people," and the young women "are some of them very comely, having good features, their faces plump and round" (Lindholdt 89). Josselyn also admired their technical abilities in making wampum: "these they work out of certain shells so cunningly that neither *Jew* nor Devil can counterfeit, they dril them and string them, and make many curious works with them" (Lindholdt 101).

On the other hand, the tone of the European accounts frequently smacks of cultural superiority. Champlain's description of the "savages from the Island Cape" exemplifies one issue, that of modesty:

Their robes are made of grasses and hemp, scarcely covering the body, and coming down only to their thighs. They have only their sexual parts concealed...all the rest of the body being naked. Whenever the women came to see us, they wore robes which were open in front (Champlain 73).

Comely as the Indians might be, the Europeans felt their propriety threatened by the show of so much bare skin.

The idea of using raw materials with a minimum of processing was another issue phrased in culturally superior overtones. Josselyn, with a hint of disdain, said: "Their apparel before the *English* came amongst them, was the skins of wild Beasts with the hair on" (Lindholdt 92). Roger Williams commented on the lowly origins of the fur fashions which were so desirable in Europe: "What treasures are hid in some parts of *America* and in our *New English* parts, how have foul hands (in smoakie houses) the first handling of those Furres which are after worne upon the hands of Queens and heads of Princes?" (166).

The fact that the Indians did not know the European methods of fabricating textiles (i.e., weaving, knitting) from agriculturally-produced fibers (i.e., wool, silk, linen, cotton) added to the impression that the Indians were "uncivilized." Instead, the Indians employed the off-loom techniques of plaiting and twining to process uncultivated plant fibers into capes, mats, and bags.

The lack of knowledge of European methods of clothing assemblage was also repugnant: "The women make all the garments, but not so exactly that you can see the flesh under the arm-pits, because they have not the ingenuity enough to fit them better" (Champlain 55). Skins and furs draped on the body with little attention to fit were reminiscent of other "barbarous" peoples known to the English, such as the Irish (Morton 29, Wood 84).

To the Europeans, lack of modesty, use of raw materials with little processing, and absence of tailoring skills placed the American Indians in the categories of "savage" and "uncivilized" peoples. Additionally, to the Puritan mind, the Indian love of ornament signified "sparks of natural pride." This perceived vanity was opposed to Christian ideals and was ripe for cynical commentary:

A sagamore with a humbird in his ear for a pendant, a black hawk on his occiput for his plume,...good store of wampomeag begirting his loins,...thinks himself little inferior to the great Cham (Wood 85).

For the Puritans the most negative connotation of Indian appearance was that it belonged to people who were "heathens" and "infidels," not Christians. The English who settled in New England were not content to live in harmony with native Americans who practiced Shamanism, wore skins and grasses, and adorned themselves with gaudy trinkets and birds' feathers. Attempts to Christianize the Indians of New England included persuading them to dress in European-style clothing.

The missionaries were successful in transforming the appearance of Indians in the praying towns. Gookin, writing in 1674, records that: "The Christian and civilized Indians do endeavor, many of them, to follow the English mode in their habit" (152). This meant the wearing of cloth suits, stockings, and cobbled shoes. It was not just the clothing that signified a "civilized" Indian, but the hairstyle as well. Long hair symbolized Indian identity to Indians and colonists alike. An Indian's willingness to cut his hair indicated his desire to live a Christian, English-style life (Axtell, *Invasion Within* 59).

The English were not completely successful at anglicizing Indian appearance, however, for perception of appearance is dependent on manner and deportment as well as apparel. Thomas Morton found Indians in traditional dress "to be handsomer, then when they are in English apparel, their gesture being answerable to their one habit and not unto ours" (Morton 30).

Change occurred not only in clothing but in the entire lifestyle of the converted Indian. According to Josselyn, the Indians living in the praying towns founded by John Eliot:

go clothed like the *English*, live in framed houses, have stocks of Corn and Cattle about them, which when they are fat they bring to the *English* Markets, the Hogs that they rear are counted the best in *New-England*. Some of their Sons have been brought up Scholars in *Harvard* Colledge (Lindholdt 105).

Not all Christian Indians changed to the English style of life in the seventeenth or even the eighteenth century, but, for the most part, in New England "you could often tell a convert by his cover" (Axtell, *European and Indian* 59).

To traditional Indians, native Americans who appeared in English styles sometimes were negatively perceived. In one telling incident about the effects of epidemics on Indian communities, three Indians ran into the house in which Josselyn was staying, crying out that they would die, that Cheepie, the Indian devil, had appeared to them gliding in the air with a rope. When asked what Cheepie looked like, the Indians replied that he was dressed as an "Englishman, clothed with hat and coat, shoes and stockins" (Lindholt 95). Beards, as was the English fashion, came under special attack. Wood tells us that Indians considered beards an "opprobrious excrement" and "call him an Englishman's bastard that hath but the appearance of a beard" (83).

Despite Indian resistance, sartorial changes were inevitable. In the years between the arrival of the colonists and King Philip's War, even the Indians who retained their tribal identities gradually expanded their traditional material culture with goods available from the Europeans. The acquisition of clothing by the Indians through gift or trade was common throughout the seventeenth century. Coats were mentioned most often in colonial records, particularly red ones. Stockings, shoes, and shirts were also important.

At first, it seems that the Indians did not take to the tailored clothing of the Europeans. Champlain tells us that when Onemechin, chief of Choüecot, was given a coat "he did not keep it long, gave it to another, as he couldn't adapt himself to it" (91). While Onemechin may have disliked the confining nature of tailored European clothes, he also may have simply given the coat away out of generosity. A century earlier Verrazano observed that the Indians he met at Narragansett Bay were "very generous" and gave away all that they had (Wroth 138). After the Pilgrims arrived, however, it is clear that the Indians began to view the coats as status markers (Brenner 173). Mourt tells us that in 1621 the great Wampanoag chief Massasoit was presented with a red coat trimmed with lace and a gold chain. After "having put the coat on his back and the chain about his neck, he was not a little proud to behold himself, and his men also to see their King so bravely attired" (Mourt 65). Thereafter, coats appear repeatedly in the records functioning like state gifts.

Coats and other trade goods also were treated as items to be bartered for land. Prudence Island, for example, was sold to Roger Williams and John Winthrop for "20 fathom wampum and two coats" (Potter 29). William Pynchon, founder of Springfield, Massachusetts, paid to the Indians in 1636 18 coats (in addition to hoes, hatchets, and knives) for a quitclaim to land he wished to acquire (Thomas 136).

This view of European clothing as being increasingly valuable within the Indian community is endorsed by incidents of theft of English-style clothing by Indians. In Springfield, Massachusetts, Indians stole two pieces of cloth and 13 coats from Pynchon's trading post in 1639 (Thomas 147). In 1650 a "best" red kersey petticoat was stolen from a private house by an Indian visiting the Springfield area from New Haven (Thomas 152). Although petticoats were not the usual garb of Indian women in the mid-seventeenth century, a Wampanoag squaw was reported as wearing a "kersey [petti-] coat" laden with wampum girdles in 1676 (Rowlandson 66).

Mary Rowlandson's captivity account supports the assumption that European clothing was viewed as an item of exchange among the Indians. Her narrative is replete with incidents where clothing items were gathered and traded among the Indians, bartered between captors and captives, and requested as ransom. If her account is accurate, dead Englishmen were routinely stripped of their apparel by Indian warriors both as proof of victory and for their intrinsic value (Rowlandson 34, 59, 64). Mary herself was presented with a silk handkerchief, a hat, and an apron for completing a sewing task for her captors (61). Trade cloth (66) and two coats (67) figured in her ransom. When Mary finally departed from the Indians, they gave her a cloak and riding hood for the journey home (70).

Except for the Indians at the praying towns, New England's native Americans did not wear English-style dress on a daily basis. Ready-made tailored items were confining, difficult to clean, and not durable enough for the Indian way of life. Roger Williams, speaking of the Narragansetts in the 1640s, tells us:

Our English clothes are so strange unto them, and their bodies inured so to indure the weather, that when (upon gift & c.) some of them have had English cloathes, yet in a showre of raine, I have seen them rather expose their skins to the wet then their cloaths, and therefore pull them off, and keep them drie (Williams 121).

Wood, writing in 1635, explained: "They love not to be imprisoned in our English fashion." He went on to say: "They love their own dog fashion better (of shaking their ears and being ready in a moment)," and that the real reason they could not conform to English clothing was "because their women cannot wash them when they be soiled, and their means will not reach to buy new when they have done with their old" (84).

New England's Indians must have understood very early that when they wished to approach the English to trade, they would be perceived of as "friendly" rather than "hostile" if at least one of the Indian party was dressed in European apparel. In 1602, 18 years before the Pilgrims landed at Plymouth, an Indian came to Bartholomew Gosnold's ship "apparelled with a waistcoat and breeches of black serdge, made after our sea-fashions, hose and shoes on his feet" (Brereton 4). Williams said of the Narragansetts that: "While they are amongst the *English* they keep on the *English* apparel, but pull of all, as soon as they come again into their owne Houses, and Company" (121).

Governor John Winthrop of the Massachusetts Bay Colony had a noteworthy sartorial relationship with Chickatabot, the Sachem (tribal chief) of Neponset. One night in 1631, Chickatabot visited Winthrop. Because he was "in English clothes, the governor set him at his own table, where he behaved as soberly, etc., as an Englishman" (Winthrop 59). Later, at Chickatabot's request, the governor sent for his tailor to make a suit of clothes for him (Winthrop 62). Chickatabot died in the small pox epidemic of 1633; one wonders if he was buried with his English clothes. Archaeological textiles from Narragansett and Mashantucket Pequot burial grounds of the second half of the seventeenth century indicate that fine wool cloth was buried with at least a few individuals, indicating possible interment of English clothes with the deceased (Welters, Ordoñez, and Tarleton 74).

Indian acceptance of certain types of European fabrics, such as thick woolen cloth, served as a substitute for garments formerly made of skins. Wood states: "If their fancie drive them to trade, they choose rather a good coarse blanket, through which they cannot see, interposing it between the sun and them; or a piece of broad cloth, which they use for a double end, making it a coat by day and a covering by night" (84). Josselyn informs us that "since they have had to do with the English they purchase of them a sort of Cloth called trading cloth of which they make Mantles, Coats with short sleeves, and caps for their heads which the women use" (Lindholt 93). Regarding the Narragansetts, Williams said: "They all generally prize a Mantle of English or Dutch Cloth before their owne wearing of Skins and Furres, because they are warme enough and Lighter" (160). Gookin described in 1674 the fabrics in use by the Indians for apparel:

But, for the most part, they sell the skins and furs to the English, Dutch and French, and buy of them for clothing a kind of cloth, called duffils, or trucking cloth, about a yard and a half wide, and for matter, made of coarse wool, in that form as our ordinary bed blackets are made, only it is put into colours, as blue, red, purple and some use them

Fig. 2. *Portrait of Ninigret II. Son of Ninigret I, Chief of the Niantic Indians,* ca. 1681. Museum of Art, Rhode Island School of Design. Gift of Mr. Robert Winthrop.

white. Of this sort of cloth two yards make a mantle, or coat, for men and women, and less for children. This is all the garment they generally use, with this addition of some little piece of the same, or of ordinary cotton, to cover their secret parts (Gookin 152).

Numerous examples of coarse woolens known as trading cloth, trucking cloth or duffle, have survived in fragment form in Wampanoag, Narragansett, and Mashantucket Pequot cemeteries of the period (Dillon; Welters, Ordoñez and Tarleton).

That the Indians seemed to use the cloth "as is" rather than to manipulate it into European-style clothing is noteworthy. As the skins worn in traditional clothing were being depleted through the fur trade, heavy woolens were substituted without changing the form of the garments. The portrait of Ninigret II (Fig. 2) shows the Chief of the Niantic Indians in a breech clout and mantle made of trade cloth, while his legwear, ornaments, and hairstyle are of native manufacture.

The process of acculturation operated almost entirely in one direction in regard to dress—from the Europeans to the Indians. At least one aspect of traditional Indian attire, however, was adopted by the New England colonists, and that was footwear. Roger Williams, speaking of the leather moccasins and leggings of the Narragansetts, praised their virtues:

Both these, Shoes and Stockins they make of their Deere skin worne out, which yet being excellently tann'd by them is excellent for to travell in wet and snow; for it is so well tempered with oyle, that the water cleane wrings out; and being hang'd up in their chimney, they presently drie without hurt as my selfe hath often proved. (120)

Indian war parties heading for white settlements reportedly carried extra pairs of moccasins for their captives to wear on the journey back to tribal lands (Axtell, *European and Indian* 297).

Another item of footwear adopted by Europeans was the snowshoe, which Josselyn described as follows: "In the winter when the snow will bear them, they fasten to their feet their snow shooes which are made like a large Racket we play at *Tennis* with, lacing them with *Deers*-guts and the like" (Lindholt 92). Colonists adopted moccasins and snowshoes to travel easily over the snow (Axtell, *European and Indian* 296).

On the eve of King Philip's War, both ethnic groups had adopted some sartorial traits of the other, although the balance was certainly uneven. The colonists had transported the English fashion system across the Atlantic and rooted it in American soil. The only Indian clothing items worn by the English were moccasins and snowshoes, and these were for their functional superiority to cobbled shoes under certain conditions. Christian Indians communicated their adoption of English ways through their dress. The unconverted Indians appeared in distinctly Indian garb, although their clothing was sometimes fashioned from European materials. The overall message conveyed to both the Indian and Anglo communities by the majority of native Americans in southern New England through their appearance was "I am Indian."

King Philip's War to the American War of Independence: 1675-1783

Metacom, also known as King Philip, was the chief of the Wampanoag tribe. He led a last fatal uprising against the English in 1675 with the aid of other New England tribes. While the Narragansetts joined Metacom, the Pequots and the missionized Wampanoags at Mashpee did not. Accounts of King Philip's War, which the Indians refer to as their War for Independence, give us glimpses of southern New England's Indians proclaiming their ethnic identity through appearance before they were finally beaten into submission by the English.

Metacom and his allies knew how to dress to impress, judging by contemporary descriptions of their appearance. Josselyn, who met Metacom in Boston before he sailed for England in 1671, described him in these terms: "Prince *Phillip*...had a Coat on and Buskins set thick with these Beads [wampum] in pleasant wild works and a broad Belt of the same, his Accouterments were valued at Twenty pounds" (Lindholdt 101). Mary Rowlandson, captured by the Wampanoag in 1676, witnessed a celebratory dance in which her master, the sagamore Quanopin (related to Metacom through marriage) was "dressed in a Holland shirt with great laces sewed at the tail of it; he had his silver buttons, his white stockings, his garters were hung round with shillings, and he had girdles of wampum upon his head and shoulders" (Rowlandson 66). Quanopin's squaw, Weetamoo, who was Mary's mistress, was "a severe and proud dame" like "any of the gentry of the land" who powdered her hair, painted her face, and bedecked herself with wampum jewelry (Rowlandson 61). The attire of Indian leaders at this time was a mix of English styles and native-made goods, yet the message was still a declaration of identity as an Indian.

The English seemed especially impressed by the wampum. When King Philip was killed in 1676, the belt he was wearing was described as "wrought with black and white wompom in various figures and flowers, and pictures of many birds and beasts" (Church 170). Paul Revere's engraving of King Philip (Fig. 3) shows him in a European-style linen shirt and woolen mantle with a wampum girdle and headband decorated with images of birds and beasts. The

PHILLIP alias METACOMET of Pokanoket.
Engraved from the original as Published by Church.

Fig. 3. *Portrait of King Phillip. Alias Metacomet of Pokanoket.* (RHi x3 771).
Courtesy of Rhode Island Historical Society.

moccasins are in the style of the Mohawk, as the source for Revere's image is undoubtedly the portrait of Mohawk King Ho Nee Yeath Taw No Row, painted in 1710 when four Indian sachems visited London (Saunders 85-87). Mezzotints made from the portraits received great visibility in the colonies. Revere must have read Church's 1716 account of King Philip's War and added the appropriately decorated wampum belt.[3]

Mary Rowlandson's account reveals that the Indians were hard pressed to utilize the European cloth they acquired through trade or raids. Mary was asked to make stockings, shirts, caps, shifts, and breech clouts out of textiles the Indians did not know how to manufacture into garments themselves. Philip himself asked her to make a shirt and cap for one of his boys (47). Mary even unravelled a pair of stockings and reknitted them to fit the owner (55). For such tasks she sometimes received fashionable items of apparel for which the Indians had no use: "Then came an Indian and asked me to knit him three pair of stockings, for which I had a hat and a silk handkerchief" (Rowlandson 61).

During the skirmishes of King Philip's War, clothes served as a disguise for both the Indians and the colonists. In Mary Rowlandson's travels, her group once encountered a band of Indians on horseback "dressed in English apparel, with hats, white neckcloths, and sashes about their waists, and ribbons upon their shoulders" (58). So successful was their disguise that even Mary mistook them for Englishmen until they moved close enough so she could see their faces. At the same time, colonial soldiers wore moccasins to minimize evidence of their presence in Indian territory (Axtell, *European and Indian* 300).

At the conclusion of the war, the colonists were as Eurocentric as ever. In their minds, the Christians had prevailed over the infidels. The murder of King Philip was seen as the slaying of a "naked, dirty beast" (Church 154). The old appellation of "King" Philip for Metacom was touted as inane for "a squalid savage, whose palace was a sty; whose royal robe was a bearskin or a coarse blanket, alive with vermin" (quoted in Washburn 94).

Missionary work resumed with renewed zeal after the war. By the middle of the eighteenth century, missionaries had been sent to most of New England's tribes courtesy of groups organized for the religious education of native Americans. The successful praying towns of Massachusetts were held up as a model, including the English-style dress of the inhabitants. In 1698, a delegation from the Society for the Propagation of the Gospel visited Mashpee and reported that the 263 Indians were "in general well clothed" (Campisi, *Mashpee* 80-81). Being "well clothed" meant being dressed in English-style clothing.

Education of Indian school-aged children was one of the main activities of the missionaries. Teaching Indian children how to read and write was seen as the road to their salvation. To attract children to the schools in the eighteenth century, present-giving became a necessary part of educational programs. Stroud blankets, manufactured and dyed on the River Stroud in Gloucestershire, England, were issued as regularly as school books. For one recruit who pledged to become a minister, the New England Company furnished a "Homespun Coat, Jacket, and Breeches, two shirts, Stockings, Shoes and Hat, after the English Fashion" (quoted in Axtell, *Invasion* 188).

Samson Occum (1723-1792), a Mohegan Indian, became a successful Presbyterian minister to the Indians in southern New England. He eventually led the Indian movement to Brothertown, New York around the time of the Revolutionary War which attracted followers from the Mashantucket Pequots (McBride, "Historical Archaeology" 112) and the Narragansetts (Conkey, Boissevain, and Goddard 181). A surviving portrait of Occum, dated 1768, shows him in a coat, waistcoat, knee breeches, and preacher's collar, just like any other Protestant minister of the day (Conkey, Boissevain, and Goddard 182).

How did the Indians who remained on the reservations live at this time? Were they really clones of the English, as the proponents of the missions would have us believe? The Indians typically did not practice English-style farming, instead selling wood from their forests or leasing farm land to their Anglo-American neighbors. Although some of them continued to hunt and fish, others found work as farm hands, stone masons, and seamen. Indian children were bound out as servants, or apprentices in crafts such as cordwaining (Conkey, Boissevain, and Goddard 184). Evidence shows that many Indians retained indigenous cultural traits despite their status as praying Indians. By the middle of the eighteenth century the Mashpees did not understand sufficient English to comprehend sermons; as a result, they requested a minister who could preach in Algonquian (Hutchins 88). As regards architecture, in 1767 nearly three-quarters of the dwellings in Mashpee were wigwams rather than English-style houses (Hutchins 78). On the Mashantucket Pequot reservation many of the houses were wigwams as well (McBride, "Historical Archaeology" 109). Most likely clothing was not uniformly English either.

Evidence from a recently excavated Mashantucket Pequot cemetery dated 1670-1720 indicates that this group of Indians retained their traditional way of life despite being surrounded by English colonists. Intentionally isolated from Euro-American culture, they continued to bury their dead in the traditional manner in a flexed position with grave goods (McBride, "Pequot Lifeways"). The textile fragments from this site support that traditions were preserved. The fragments were of a medium to heavy woolen variety (i.e., duffels, trading cloth) used by native Americans in the mid-seventeenth century for breech clouts and mantles. Milling and napping finishes were still evident in many samples. Changes, however, occurred gradually throughout the eighteenth century so that by 1783-84, Francesco de Miranda described the "Indians that still kept themselves here" as "moderately well dressed" (as quoted by McBride, "Pequot Lifeways"). To Europeans, "well dressed" still meant attired in European-style clothing.

The changeover to English-style dress by the mid-eighteenth century is supported in the accounts of other travelers. In 1744 Alexander Hamilton visited the Narragansett King, George Ninigret, at Charlestown. King George lived like the colonial gentry. He had property of 20,000-30,000 acres, some of which he leased out to tenants. He served Hamilton good wine and introduced his wife who was dressed "like an Englishwoman" in fashionable silks, hoops, and stays (as quoted in Axtell, *Invasion* 172).

Southern New England's Indians fought in the American War of Independence alongside American colonists. Soldiers from Mashpee served in regiments from Barnstable, Falmouth, and Sandwich (Peters 48). The last hereditary sachem of the Narragansetts died in the war (Conkey, Boissevain, and Goddard 181). An ironic sartorial contribution to the war effort was the Indian clothing donned by the perpetrators of the Boston Tea party. It was not merely a disguise, but a symbol of the fierce determination which had survived in the colonial imagination since King Philip's War a century earlier (Axtell, *European and Indian* 299).

At the beginning of this period Indians were attired in a mixture of European and Indian-made goods. As the eighteenth century progressed, English cultural traits gradually made more and more inroads, mainly in the guise of Christianity. What few records remain from this period indicate that by the late eighteenth century the Indians in southern New England wore the same clothing as other Americans in a similar socio-economic bracket.

New Republic through the Victorian Era: 1789-1899

Native Americans who fought in the American War of Independence believed that they were fighting for the rights of all men. Instead, Indians found themselves on the bottom of the social order in New England. According to an 1822 report on Indian Affairs, even the "free negro population" in Mashpee fared better than the Indians since African-Americans in Massachusetts had the

Fig. 4. *Fragment of a knitted wool stocking,* archaeological textile from an unmarked Indian grave in Mashpee, late 18th or early 19th century. Historic Textile and Costume Collection, University of Rhode Island.

right to vote and run for office. The 320 Indians at Mashpee, the 429 Narragansetts at Charlestown, and the 50 Mashantucket Pequots at Groton were governed by overseers named by state governments. The Indians' "intemperate use of ardent spirits" made them "poor and miserable," and easy prey for opportunistic whites. Encroachment on reservation land was renewed to the point where a plan to remove the Mashpee Wampanoags and Narragansetts to a "wild country" in the American West was considered (Morse 68-75).

Evidence shows that in the early nineteenth century, southern New England's Indians were more attuned to Euro-American ways than ever before. At Mashpee, they had "altogether adopted the habits of civilized life," "forgotten their ancient names, and indeed their language too" (Morse 69). Few wigwams were left on any of the three reservations. The Indians had gardens and cultivated the reservation land as well as sold wood for income. Young Indian men were valued as whalemen. Churches were active, and for the most part children were being taught to read and write (Conkey, Boissevain, and Goddard 184; Morse 69-75). Only through the manufacture of traditional crafts, such as baskets and brooms, were native traditions expressed (Morse 75; Apes, *Son of the Forest* 10).

As far as clothing was concerned, the Indian women at Mashpee were "many of them good spinsters, combers and weavers." They clothed themselves and their husbands "in everyday homespun...in the English mode" making "very decent and showy" apparel for Sunday services (Hutchins 68).

Archaeological textiles from a late eighteenth- or early nineteenth-century burial at Mashpee confirm that the Indians at this time wore clothing similar to that of other Americans of the same social standing (Fig. 4).[4] Surviving fragments of wool textiles revealed hand sewing, seam allowances, braided trims, knotted tape closures, fabric-covered ball buttons, a possible garter, darning in the heel of a stocking, and knitted shaped stockings (Welters, Ordoñez, and Tarleton 74). No animal skins or grave goods were present, although one corpse was buried wearing a metal headband, and the hair was still long. Apparently Mashpee Indians were proclaiming their ethnic heritage with long hair and traditional headgear.

The expression of cultural traditions through hairstyle and headgear also was practiced by blacks during this period. In a study of black style in New York City, they wore the same clothing as whites but demonstrated a continuity with their African or West Indian past by wearing traditional hairstyles and headcoverings (White 32-33). Even after the middle of the century, photographs of African-Americans reveal that the tignon, a cloth head wrapper, still differentiated female black slaves from working class white women (Tandberg 12-13).

In the 1830s, leadership within the Indian community began to agitate for self-governance. William Apes, a native-American preacher of Pequot ancestry, organized a "pretended riot" at Mashpee which resulted in the passing of an act returning Mashpee to the status of an incorporated district with the power to select its own officers (Apes, *Indian*; Hutchins 108).

Apes' account of his own upbringing reflects the suffering of many southern New England Indians at this time. Relegated to reservations with limited education and few economic resources, one way out was to drown their sorrows in alcohol. Another was to enter the non-Indian world to find employment. Born in 1798 to a Pequot mother and a father of mixed blood, William suffered abuse at the hands of his own relatives before being bound out to a series of white families. He eventually ran away from his masters and sought employment on packet boats, as a soldier in the War of 1812, and as a farmhand before returning to the reservation in Groton at the ripe old age of 19. He married an Indian woman "nearly the same color as myself" and began preaching.

Clothing figures prominently in Apes' account. A presentable appearance was synonymous with dignity in his eyes. When living with his parents and grandparents, he said "our clothing was of the poorest description, literally speaking we were clothed in rags, so far as rags would suffice to cover our nakedness" (Apes, *Son of the Forest* 10). During his indentures, his appearance improved, as clothing was provided for by his masters: "I had enough to eat and wear" (16), and "In a little time I was furnished with new clothes" (35). After he set out on his own, however, clothing again became a problem. Once he tried selling his clothes to raise money; another time he was given a pair of pantaloons for two months wages. He made several attempts to return to the reservation to see his family but held back because of his ragged appearance: "I was now about one hundred miles from home, and not having clothes suitable for the season, I concluded to go to work in order to get such as would answer to make my appearance in at home" (77); and finally: "In the spring I had good clothes, and withal looked very decent, so I thought I would make another effort to reach my home" (79).

Any Indian trying to find employment in nineteenth-century America tried to diminish his or her ethnic differences by wearing styles rooted in the prevalent fashion system, even if the actual clothing was shabby and indicative of poverty. Photographs of Indians at Mashpee, Charlestown, and Ledyard from

aged 100 years

Eunice Mauwee
from a daguerreotype by Lawrence.

Fig. 5. *Portrait of Eunice Mauwee (from a daguerreotype by Lawrence),* 1852. The Connecticut Historical Society, Hartford.

(Peters 32, 34, 35; Hutchins 127, 136). The everyday dress of Indians was little different than that of other Americans. Photographs of Indian schoolchildren reveal the total adoption of fashionable dress styles. At the end of the century, little Indian boys wore Norfolk jackets and breeches, while little girls wore white lingerie dresses with bows in their hair (Peters 73).

Eunice Mauwee (1756-1860), the "Last of the Pequots," was photographed in the 1850s wearing a striped cotton dress and shawl typical of the fashion of the period (Fig. 5). The only difference between Eunice and her white contemporaries was her headband. A white cap and conservatively-trimmed bonnet would have been more in keeping with fashion. Other elderly Indians reportedly adhered to remnants of the old traditions as well. Sylvia Casco, who died in the 1870s, was the last Mashpee resident to live in a wigwam (Hutchins 135).

The dominance of fashionable dress among southern New England's Indians by the mid-nineteenth century parallels the experience of other ethnic groups in America. At Ellis Island, newly-arrived immigrants changed out of native costumes as soon as possible. Commissioner Edward Corsi observed that one-half hour after the ferry boat landed in New York City, the ferry house dressing rooms and the bushes outside had the appearance of a "junk shop" and "queer headgear lay about." New arrivals were supplied with American-style clothing by relatives and friends who did not want to be seen with a "greenhorn" in New York City (Tifft 90).

Even so, a cultural revival, of sorts, was born. Americans during the Romantic period began to show a nostalgic interest in New England's native Americans. James Fennimore Cooper wrote *The Last of the Mohicans* and Longfellow penned the poems "Hiawatha" and "The Skeleton in Armor." Scientists in the new discipline of anthropology searched for "pure-blooded" Indians. The survivors they found, like Eunice Mauwee, were labeled "the last of" their tribe. Before long, a few Indians came forward proclaiming themselves to be descendants of famous seventeenth-century sachems. Zerviah Mitchell published a book in 1878 in which she declared herself a direct lineal descendant of Massasoit, the great Wampanoag chief. She called her three daughters "princesses" and "fashioned for them shell-studded 'royal' buckskin gowns and feather tiaras" (Hutchins 146-47). Terwileema, reportedly the last female descendant of King Philip, was photographed in the 1880s wearing an appliquéd and beaded costume with a feather headdress (Weinstein-Farson 57).

Meanwhile, moccasins appeared during the nineteenth century as an all-American fashion item for men, women, and children. The moccasin was

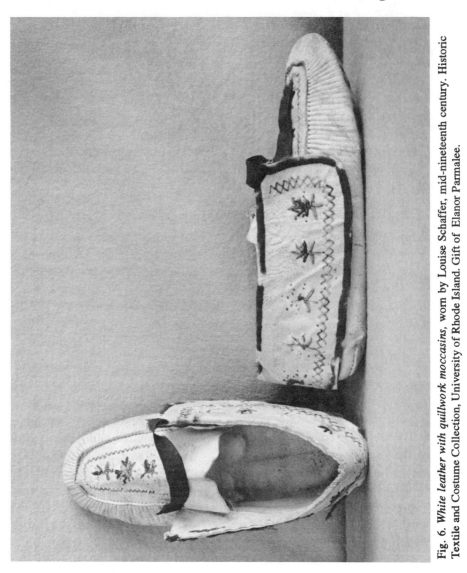

Fig. 6. *White leather with quilwork moccasins*, worn by Louise Schaffer, mid-nineteenth century. Historic Textile and Costume Collection, University of Rhode Island. Gift of Elanor Parmalee.

recommended as a house slipper. Woodland Indians soon developed cottage industries to produce and sell decorative moccasins with beadwork, quillwork, or silk embroidery. Many examples survive in New England collections. A pair of children's moccasins at the Nantucket Historical Society were worn by little Hannah Vickery, the adopted daughter of Shubael Coffin, around 1810. These moccasins were made by the Western Great Lakes Indians. At the Northampton Historical Society are a pair of men's moccasins worn by Dr. Samuel Shaw, of Plainfield, Massachusetts, when he was an invalid in the 1850s and 1860s. The University of Rhode Island owns women's moccasins, including a white leather with quillwork pair worn by Louise Schaffer in the mid-nineteenth century (Fig. 6).

The cultural shift that began in the seventeenth century was completed in the nineteenth century. After the Revolutionary War, the small number of Indians remaining in southern New England virtually disappeared into the Anglo-American landscape. Only a few ethnic markers remained to distinguish them from whites—a wigwam or two on the reservation, the manufacture and sale of traditional baskets, or the wearing of a headband. At the same time the Indian moccasin became firmly entrenched in the repertoire of classic American styles.

Revival in the Twentieth Century

The romantic stirrings which began in the Victorian era grew into a full-fledged cultural revival among the Indians of southern New England in the first quarter of the twentieth century. This revival was intensified by the growth of New England's tourist industry which created a renewed desire for choice Indian land near the growing seaside resort communities and a demand for spectacles involving "real Indians" (Conkey, Boissevain, and Goddard 185). The revival is well-documented for the Mashpee Wampanoags. Sources credit two individuals—Eben Queppish and Nelson Simons—with revitalizing Mashpee as an Indian community (Campisi, *Mashpee* 130; Hutchins 137-47; Weinstein-Farson 75). Identification as an Indian figures prominently in both of their stories.

Eben Queppish was born in Mashpee but left in 1875 at age 16 to find employment off the reservation. He worked in a series of wild West shows, including Buffalo Bill Cody's, in which he wore Indian costumes comprised of feathered headdresses, fringed shirts, and leggings. Eventually he returned to Mashpee where he earned his living as a cook at a hunting lodge and a maker of splint baskets (Hutchins 137-38; Campisi, *Mashpee* 131). Nelson Simons, born in 1886, attended the Carlisle Indian School in Pennsylvania. When he returned

Fig. 7. *Annual Tribal Pow-Wow of Narragansett Indians at Old Indian Meeting House.* Photograph by Avery Lord, August 9, 1925. Charlestown, R.I. (RHi L866 292). Courtesy of the Rhode Island Historical Society.

to Mashpee in 1914, he began appearing publicly in fringed buckskin and beaded moccasins (Hutchins 147). Both Queppish and Simons took Indian names in addition to their Christian names. Queppish's Indian name, perhaps in reference to the status coats given to New England's Indians in the seventeenth century, was Red Jacket (Campisi, *Mashpee* 131).

Queppish and Simons were exposed to Indians from all over the United States during their years away from Mashpee. This heightened their awareness of Indian culture among tribes which had preserved native traditions through the nineteenth century. Upon returning to the reservation, these two men joined forces to assert the cause of the Wampanoag Indian community. The result was the formation of the Wampanoag nation in 1928 with Indians from the communities at Mashpee, Gay Head, and Herring Pond.

The following year the first annual Wampanoag pow-wow was held. Although the Mashpee had celebrated an annual summer homecoming for centuries, the formal characteristics now associated with the pow-wow solidified in the 1920s. Traditional foodways, dances, pageants, and costumes contributed to the multi-day festivals.

The Wampanoags were not isolated in their desire to revive and celebrate ethnic heritage at this time. The Narragansetts say they have had annual pow-wows since the 1600s, yet photographs of the 1925 pow-wow at their stone church show similarities to pow-wows held by other New England tribes at this time (Fig. 7). Photographic evidence reveals that the Mashantucket Pequots also participated in this revival although only a handful of people were living on the reservation in the 1920s. A Pequot tribal photo album contains several snapshots of Lemuel Fielding, chief of the Mohegan Indian Association, in costume at a 1920 Mohegan "wigwam festival." Fielding also was photographed by Frank Speck, the American Indian anthropologist, in the same costume, parts of which he had borrowed from Lester Skeesuks, a Narragansett-Mohegan from Brothertown, Wisconsin (Conkey, Boissevain, and Goddard 186). The presence of these snapshots, contributed to the photo album by individual tribal members, indicate that the Mashantucket Pequots participated in the 1920 Mohegan "wigwam festival."

The wearing of dress which symbolized Indian identity became an important part of these ceremonial occasions. Indians referred to their ensembles as "regalia," connoting the idea of rich costumes to be paraded in front of spectators. Regalia was decidedly "pan-Indian" in that it drew upon the familiar clothing and adornment traditions of the Indians of the Great Plains and the Southwest. The adoption of Plains Indian dress in southern New England no doubt occurred after Buffalo Bill Cody made a much-publicized visit to the grave of Uncas in 1907 accompanied by Plains Indians on horseback in full costume (Conkey, Boissevain, and Goddard 185).

Males donned deerskin shirts and fringed trousers as regalia, while females wore deerskin dresses. Aprons simulating breech clouts were sometimes worn. Clothing was decorated with beadwork and appliqué, often in floral patterns which had been introduced by Europeans to Indians in the northern Midwest in the previous century. Vests, another European influence, appeared regularly with beads sewn on as decoration (Peters 27, 47, 54). Moccasins were standard footwear. Necklaces and pendants made of beads, seeds, or shells were important accessories.

The article of dress which became the ultimate symbol of the American Indian was the feathered headdress (Fig. 7). Most flamboyant was the war bonnet, which was based on the traditional headgear of the Sioux. War bonnets were usually worn by the most prominent males at a pow-wow. Another type of headdress which was common to New England Indian regalia consisted of an upright feather coronet. This headdress was worn by men, women, and children.[5] A simple alternative for the feathered headdress was a headband with or without a single feather. Feathers worn on the head were not without precedent in southern New England; the exact manner and style in which they were worn, however, is not clear.

Chief's blankets, an apparel item adopted from the Navaho, also are evident (Fig. 7; *Mashpee* 79; Peters frontispiece and 47). The Navaho had commercialized the production of their blankets in the latter nineteenth century and developed a substantial mail order business with East coast clientele, so New England Indians may have purchased blankets from fellow native Americans in the Southwest for ceremonial purposes. Several instances of blankets being incorporated into New England Indian ritual are on record. On August 9, 1925, Avery Lord photographed a Narragansett reenactment of a traditional wedding in which the groom offered wampum and a blanket to the father of the bride in exchange for the daughter. The groom then brought the bride under the blanket after concluding the transaction with the father. The blanket tradition was incorporated into real weddings among Indians as well. When Chief Red Shell married Princess Mannanata in Mashpee on January 9, 1927, at the conclusion of the Christian ceremony the bridal party went outdoors where the bride and groom "marched slowly around the sachem, the pair being wrapped in a single blanket, while the marriage dance was formed around them" (quoted in Hutchins 149). A similar blanket was used at the wedding of the Wampanoag Princess Redwing to Chief White Oak of the Mohegans in 1936 ("Pequots" 20).

Regalia was worn only for occasions when Indians wanted to celebrate their ethnic identity; it was not worn everyday. Before the 1960s, few Indians in New England wore items of clothing recognizable as Indian on a daily basis. However, a few subtle ethnic markers began to surface among cultural leaders for everyday wear during the early revival years. Some Indian men began to grow their hair long (Conkey, Boissevain, and Goddard 185; Sekatau). Indian women like Elizabeth Plouffe of the Mashantucket Pequots wore apple seed necklaces (Prince). Others revived traditional crafts, such as making moccasins (Prince).

The social upheaval of the 1960s included numerous "people power" movements. Amidst the civil rights movement, student demonstrations, and protest against the Vietnam war, came the Indian rights movement. The confrontation between the Bureau of Indian Affairs and the Sioux in South Dakota strengthened the Indian cause. Hippies flaunted the social conventions of their middle-class parents by wearing Indian-inspired fringed vests, moccasins and headbands as well as other anti-establishment "costumes."

Indian political and cultural identity was strengthened in New England in the 1970s by the emergence of several leaders. The Mashpee Wampanoags, the Narragansetts, and the Mashantucket Pequots initiated legal claims to lost land and filed applications for federal recognition of tribal status. A renewed pride in native American traditions developed, led by people like Ella Thomas Sekatau, a member of the Narragansett tribe, who helped establish the Wampanoag village at Plimoth Plantation in the 1970s. A young Mashpee woman credited Ella Sekatau with transforming her from a "beautiful powwow princess to a knowledgeable human being" (Weinstein-Farson 85). Ella Sekatau continues to serve as a cultural resource to both the Indian and the non-Indian communities in southern New England.

Southern New England's Indians once again were proud of their heritage, and they demonstrated it through their appearance at rituals. When Theresa Hayward, a Mashantucket Pequot, married Thomas Bell on August 9, 1970, the wedding party was attired in "Indian costume." The bride wore a white mini-dress decorated with beads in the traditional Pequot colors of red, black, and white. Her hair was arranged in long braids, and on her head was a beaded headband sporting a single feather. The final touch to this ethnic, yet fashionable, bridal ensemble was a pair of white leather moccasins in a boot style not unlike those worn by Ninigret II in his portrait. The Indian ceremony was officiated by none other than Princess Redwing, who revived the Indian blanket ritual from her own 1936 wedding, blanket and all ("Indian Wedding Ceremony" and "Pequots Revive Bridal Rite").

Throughout the Western world, fashionable dress became more flexible in the 1970s and 1980s, allowing greater freedom of personal expression through clothing. New England Indians started wearing beaded headbands and ties on an everyday basis to identify themselves as native Americans. Calico ribbon shirts, based on those worn in the late nineteenth century by Plains Indians, and woven wool sashes became popular (Lester 63-66). Men sometimes wore their long hair in ponytails. The era of the T-shirt offered another format for demonstrating ethnic affiliation. The Mashpee Wampanoags printed their tribal logo on baseball caps as well as T-shirts (Peters 79; Weinstein-Farson 88).

As pan-Indian clothing crept into the everyday wardrobe of the native American, the regalia worn for ceremonial occasions became more historically accurate. The attention devoted to America's cultural heritage during the Bicentennial caused the more historically conscious southern New England Indians to abandon the Plains Indian fringed buckskins and feathered war bonnets of their grandfathers for the breech clouts and fur mantles of their seventeenth-century ancestors (Lester 58-59; Peters 55).

The current state of native American cultural and economic revival in southern New England has been in the public eye recently with the February 1992 opening of the Mashantucket Pequot "Foxwoods" casino in Ledyard, Connecticut. Here the clash and compromise of America's respective costume traditions is seen in employee uniforms. Male and female employees, only a few of whom are native Americans, wear shirts in the currently fashionable colors of turquoise and pink with wampum-like braid trim. The white cocktail waitresses wear abbreviated fringed Ultrasuede tunics which are color coordinated with the other uniforms. Tribal spokesperson Theresa Bell explained that these outfits were specially designed and selected after proposals for more revealing ensembles akin to the scanty garb worn by Las Vegas and Atlantic City casino waitresses were rejected. In keeping with the Indian theme, each waitress sports a single feather in her hair. High heels rather than moccasins are required footwear for the waitresses.

Conclusion

This paper has examined the interactions between Europeans and native Americans in southern New England to determine the role appearance played in proclaiming ethnic identity. Dress and personal adornment was a clear and unmistakable marker between the world of the European and the world of the

Indian in the Contact period. English colonists viewed their own tailored clothing as that of "civilized" Christians while the skins, furs, and ornaments of native Americans were seen as the attire of "savage" pagans. Part of the mission to convert the Indians to Christianity included getting them to dress in English-style clothes. The colonists were only partially successful, however, as many Indians persisted in their traditional ways of dressing.

Within the Indian world, traditional dress in the seventeenth century conveyed differences in social status within a tribe as well as between tribes. It also could proclaim readiness to trade or conversion to Christianity. As furs and skins were depleted through trade, the Indians began to use European cloth and clothing in ways that were culturally distinctive. The New England colonists, despite their ethnocentric views, valued the functional footwear of the Indians and adopted the wearing of both moccasins and snowshoes.

During the period between King Philip's War and the American War of Independence, the much reduced native populations gradually adopted Anglo-American dress. By the end of the eighteenth century, their clothing resembled that of other Americans of similar social standing. Indications exist, however, for persistence of certain symbols of Indian identity into the nineteenth century, namely that of headgear and hairstyle. Even into the second half of the nineteenth century some Indians in southern New England wore headbands and long hair.

During the Victorian era, the dominant American culture began to romanticize the past. Soon New England's Indians, who had forgotten many of their own traditions, came forward with a host of "princesses" and "chiefs" descended from the sachems of old. By the early twentieth century, this rebirth of cultural pride grew into a full-scale revival for the Wampanoags, Narragansetts, and Mohegan-Pequots. Annual pow-wows offered each tribe the opportunity to celebrate their own ethnic heritage and to display their traditions to other Americans. The better-documented heritage of the Indians of the Plains and the Southwest provided a springboard for the invention of new traditions as exhibited in the pan-Indian regalia of the revival period.

The legal rights obtained by southern New England's tribes in recent years have strengthened appreciation of Indian cultural traditions. Being an American Indian is a state to be celebrated, and clothing is, once again, one of the main ways in which this celebration is accomplished. Indian men now wear ponytails, ribbon shirts, and beadwork neckties on a daily basis to signify their ethnic identity. Indian women proclaim their heritage through jewelry and insignia on apparel. Meanwhile, the Indian moccasin in all its variations has become an

American classic. What began as the meeting of two radically different cultures has come full circle in this age of cultural diversity.

Notes

[1]For the purposes of this paper, ethnic group can be defined as "any group of people who set themselves apart and are set apart from other groups with whom they interact or coexist in terms of some distinctive criterion or criteria which may be linguistic, racial or cultural" (Charlotte Seymour-Smith, *Macmillan Dictionary of Anthropology* [London: Macmillan, 1986], s.v. ethnic group).

[2]I selected these tribes because faculty and students of the Textiles, Fashion Merchandising and Design Department at the University of Rhode Island have analyzed archaeological textiles from late eighteenth/early nineteenth century graves in Mashpee, a Narragansett cemetery dated 1650-1670, and a Mashantucket Pequot cemetery dated 1670-1720.

[3]A similar wampum belt, attributed to the Wampanoag chief John Tyzacke (or Tyasks) and contemporary to King Philip, is on display at the Museum of the American Indian in New York City.

[4]These unmarked burials were accidentally disturbed in 1990. The Massachusetts Historical Commission conducted the overall study of the site. For more information, see Field Report, Seneca Road Burials, Massachusetts Historical Commission, May, 1990.

[5]A young Mashantucket Pequot girl named Alice Langevin, photographed on May 9, 1915, wore such a feathered coronet. The photograph is in the possession of the Mashantucket Pequot tribe.

Works Cited

Apes, William. *A Son of the Forest*. New York: Published by the Author, 1829.

_____. *Indian Nullification of the Unconstitutional Laws of Massachusetts Relative to the Marshpee Tribe: or, The Pretended Riot Explained*. Boston: P of Jonathon Howe, 1835.

Axtell, James. *The European and the Indian*. New York: Oxford UP, 1981.

_____. *The Invasion Within: The Contest of Cultures in Colonial North America*. New York: Oxford UP, 1985.

Brasser, T.J. "Early Indian-European Contacts," in *Handbook of North American Indians, Vol. 15: Northeast*. Ed. Bruce G. Trigger. Washington, D.C.: Smithsonian Institution, 1978: 78-88.

Brenner, Elise M. "Sociopolitical Implications of Mortuary Ritual Remains in 17th-Century Native Southern New England," in *The Recovery of Meaning: Historical Archaeology in the Eastern United States*. Eds. Mark P. Leone and Parker B. Potter, Jr. Washington, D.C.: Smithsonian Institution P, 1988: 147-88.

Brereton, John. *Discoverie of the North Part of Virginia* (1602). Ann Arbor: University Microfilms, Inc., 1966.

Campisi, Jack. "The Emergence of the Mashantucket Pequot Tribe, 1637-1975," in *The*

40   Dress in American Culture

Pequots in Southern New England. Eds. Laurence M. Hauptman and James D. Wherry. Norman: UP of Oklahoma, 1990, 117-40.

_____. *The Mashpee Indians: Tribe on Trial*. Syracuse, N.Y.: Syracuse UP 1991.

Champlain, Samuel de. *Voyages of Samuel de Champlain 1604-1618*. Ed. W.L. Grant. New York: Charles Scribner's Sons, 1907.

Church, Benjamin. *Diary of King Philip's War 1675-76*. Chester, CT: The Pequot P, 1975.

Conkey, Laura E., Ethel Boissevain and Ives Goddard. "Indians of Southern New England and Long Island: Late Period," in *Handbook of North American Indians, Vol. 15: Northeast*. Ed. Bruce G. Trigger. Washington, D.C.: Smithsonian Institution, 1978: 177-189.

Dillon, Phyllis. "Trade Fabrics," in *Burr's Hill: A 17th Century Wampanoag Burial Ground in Warren, Rhode Island*. Ed. Susan G. Gibbon. Bristol, R.I.: The Haffenreffer Museum of Anthropology, 1980: 100-107.

Goddard, Ives. "Eastern Algonquian Languages," in *Handbook of North American Indians, Vol. 15: Northeast*. Ed. Bruce G. Trigger. Washington D.C.: Smithsonian Institution, 1978: 70-77.

Gookin, Daniel. *Historical Collections of the Indians in New England*. Massachusetts Historical Society Collections, Part 1. Vol. 1, 1792.

Hutchins, Francis G. *Mashpee: The Story of Cape Cod's Indian Town*. West Franklin, N.H.: Amarta P 1979.

"Indian Wedding Ceremony is Unusual and Impressive." *The Day* New London: 10 August 1970:22.

Lester, Joan A. *We're Still Here*. Boston: The Children's Museum, 1987.

Lindholdt, Paul J., Ed. *John Josselyn, Colonial Traveler*. Hanover, N.H. UP of New England, 1988.

McBride, Kevin A. "The Historical Archaeology of the Mashantucket Pequots, 1637-1900," in *The Pequots in South New England*. Eds. Laurence M. Hauptman and James D. Wherry. Norman: UP of Oklahoma, 1990, 96-116.

_____. "Pequot Lifeways." *Algonkians of New England: Past and Present*. The Dublin Seminar for New England Folklife. Deerfield, MA: 29 June 1991.

Morse, Jedediah. *A Report to the Secretary of War of the United States on Indian Affairs* [1822]. New York: Augustus M. Kelley, 1970.

Morton, Thomas. *New English Canaan or New Canaan*. [1637]. American Culture Series. Ann Arbor, MI: University Microfilms.

Mourt, G. *A Journal of the Pilgrims at Plymouth, Mourt's Relation* [1622]. Ed. Dwight B. Heath. New York: Corinth Books, 1963.

"Pequots Revive Bridal Rite." *The Day*. New London: 10 August 1970: 20.

Peters, Russell M. *The Wampanoags of Mashpee*. Somerville, MA: Media Action, 1987.

Potter, Elisha. *The Early History of Narragansett*. Collections of the Rhode Island Historical Society, Vol. 3. Providence, R.I., 1835.

Prince, Charlene. Interview. Ledyard, CT. 16 January 1992.

Rowlandson, Mary. "The Sovereignty and Goodness of God" [1682], in *Puritans Among the Indians*. Eds. Alden T. Vaughan and Edward W. Clark, Cambridge, MA: The Belknap P of Harvard UP, 1981: 31-75.

Salwen, Bert. "Indians of Southern New England and Long Island: Early Period," in

Belknap P of Harvard UP, 1981: 31-75.

Salwen, Bert. "Indians of Southern New England and Long Island: Early Period," in *Handbook of North American Indians, Vol. 15: Northeast.* Ed. Bruce G. Trigger. Washington, D.C.: Smithsonian Institution, 1978: 160-176.

Saunders, Richard S. and Ellen G. Miles. *American Colonial Portraits: 1700-1776.* Washington, D.C.: Smithsonian Institution P, 1987.

Sekatau, Ella Thomas. "Cultural Lifestyle of the Narragansett Indians." Lecture, North Kingstown Free Library, No. Kingstown, R.I. 23 September 1991.

Simmons, William S. "Narrangansett," in *Handbook of North American Indians, Vol. 15: Northeast.* Ed. Bruce G. Trigger. Washington, D.C.: Smithsonian Institution, 1978: 190-97.

Tandberg, Gerilyn. "Decoration and Decorum: Accessories of Nineteenth-Century Louisiana Women," *The Southern Quarterly,* 27:1, 1988, 9-31.

Thomas, Peter Allen. "In the Maelstrom of Change: The Indian Trade and Cultural Process in the Middle Connecticut River Valley, 1635-1665." Unpublished Doctoral Dissertation, University of Massachusetts, 1979.

Tifft, Wilton S. *Ellis Island.* Chicago: Contemporary Books, 1990.

Washburn, Wilcomb E. "Seventeenth-Century Indian Wars," in *Handbook of North American Indians, Vol. 15: Northeast.* Ed. Bruce G. Trigger. Washington, D.C.: Smithsonian Institution, 1978: 89-100.

Welters, Linda. Margaret Ordoñez, and Kathryn Tarleton. "Textiles from New England Indian Burial Sites," in *Book of Papers, 1991 International Conference and Exhibition,* October 8-11, 1991, 71-75. (Research Triangle Park, N.C.: American Association of Textile Chemists and Colorists).

Weinstein-Farson, Laurie. *The Wampanoag.* New York: Chelsea House Publishers, 1989.

White, Shane. "A Question of Style: Blacks in and around New York City in the Late 18th Century," *Journal of American Folklore,* 102: 403, 1989, 23-44.

Williams, Roger. *A Key into the Language of America* [1643]. 5th ed. Providence: The Rhode Island and Providence Plantations Tercentenary Commission, 1936.

Winthrop, John. *History of New England, 1630-1649.* Vol. 1 Ed., James K. Hosmer. New York: Charles Scribner's Sons, 1908.

Wood, William. *New England's Prospect* [1635]. Ed. Alden T. Vaughn. Amherst: U Massachusetts P, 1977.

Wroth, Lawrence C. *The Voyages of Giovanni de Verrazzano, 1524-1528.* New Haven, CT: Yale UP, 1970.

Dress for the Ohio Pioneers

Carolyn R. Shine

Westward Expansion in America

What people wear would seem to be of little significance to the tide of history, but the economic aspects of the production and distribution of clothing have always been of enormous significance. In the seventeenth and eighteenth centuries competition for trade in a lucrative clothing material—fur—fuelled the bitter fighting between the English and the French that accompanied the westward expansion of the British colonies in North America. This same fur trade promoted exploration of the continent farther and farther west as the eastern populations of fur-bearing animals were diminished by excessive trapping and by the destruction of their habitats as the forests were cut down for the sake of agriculture (Phillips xx-xxi). Thus, fur traders, trappers and hunters were the advance scouts for the westward expansion of the frontier. The settlers who followed them were often obliged to turn themselves into hunters and trappers to keep afloat economically until they had cleared land and established marketable crops.

By the time of the Revolutionary War, settlements were already struggling to survive on the western side of the Appalachian Mountains in the westernmost counties of Pennsylvania, Maryland and Virginia. These settlements were devastated periodically by the wars between the French and the English, and then between the English and their rebellious American colonists. In these eighteenth-century wars, both the English and the French made use of native American tribes who had their own reasons for fighting ferociously against the swelling tide of settlement. Native Americans kept up the war even after the Americans and the English signed their treaty in the winter of 1782-83 so that the pioneers had to go on fighting in order to rebuild their burnt-out settlements from Georgia to New York. Nevertheless, settlers doggedly pressed on westward into Kentucky and the Territory of the United States Northwest of the River Ohio, in spite of conflict with native Americans at this new frontier, a

42

conflict which repeated the blood-drenched scenario of the Appalachian frontier.

Bowing to this westward pressure, Congress opened the Northwest Territory to settlement in 1787, and in the Spring of 1788 land speculators and settlers from around Boston took up a site on the Ohio River near the Pennsylvania border which they called Marietta. A few months later another group of pioneers, mostly from New Jersey, advanced some three hundred miles downriver, establishing the villages of Columbia, Cincinnati and North Bend, collectively known as the Miami Purchase, on a twenty-five mile stretch of the Ohio between the Great and Little Miami Rivers. Surrounding these first settlements was a forested expanse so extensive that when the Northwest Territory was divided into states in the nineteenth century it made no less than five states: Ohio, Indiana, Illinois, Michigan and Wisconsin.

In the midst of this "howling wilderness," with their nearest neighbors a hundred miles away in Lexington, Kentucky, itself a pioneer village, the settlers in the Miami Purchase were a long way from supplies for everyday living such as axes, hoes, cooking utensils and textiles for clothing and bedding (May, Journals 135; Grant 1:80). The pioneers brought as much as they could with them, but the meager space afforded by a wagon or the saddle bags of pack animals drastically restricted their belongings. Essential shoes had to compete for space with the indispensable axe—and were of almost equal value. At Redstone on the Monongahela, where the pioneers bought flatboats for the Ohio River passage, shoes sold for twelve to fifteen shillings in 1788, axes for fifteen to twenty (Shepard 318). In accounts for the Boston household of John May, one of the Marietta pioneers, shoes are recorded from four to six shillings and a pair of boots at five shillings (May, Account Book). These prices cast some light on the price inflation due to distance and scarcity.

Fashions in the East: What the Pioneers Left Behind

The clothing the pioneers took with them was, of course, what was commonplace in the eastern communities they were leaving, but as they moved westward their clothing was increasingly influenced by the requirements of hard manual labor and by diminishing access to supplies. In the eastern communities there was a considerable range of clothing from high fashion and costly to practical and inexpensive. John May, riding from Boston to Marietta in 1788, wrote in his diary that in Philadelphia "some of the ladies appear sensible and dress neat, and some appear by their garb to be fools. I have seen a headdress in this city at least three feet across" (May, Journals 29). At that time fashionable dress for men, as well as women, had reached a peak of extravagance in Paris and London society which was echoed in Philadelphia, Boston and New York. Fashions crossed the Atlantic in a matter of months, particularly since the 1770s and 1780s had seen the inauguration of fashion periodicals like *The Lady's Magazine* from London and *La galerie des modes* from Paris. Also, dolls dressed in the height of fashion were still used to disseminate the latest fashions (Walpole 12:316; 15:221).

In the newspaper, *Massachusetts Centinel*, Boston merchants advertised costly imported silks such as Lustrings, Sattins, Taffeties, French Stripes, Gauzes, Gauze Handkerchiefs, and Tiffany Aprons which were laced in here and puffed out there with Girths, Stuffing, Hippers, Rumpers, Spiders and Hoops (*Massachusetts Centinel* 18 Oct., 3 Dec. 1788; 11 Feb. 1789). In 1782, Mrs. Henry Knox, wife of the Secretary of War, was described by the Reverend Manasseh Cutler as "very gross...her hair in front is craped at least a foot high much in the form of a churn bottom upward and topped off with a wire skeleton in the same form covered with black gauze which hangs in streamers down her back. Her hair behind is in a large braid, turned up and confined with a monstrous large crooked comb" (Cutler 231). That Rev. Cutler was not exaggerating can be seen in many of the portraits of the time.

For the pioneers from New Jersey, the center of fashion was Philadelphia. As John May observed, not all Philadelphians dressed in the extravagant style favored by Mrs. Knox. Many Philadelphians belonged to the Society of Friends, the Quakers, who made it a rule to dress simply. Many Philadelphians who were not Quakers also dressed simply. The portraits of Mr. and Mrs. Francis Bailey (Figs. 1, 2), painted by Charles Willson Peale in 1791, show what was being worn by the conservative, industrious middle class to which most of the pioneers belonged or aspired to belong. Mrs. Bailey was, in fact, one of those who migrated to Cincinnati, though not in the first wave.

The clothes seen on the Baileys, though not high-style, were still "Best Clothes," clothes to sit for your portrait in, and not very suitable for conquering the wilderness. Mr. Bailey's coat was probably superfine woolen broadcloth imported from England and his neckcloth imported from the Netherlands which produced the finest linen cambric (named for the town of Cambrai, now in northern France). Mrs. Bailey's gown was probably silk, glazed wool or a silk and wool mixture imported from England or the Continent, and her kerchief and cap might be made from cotton imported from India which produced the finest cotton.

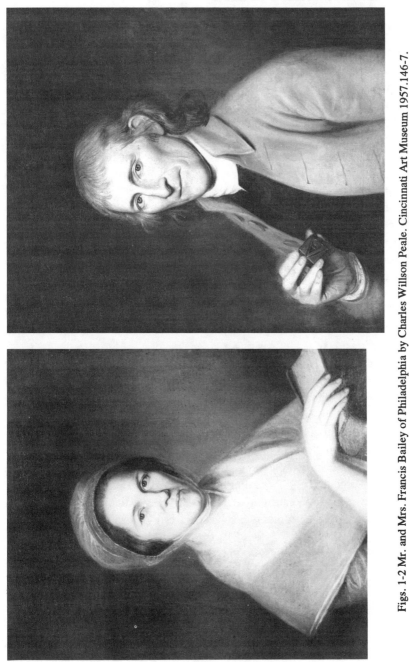

Figs. 1-2 Mr. and Mrs. Francis Bailey of Philadelphia by Charles Willson Peale. Cincinnati Art Museum 1957.146-7.

Work Clothes Worn in the Colonies

America's production of textiles in the eighteenth-century was almost entirely limited to coarse home-spun and home-woven linen, wool and linsey-woolsey, (a fabric woven with a wool weft and a linen warp for economy's sake since wool was more costly than linen), with some cotton in the southern colonies. Optimistic attempts to produce silk in all the colonies seem to have had little success. It is reasonable to assume that the pioneers wore what could be called work-clothes of the least expensive materials, with an emphasis on warmth and toughness since the protective function of clothing would outweigh the social-identifier function when it came to mountain trails and forest underbrush.

The man-in-the-street at that time generally wore breeches of leather, linen, and grades of wool less expensive than broadcloth, or a wool substitute like linsey-woolsey. In winter the breeches were often lined with leather; in summer linen trousers were common. Shirts were of linen of various grades, or wool in white, checked or striped motifs. A waistcoat or jacket, with or without sleeves, could be of wool, leather, linen or calico, plain or striped. Not everyone had a coat; sometimes the long-sleeved waistcoat served as a coat. Some men did have coats, usually of an inexpensive grade of wool, though there are occasional newspaper reports of a thief wearing a stolen coat of good broadcloth.

One of the best sources of information on the lowest common denominator in clothing comes from newspaper ads for runaway indentured servants and apprentices. Additional information comes from reports and correspondence of field officers of military units. Most uniform clothing came from England at very uncertain intervals so that the soldiers, that is the privates, did a lot of their fighting in civilian clothes (Dinwiddie III:413, 462, 520; IV:581). This usually meant shirt, breeches or trousers, waistcoat and a blanket to sleep in and serve as a cloak (Pargellis 141). According to The Papers of Henry Bouquet, rangers who were assigned to scout the woods often wore Indian dress: long Indian leggings, moccasins, shirt and either breeches or a breech clout and war paint (Bouquet II 124).

One of the few descriptions of the clothing of pioneer women comes from the Reverend Joseph Doddridge. Looking back, in 1824, to his family's pioneering at the western extremity of Pennsylvania where they settled in 1773, Doddridge said the women wore a linsey petticoat and bed gown with a homemade handkerchief and a linen sunbonnet (116). The handkerchief mentioned by Doddridge was the large kerchief worn on the shoulders as is shown in the portraits of Mrs. Bailey and Mrs. Woods, the other kind usually being called a pocket-handkerchief. An item of clothing not mentioned by Doddridge was the apron, worn in the eighteenth century both for utility and for fashion (Gehret 57-63). The petticoat was not underwear—that was the eighteenth-century word for a skirt. The bed gown was an overblouse, approximately hip length and one of the class of garments called variously bed gowns, short gowns or jackets (Garsault 51-52). Contemporary documentation of clothing is always somewhat ambiguous unless the context is absolutely explicit because names of garments shifted from one garment to another, and a single garment might be called by several different names.

Whatever details distinguished the bed gown, short gown and jacket from one another, they probably were alike in being no more than about hip length, thus affording a considerable saving in the cost of material as compared with a full-length gown, as well as allowing greater freedom of movement for women who had work to do (Kidwell 30-65). John F. Watson wrote in *Annals of Philadelphia* that petticoat-and-short-gown was the uniform of the serving girl (189), but a middle-class Boston woman wrote in her diary on a hot day, "I soon dis-robed myself and putting on a little short-gown sat down to enjoy the easy wind...." (May, Orderly Book). "Dis-robed" almost certainly meant, not that she undressed completely, but that she removed her full-length robe, tight-fitting in the bodice and open in front over her petticoat (Fig. 3). She is echoed by Janet Schaw writing of the heat in North Carolina, "we lie panting...dressed in a single muslin petticoat and short gown" (182).

Even the most modest clothing could be quite colorful. Ads in the *Pennsylvania Gazette* for runaway serving women mention such garments as a striped linsey petticoat, a red petticoat, a gown with broad red stripes, a blue stuff jacket and petticoat, a brown shalloon gown and blue stockings.

Doddridge said the women wore coarse shoes, or moccasins copied from the Indians, or shoepacks (similar to moccasins) and in summer went barefoot. The Reverend Charles Woodmason, visiting remote congregations in North Carolina in 1768, noted that the women attended church barefoot and wearing only a shift and a short petticoat (31, 61). Illustrations of frontier America in the eighteenth century are scarce, but a French spy, Victor Callot, made a drawing of a frontier log cabin while on a trip down the Ohio in 1796. The drawing shows a woman who appears to be wearing a petticoat and short gown, kerchief and cap (Fig. 4).

Frontier Fashions: Hunting Shirts and Moccasins
The extant letters and diaries from the early years of settlement in the

Fig. 3 Mrs. William Woods, 1793, wearing a full-length gown, by Charles Peale Polk. Cincinnati Art Museum 1957. 453.

Fig. 4. Illustration of a log cabin from *A Journey in North America* by Georges Henri Victor Collet who visited this country in 1796. Cincinnati Historical Society.

Miami Purchase say almost nothing about clothing. It was not until the survivors came to record their memories of the heroic days that information about clothing emerges. Mary Gano said her husband felled a buckeye tree and hewed with his axe two large wooden trays. One she used for food; in the other she washed their clothes, and when they had been ironed, the tray "answered the purpose of a Beureaugh" (Drake Papers). This suggests a very small quantity of clothing for two adults and three children. She did not, however, give any description of that clothing.

One of the earliest backward glances to appear in print was Cincinnati's first city *Directory* of 1819, which stated in its sketch of the town's history: "The men wore hunting shirts of linen and linsey-woolsey, and round these a belt in which were inserted a scalping knife and tomahawk. Their moccasins, leggins and pantaloons were made of deer skins. The women wore linsey-woolsey manufactured by themselves" (22). This information was said to come from participants in the original settlement, many of whom were still alive and flourishing in 1819. The clothing that really stood out in their memories was the dress of the woodsmen—trappers and hunters. Yet not all frontiersmen conformed to this style of dress. In John May's diaries of his trips to Marietta, he does not mention wearing or even seeing the woodsman's garb of hunting shirt, leggings and moccasins. On 29 May, 1789, he wrote that he wanted to get his flannel underwaistcoat washed because it had reached a state of "high repute" from continuous wearing in the chilly mountain passes. On 3 December he excused himself from attending church because of a hole in his "briches." And he took along with him the kind of goods he thought likely to find a ready market: calico, tow cloth (a low-grade of linen) and shoes (May, Accounts).

The hunting shirt, however, figured in most Cincinnati memoirs. It had probably evolved from the loose-fitting coat or outer garment called a frock, once worn in England by country laborers and shepherds (Johnson, Bailey), and later modified and upgraded to fashionable attire in the eighteenth century. The hunting shirt may also have evolved from the sleeved waistcoat of the mid-eighteenth century. Although the American hunting shirt or frock was a backwoods garment of hunters, trappers and other woodsmen, the success of three companies of frontier riflemen in the Revolutionary War gave their woodsmen's dress considerable cachet. The Riflemen's shirts were a deep ash color, according to Judge John Joseph Henry's account of the expedition to Quebec in which he took part (Roberts 301). Biographies of Daniel Morgan, who led one of the Rifle Companies, state that the shirts were brown or dry-leaf color—all good camouflage (Graham 63; Higginbotham 17). The engraving of

Morgan, the frontispiece of James Graham's biography of Morgan (Fig. 5), indicates that Morgan was famous for wearing the woodsman's dress and, vice versa, that the woodsman's dress became famous for being worn by that formidable warrior. The engraving was copied from John Trumbull's painting (not painted until 1821) of the victorious American generals after the battle of Saratoga. In the Trumbull painting, Morgan wears woodsman's dress while everyone else wears regimental uniforms. Trumbull stated that he based his portrait on a miniature that he had painted of Morgan around 1792 which, in fact, he had copied from an earlier Peale portrait (Cooper No. 73; Sellers 145). In the Peale portrait, however, Morgan wears a regular uniform. This leaves the source of Trumbull's version of woodsman's dress undocumented. It does not agree very closely with the description left by Reverend Doddridge, and it certainly does not fit Judge Henry's report that Morgan led his men in breech clout and leggings with his thighs naked and scratched by underbrush (Roberts 327).

Reverend Doddridge's parents settled west of present-day Pittsburgh in 1773, in the no-man's land that was claimed by Virginia and Maryland as well as by Pennsylvania. It was from this frontier that Daniel Morgan and two other frontiersmen recruited their riflemen and took them to George Washington's headquarters in 1775, wearing the hunting shirt and leggings that Doddridge, writing the history of the area in 1824, called the ordinary working dress of the frontiersman, particularly when "hunting and going on scouts and campaigns." Doddridge described the hunting shirt as "a kind of loose frock reaching halfway down the thighs, with large sleeves." It opened down the front, was double-breasted, with the overlap serving as a pocket in which to carry food and other supplies, and was secured by a sash or belt. It evidently had no buttons which meant that it was easier to make and cheaper than a tailored coat. It had a large "cape" (which at that time generally meant a collar) sometimes embellished with fringe, if only of ravelled cloth. "The hunting shirt was generally made of linsey, sometimes of coarse linen, and a few of dressed deer skins. These last were very cold and uncomfortable in wet weather." A shirt and jacket or waistcoat could be worn under the hunting shirt. On their legs men wore leggings or gaiters and breeches, or a breech clout and thigh-length leggings (113-16).

It is clear that the pioneers borrowed garments of the native Americans to wear with the hunting shirt, shirt and waistcoat which were of European origin. Yet, it must be noted that Native Americans also wore shirts which they accepted from the Europeans in trade for their furs. When on the warpath, the

GENERAL DANIEL MORGAN.

FROM THE ORIGINAL PICTURE IN THE ROTUNDA OF THE CAPITOL, WASHINGTON.

Fig. 5. Engraving of Daniel Morgan from James Graham's biography of Morgan. Cincinnati Historical Society.

native Americans frequently stripped down to breech clout, leggings and paint. On their feet they wore moccasins which could be stitched up from deer skin in an hour or two. The pioneers adopted native moccasins because they could be acquired easily from a readily available forest product and cost nothing but a little labor. Like buckskin hunting shirts, however, they soaked up water, and therefore were seen as the cause of rheumatism, a malady which afflicted most hunters (Doddridge 113-16).

Daniel Morgan's Riflemen were not the only ones to go to war in woodsman's dress. In 1775 George Washington himself called for 10,000 hunting shirts to clothe his troops, but as early as 1758 he was ordering from Philadelphia cloth for "Indian stockings" and breech clouts for the men under his command in the campaign against Fort Duquesne (where Pittsburgh is now) (2: 190, 240). A British officer of the garrison of Quebec in December 1775 was astonished to see the American troops clad only in "canvas frocks" (Aimslie 25).

It is significant that throughout Washington's military career he was perpetually begging the authorities—the colonial governors of Virginia and later the Continental Congress—for clothing for his men. Over and over he wrote "the men are almost naked," a complaint made by other officers as well. This suggests that clothing was hard to acquire for those not rich, and particularly if they were far from centers of supply.

When settlers moved westward after the American Revolution, they took with them the clothing they already had, and they encountered many of the problems and shortages that had plagued the soldiers. Like Doddridge, many early Cincinnatians associated the woodsman's dress chiefly with "hunting and going on scouts and campaigns." Jacob Fowler said that in 1791 he had dressed deer skins for moccasins for General St. Clair's troops at Fort Hamilton near Cincinnati (Cist 78), but in 1793 Anthony Wayne, nagging the War Office for supplies, complained that two pairs of moccasions were worth less than one pair of common shoes (309). Army Regulations of 30 April, 1790, specified that each soldier be issued annually a hat or helmet, coat, vest, overalls, shirts, four pairs of shoes, two pairs of socks, blanket, stock and clasp, and a pair of buckles. This contradicts the hunting-shirt-leggings-moccasins picture, but as General Wayne repeatedly reminded the War Office, there was a gap between the issue of Directives at the War Office and the issue of actual garments at the frontier, which frequently had to be filled with locally supplied substitutes.

Benjamin Van Cleve of Cincinnati said in his "Memoirs" that he had accompanied a military expedition down the Ohio River in 1794 as contractor

SPENCER TAKEN PRISONER.

Page 41.

Fig. 6.   Illustration from O.M. Spencer's *Indian Captivity* showing his capture by the Indians.   Cincinnati Historical Society.

for supplies, "my gun in one hand & tomahawk in the other, a knife eighteen inches long hanging pendant at my side dressed in a hunting frock breech cloth and leggins..."(61). And the Reverend Oliver M. Spencer described a company of Volunteers from Columbia as "well mounted and armed with rifles, knives and some even with tomahawks, and dressed in hunting shirts" (15).

On the other hand, Spencer said that when, in 1792 at the age of eleven, he was captured by Indians between Cincinnati and Columbia (Fig. 6), he was wearing a plain summer roundabout (short jacket) and pantaloons with "covered mould buttons," and a blue silk vest with two rows of plated sugar loaf buttons—which his Indian captor ripped off and tied round his own legs. Spencer was rescued by a fur trader and restored to his family the following year via Detroit, where his Indian rags were replaced with another roundabout from the wardrobe of an Ensign, and a pair of stockings and slippers—from one of the women there (86,131). We do not know what those slippers looked like, but whatever they were, they were available, and availability counted heavily at the frontier.

The pioneers made use of as many locally growing natural products as possible to ease shortages of goods and of the money to buy them. There is a tradition that nettle fibers were spun into a substitute for linen (McBride 1:202); and that when a buffalo was shot for food, wool could be sheared from the hide to substitute for sheep's wool, the hide being used for shoes (Martzolff 194; Denny 237; Byrd, *Prose Works* 140, 149). No substitution was involved, however, in the case of buckskin breeches. Deer hides were, in fact, a profitable commercial item and one of the few dependable early sources of income for the settlers. Like the frock, buckskin breeches were first worn by workingmen. In the eighteenth century they were adopted by the English upper classes for hunting, and thus became fashionable.[1] In addition to leggings, moccasins and breeches, buckskin was also used for overalls.[2]

In spite of the need for hard-wearing clothing and in spite of scarcity of possessions, there is evidence that the pioneers never quite lost sight of keeping up appearances. Silk stockings can be documented in Cincinnati as early as 1793. They appear on a bill (Fig. 7) from the merchants Smith and Findlay to Lieut. Isaac Younghusband at Fort Washington, and also in a theft from a Thomas Goudy.[3] Furthermore, the Goudy theft included a man's silk breeches and waistcoat.

Pioneer Merchants
Although Thomas Goudy probably brought his dress clothes with him, there

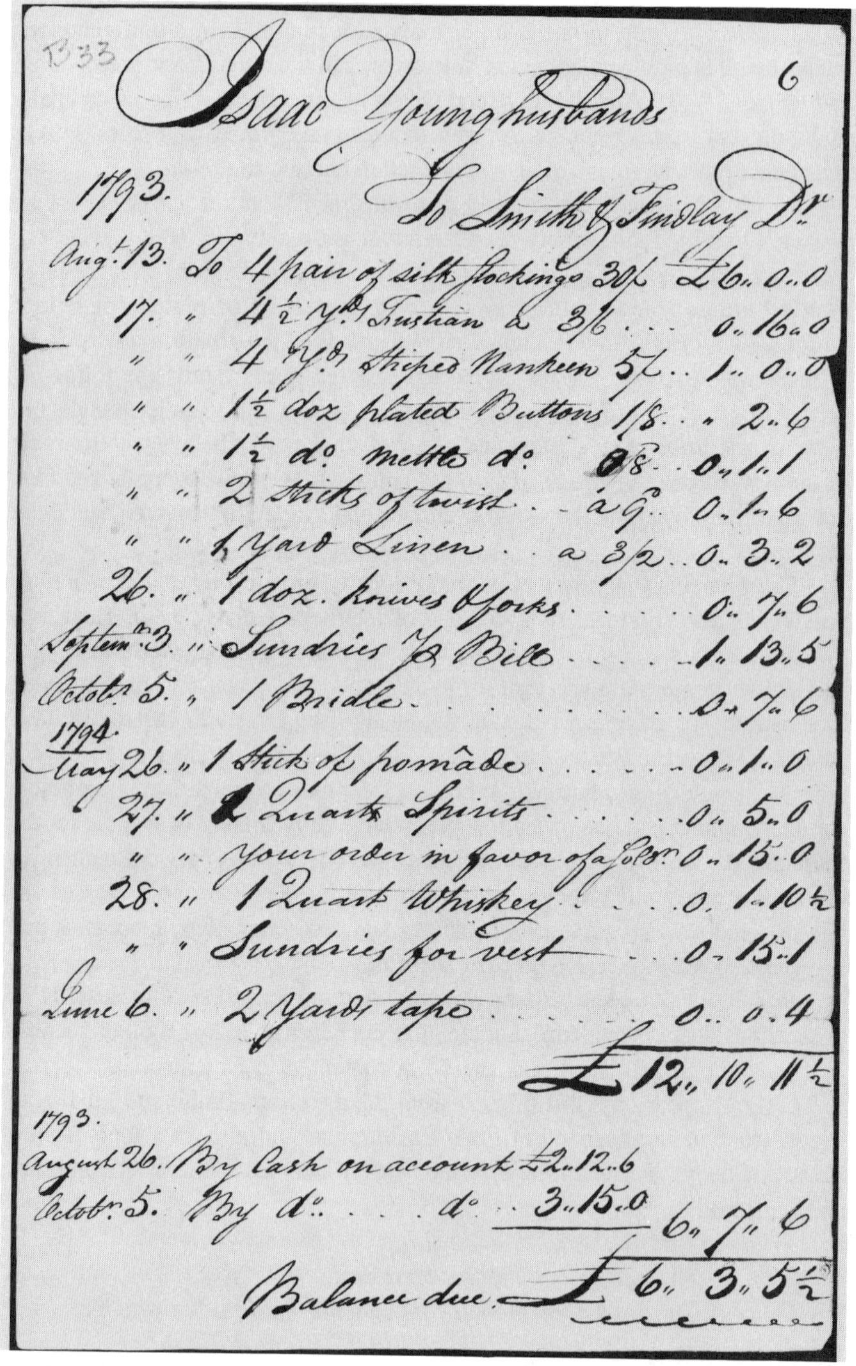

B33

6

Isaac Younghusbands

1793.   To Smith & Findlay Dr

Aug.ᵗ 13.	To 4 pair of silk stockings 30/		£6.. 0..0
17.	" 4½ yᵈˢ Fustian a 3/6 ...		0..16..0
"	" 4 yᵈˢ striped Nankeen 5/ ...		1.. 0..0
"	" 1½ doz plated Buttons 1/8 ...		" 2..6
"	" 1½ do. mettle do. 8 ...		0..1..1
"	" 2 sticks of twist .. a 9 ..		0..1..6
"	" 1 Yard Linen .. a 3/2 ..		0.. 3..2
26.	" 1 doz. knives & forks		0.. 7..6
Septemᵇ 3.	" Sundries ⅌ Bill		1.. 13..5
Octobᵣ 5.	" 1 Bridle		0.. 7..6
1794.			
May 26.	" 1 Stick of pomâde		0..1..0
27.	" 2 Quarts Spirits		0.. 5..0
"	" Your order in favor of a John.ᵈ		0.. 15..0
28.	" 1 Quart Whiskey		0. 1..10½
"	" Sundries for vest		0.. 15..1
June 6.	" 2 Yards tape		0.. 0.4
			£12.. 10.. 11½

1793.
Auguˢᵗ 26. By Cash on account £2..12..6
Octobᵣ 5. By do .. do. 3..15.0   6.. 7.. 6

Balance due ..   £ 6.. 3.. 5½

Fig. 7. In August 1793 Lieut. Isaac Younghusband bought four pairs of silk stockings from the Cincinnati merchants Smith & Findlay. Cincinnati Historical Society.

was a tailor in Cincinnati as early in 1790, (*Directory*) and like John May some settlers may have brought in clothing material to sell or trade. By 1790 there were already merchants attempting to make a living out of hauling eastern goods to the goods-hungry frontier. The merchant, William Stanley, for instance, wrote in his journal that when he arrived in Cincinnati in 1790, another merchant, John Bartle, already had a store there. Philadelphia and Baltimore were the chief sources of goods for settlements along the Ohio and for Kentucky. The freight wagons took about twenty-three days from Philadelphia to Redstone on the Monongahela where the goods were transferred to flatboats for the river passage (Fig. 8). Some merchants used the boats as floating stores, others established stores in one or more communities, or sold on a temporary basis out of a room in a tavern. Taverns were almost the only buildings in frontier villages which had space available for traveling merchants and for community activities such as auctions, meetings and entertainments.

Among the Torrence Family Papers, a typical invoice of 1790 from a Cincinnati merchant, includes among other items: china and bone knives and forks, Barlow knives at twelve shillings sixpence, Drab Cloth at thirteen shillings twopence a yard, "Nitting pins" at twopence each, snaffle bits, narrow black ribbon, seven pairs of spectacles at two shillings threepence each, two scarlet cloaks at one pound sixpence each, a cask of powder, handsaw files, six Hatts No. 5 at four shillings tenpence each, buck shot, sad irons, frying pans, flints, etc. The Drab Cloth would be for a tailor to make up into a man's suit. The color drab appears frequently in invoices and apparently was very modish at that time. The word "cloth" almost invariably signified cloth made from wool and was expensive. A 1794 invoice lists fine cloth at twenty-two shillings sixpence a yard whereas linen was only three shillings ninepence a yard.

A 1791 invoice lists Indian calico, striped chintz, two purple calico, cotton and linen check, large cotton shawls, ten and a half dozen coat buttons, horn combs, beaver fustian, blue strouding, superfine cloth, brown cloth, worsted and cotton hose, olive sattinet and printed linen. These are the makings for men's and women's clothing, curtains, chair covers etc., and almost all those materials were imported. In 1788 when a textile manufactory opened in Beverly, Massachusetts, to produce "cotton velvets, curduroy, jean, fustian, denim, marseilles quilting, dimity, muslinett," etc. it was front page news in the *Massachusetts Centinel* 30 April.

The pioneers in the Miami Purchase traded furs, deer skins and wild ginseng for goods from the merchants—it was almost wholly a barter economy.[4] Hard money was scarce all over the country, but particularly at the frontier; and

Fig. 8. Illustration of one of the flatboats used to float people, goods and stock down the Ohio River, from Collot's

merchants had to take payment in local products and cart them back across the mountains or float them down to New Orleans which was in the hands of the Spanish. Although the Spanish intermittently closed the port to Americans, some goods did get through (Phillips 11). Wheat, corn, whiskey, tobacco, country linen and other agricultural products were fed into the system as they became available. As noted in the Cincinnati newspaper *Liberty Hall*, in 1814 you could still pay in wheat for a subscription to that newspaper, and as late as 1821, J. B. Robinson would accept wheat, corn, flax, wool, sugar, beeswax, tallow or frosted potatoes in payment for carding wool (*Liberty Hall* 15 Nov. 1814; 14 Nov. 1821).

Ready-made Clothing

Except for fit—every-one garments like shawls, cloaks,—and oddly enough, shoes,—Cincinnati papers and merchants' records mention almost no ready-made clothing until 1817, although in the east, ready-made waistcoats and shirts were being advertised in the *Massachusetts Centinel* in 1788. Indeed in 1789 Congress was debating a tariff on imported ready-made clothing.[5] Ready-made clothing had been imported into North America at an early date. For instance, William Byrd wrote to Arthur North in London in 1686, "Send mee about ten or a dozen suits of servants cloths ready made for tryall..." (*Correspondence* 62). In 1709 John Lawson mentioned ready-mades for men and women among other imports (88). In 1768 a New England merchant advertised ready-made clothes for men: coats, silk jackets, shapes and cloth ditto, stocking breeches, velvet cotton thickset, duroy everlasting and plush breeches, sailors great coats, outside and inside jackets, check shirts, frocks, long and wide trowsers, Scotch bonnets and blue milled shirts (Earle 321). In the Canadian campaign of 1756, Sir William Johnson was ordering shirts, coats and other garments from London in lots of a hundred and two hundred at a time, to give or sell to native Americans (William Johnson 2:898-9). In the eighteenth century most clothing, however, was made to measure and sewn by hand, either at home or by a professional tailor or seamstress. An invoice of 1705 charged Major Winslow, stationed at Fort Washington in Cincinnati, for linen, for thread and for making shirts (Torrence Papers).

Frontier Fashion

In November 1793 the Territory's first newspaper, *Centinel of the North- western Territory*, began publication in Cincinnati, cramming into only four small pages local, territorial, national and international news, editorials, merchants' ads, personals, marriage and death notices. It was in the *Centinel* of 23 November that Thomas Goudy advertised that his house had been robbed of a black silk waistcoat and breeches, three other waistcoats of black Florentine, of buff cassimere (or kerseymere), and of purple and white stripes, a pair of yellow ribbed worsted breeches, a pair of kneebuckles with purple and white "paist" (glass) stones, nine ruffled shirts, two pairs of silk stockings, two pairs of striped silk and cotton stockings, one pair of cotton stockings, two pairs of shoes and a red cotton handkerchief with white spots.

Goudy's wardrobe seems dressy for a village of log houses still under attack by Indians, but perhaps he wore the satin breeches to the balls given by the officers at Fort Washington to celebrate Washington's birthday in 1791 and Fourth of July in 1792. Dr. Allison, the Army surgeon, also gave a Christmas ball in 1795 (*Centinel* 26 Dec. 1795). As noted previously eleven-year-old Oliver Spencer was on his way home from the 1792 July Fourth event when the Indians captured him, dressed, not in hunting shirt, but in roundabout and blue silk vest with plated buttons (Spencer 29, 35). And the *Centinel* of 26 April, 1794, contained both a report on recent Indian raids and an ad for a hairdresser and perfumer by the name of Peter Welsh. Ads in the *Centinel* for a lost gold English watch, a gold enameled mourning breast pin and a green surtout (a man's fashionable fitted overcoat) are further evidence that the pioneers were doing their best to dress respectably.

After the battle of Fallen Timbers in August 1794, which put an end to organized Indian resistance in Ohio, there came an immediate increase in material well-being which is reflected in the pages of the *Centinel*. On 14 November, 1795, G. Turner's household goods advertised for sale included books, furniture, chinaware, carpets, a "superb secretaire of zebrawood richly ornamented with gilt brass," walnut window and door frames and turned pillars. Queen's Ware, Josiah Wedgwood's popular cream-glazed earthenware, began to be advertised in Cincinnati in December 1794.

While some pioneers made their own shoes, the 1819 Cincinnati *Directory* revealed that Cincinnati had a shoemaker as early as 1790, though it did not identify him (Martzolff 194). Jacob Fowler was making moccasins for the soldiers in 1791, and the *Centinel* for October 1794 yields an ad for a newly arrived shoemaker by the name of John Finnyhon. In Lynn, Nahant and Reading, Massachusetts, however, a ready-made shoe industry was well established and in 1788 was turning out nearly half a million pairs a year (*Columbian Centinel* 9 March 1793; Warville 265). When John May set out for Marietta in 1789, he took along 128 pairs of shoes to sell. In 1795 Smith &

Findlay of Cincinnati listed two pairs of shoes on a January bill (Torrence Papers), and in October, Daniel Mayo was advertising wines, groceries, cotton, boots and bootees (short boots for men) as well as men's and women's shoes. Since Smith, Findlay and Mayo were merchants, not shoemakers, these were ready-mades. Within a short time many other Cincinnati merchants were advertising shoes.

Hats too were available ready-made. The 1790 Smith & Findlay bill listed "6 Hatts No. 5." Unfortunately the bill did not specify whether these were the old familiar broad-brims or tricornes, the new stovepipes, or military uniform hats. Hats were also among the items listed for sale at Samuel Freeman's House in the *Centinel* of 21 June 1794 (Fig. 9). This list also included several kinds of woolen material suitable for men's tailored clothes: "Forrest Cloth, Brown Halfthicks and Gray Coating." For women the list included printed cottons and silk.

While the availability of fabrics and other goods increased after 1794, the hunting shirt was still being worn. Indeed the hunting shirt had great meaning in the wardrobes of the frontiersmen. Like blue jeans today that started as work clothing, were glamorized and then sentimentalized as symbolic of a certain life style, the hunting shirt started as work clothing, was glamorized by its role in the Revolutionary War and then was sentimentalized as symbolic of the intrepid woodsman and explorer. Hunting shirts were work clothes that were glamorized by their role in the Revolutionary War and then became sentimentalized as symbolic of a certain life style. According to Thomas Jefferson, Patrick Henry loved to get into a hunting shirt and go hunting in the piny woods and sit around a campfire with his cronies cracking jokes (Randall 1:40). The hunting shirt continued to be worn in Cincinnati as part of the uniform of the First Regiment of Ohio Militia until at least 1812, even though the frontier had advanced well to the west of Cincinnati by that time (*Liberty Hall* 6 Oct 1812).

In February 1796 the clothing materials advertised in the *Centinel* were still from the thrifty end of the scale—Coatings, Swanskins, Baizes, Halfthicks, Thicksetts and Corduroys. By April, however, David Ziegler was offering "Beautiful Vest Patterns, Pour le Roi, Pour Princes and Pour Signeur," and two weeks later J. Forguson, just arrived from Philadelphia, was offering India Nankeens and Muslins, both fashionable fabrics. The *Centinel* on 22 March 1795 carried an advertisement by a professional skin dresser offering to make buckskin breeches, gloves and overalls. And there were no fewer than nineteen merchants or merchant partnerships advertising dry goods, groceries and hardware in the *Centinel* from 1794 through 1796. Other business

WILL be fold at public Auction on Tuef-
day the 24th inft. at the houfe of Mr.
Samuel Freeman, (for cafh only) the follow-
ing articles, viz :
Rofe Blankets, No. 1 and No. 2
Indian ditto, No. 1
Forreft Cloth
Printed Cottons
Barrowthrees
Blue Strouding, No. 104
Brown Halfthicks
Gray Coating
Silk & Twift
Coloured Thread
Coat Buttons
Veft ditto
Croffcut Files
Handfaw ditto
Looking Glaffes
Ribbons and Gold Cord
Table Spoons
Tea ditto
Shot & Lead
Sattin and
Hats

B O O K S
Carrs Sermons——2 Vol.
Paradife Loft
Modern Chivalry, by H. H. Brackenridge 2 vol
The Sexator or Parliamentory Chronicle
Senacas Morals
Rollins Belles Letters
Prince of Abiffinia
The Idler, by Dr. Johnfton
Cincinnati, June 19, 1794.
N. B. The fale commences at 10 o'clock
A M.

Fig. 9. Advertisement in the *Centinel of the North-western Territory*, 21 June 1794. Cincinnati Historical Society.

enterprises included a couple of tanyards, a ropewalk, two potters, a brewery, blacksmiths and whitesmiths, cabinet makers, a maker of Windsor chairs and spinning wheels, a baker, a mason, saddlers and evidently a sawmill since a frame house was advertised in the *Centinel* of 4 January and others on 11 January and 22 February. Cincinnati was, in fact, booming. The lists of goods advertised by the merchants became longer, more fashionable and more expensive and included fans, jewelry and other luxuries. More advertisements for tailors and mantua-makers appeared, so that by the turn of the century, Cincinnatians could dress pretty much like their counterparts in the eastern states.

A Cycle Completed

The pioneers of the Northwest Territory, especially the Miami Purchase, plunged into the wilderness dressed in work clothes. Yet they carried with them some articles of fashionable dress to remind themselves of the past, and to look forward to better times to come. They got along as best they could with limited supplies eked out with available natural resources—buckskin, buffalo wool, and nettle fiber. But they did not suffer without goods very long, for hardly more than a year after the pioneer settlers arrived in the Miami Purchase, merchants followed to connect them to the main stream of life in the eastern United States.

Notes

[1]Buckskin breeches worn in polite society are mentioned in Horace Walpole's *Letters* as early as 1741, and frocks as early as 1715-20.

[2]Noah Webster in *A Compendium of the English Language* defines overalls as "a kind of long close trowser." A bib is not mentioned.

[3]Torrence Papers; *Centinel* [Cincinnati] 23 November 1793.

[4]May, *Western Journals* 131, 148, 150; *Centinel* 16 November 1793, 18; 22 February 1794.

[5]*Massachusetts Centinel* 9 July 1788, 21 January 1789; Maclay 61.

Works Cited

Ainslie, Thomas. *Canada Observed. The Journal of Captain Thomas Anslie*, Ed. Sheldon S. Cohen. New York: New York University Press, 1968.

Bouquet, Henry. *The Papers of Henry Bouquet*, Ed. S. K. Stephens, D. H. Kent, A. L. Leonard. 2 vols. Harrisburg: Pennsylvania Historical Commission, 1951.

Byrd, William. *The Correspondence of the Three William Byrds of Westover, Virginia,*

Ed. Marion Tinling. Charlottesville: University Press of Virginia for Virginia Historical Society, 1977.

_____. *The Prose Works of William Byrd of Westover*. Ed. Louis B. Wright. Cambridge: Harvard University Press, 1966.

Centinel of The Northwestern Territory [Cincinnati]

Cist, Charles. *Sketches and Statistics of Cincinnati in 1859*. Cincinnati, 1859.

The Cincinnati Directory. Cincinnati, 1819.

Columbian Centinel [Boston].

Cooper, Helen A. *John Trumbull: The Hand and Spirit of a Painter*. New Haven: Yale University Art Gallery, 1982.

Cutler, Manasseh. *Life, Journals and Correspondence of Rev. Manasseh Cutler, L.L.D., by His Grandchildren William Parker Cutler and Julia Cutler*. Cincinnati, 1888.

Dinwiddie, Robert. "Official Records of Robert Dinwiddie." *Collections of the Virginia Historical Society*. Richmond, 1833.

Doddridge, Joseph. *Notes on the Settlement and Indian Wars of the Western Parts of Virginia and Pennsylvania*. Wellsburg, VA, 1824.

Denny, Ebenezer. *Military Journal of Major Ebenezer Denny*. Philadelphia, 1859.

Drake Papers, Draper Collection. Madison: State Historical Society of Wisconsin.

Earle, Alice Morse. *Customs and Fashions in Old New England*. New York: Scribner, 1968, First ed., 1893.

Garsault, Francois Alexander de. "L'Art du tailleur." *Description des arts et metiers*. Paris, 1769.

Graham, James. *The Life of General Daniel Morgan*. New York, 1856.

Grant, Anne. *Memoirs of an American Lady*. Vol. 1. London, 1809.

Gehret, Ellen J. *Rural Pennsylvania Clothing*. York, PA: Liberty Cap, 1976.

Higginbotham, Don. *Daniel Morgan, Revolutionary Rifleman*. Chapel Hill: University of North Carolina Press for the Inst. of Early American History and Culture, Williamsburg, 1961.

Johnson, William. *The Papers of William Johnson*. Ed. James Sullivan. Vol. 2. Albany: University of the State of New York, 1921.

Kidwell, Claudia. "Short Gowns." *Dress* 4 (1978): 30-65.

Lawson, John. *A New Voyage to Carolina*. London, 1709.

Liberty Hall [Cincinnati].

Maclay, William. *The Journal of William Maclay United States Senator from Pennsylvania 1789-1791*. New York: Boni, 1927.

McBride, James. *Pioneer Biography*. Vol. 1. Cincinnati, 1869.

Martzolff, Clement L., ed. "Reminiscences of a Pioneer." *Ohio Archaeological And Historical Publications* 19 (1910).

Massachusetts Centinel [Boston].

May, John. Account Book. John May Papers. Cincinnati Historical Society.

May, John. Orderly Book. John May Papers. Cincinnati Historical Society.

May, John. *The Western Journals of John May 1788-1789*. Ed. Dwight L. Smith. Cincinnati: Historical and Philosophical Society of Ohio, 1961.

Pargellis, Stanley, ed. *Military Affairs in North America 1748-65*. London, New York: Appleton Century, 1936.

Phillips, Paul Chrisler. *The Fur Trade*. Norman: University of Oklahoma, 1961.

Randall, Henry Stephen. *The Life of Thomas Jefferson.* Vol. 1. New York, 1858.

Roberts, Kenneth, comp. *The March to Quebec, Journals of the Members of Arnold's Expedition.* New York: Doubleday, 1938.

[Schaw, Janet]. *Journal of a Lady of Quality.* New Haven: Yale UP, 1922.

Sellers, Charles Coleman. "Portraits and Miniatures by Charles Willson Peal." *Transactions of the American Philosophical Society* 42, pt. 1. Philadelphia: 1952. No. 568.

Shepard, Lee. "News from North Bend." *Bulletin of the Historical and Philosophical Society of Ohio, Cincinnati* 15 (1947).

Spencer, Reverend O. M. *Indian Captivity.* New York, 1835.

Stanley, Major William. Diary, Cincinnati Historical Society.

Torrence Family Papers. Correspondence and other papers of the Torrence Family. Cincinnati Historical Society.

Van Cleve, Benjamin. "Memoirs of Benjamin Van Cleve." Ed. Beverly W. Bond, Jr., *The Quarterly Publication of the Historical and Philosophical Society of Ohio, Cincinnati* 17 (1922).

Walpole, Horace. *Letters of Horace Walpole.* Ed. Mrs. Paget Toynbee. Vol. 12. Oxford: Clarendon, 1904.

Warville, J. P. Brissot de. *New Travels in the United States of America* [1792]. Bowling Green, OH: Historical Publications, 1919.

Washington, George. *The Writings of George Washington from Original Manuscript Sources 1745-1799.* Ed. John C. Fitzpatrick. Vol. 2. Washington: U.S. Govt. Printing Office, 1931.

Watson, John. *Annals of Philadelphia* [1842]. Philadelphia, 1856.

Wayne, Anthony. *A Name in Arms.* Ed. Richard C. Knopf. Pittsburgh: University of Pittsburgh Press, 1960.

Webster, Noah. *A Compendium of the English Language.* Hartford, New Haven, CT, 1806.

Woodmason, Charles. *The Carolina Country on the Eve of the Revolution. The Journal and Other Writings of Charles Woodmason, Anglican Itinerant.* Ed. Richard J. Hooker. Chapel Hill: University of North Carolina Press, 1953.

Nineteenth-Century African-American Dress

Barbara M. Starke

Clothing of the wealthy, politically prominent, or famous have been well documented in art and literature throughout American history. Indeed, the history of apparel in general has been largely recorded from the viewpoint of the advantaged and those thought worthy enough to be remembered. There have been few records kept of working class dress. Still less is known about the meaning and functions of apparel worn by African-American slaves and other immigrant groups who played a role in the development of America. We know little about their experiences. There is merit, therefore, in noting the collective contributions of immigrant groups and in looking at each group separately. The clothing worn by these groups reflects their place in American society, how they viewed themselves and in turn, how others perceived them. Perhaps no immigrant experience is less understood than that of African-American slaves and the role played by clothing in the development of their personal and social identities[1] (Fig. 1).

Humanistic notions for African-Americans in the nineteenth century were a mere dream yet to be realized because they were thought of by others, and by themselves, as merely the property and labor force of the advantaged class of people. Individualization of personal style in dress was dangerous and difficult to accomplish because the master determined what types of clothing could be worn, when it could be worn, and who could wear it. Independent thinking and personal actions regarding clothing behavior could be severely punished. Few African-Americans challenged their masters' authority. Thus, uniqueness of style as expressed through clothing developed slowly as African-Americans became more able to deal with their circumstances, and their masters' expectations of them.

Today African-Americans, if they choose to, are readily able to use their attire to express values, beliefs, attitudes, personality type, knowledge and social position. This need for the opportunity to express one's individual style is not unique to the present but grew out of the struggle for identity and freedom

66

Fig. 1. "Negro Family Group: Several generations of a negro family all born on J.J. Smith's Plantation, Beaufort, S.C." T.H. O'Sullivan (1862).

in the nineteenth century. The African-American struggle for clothing identity actually began when they were transported involuntarily as naked slaves. A once proud African people were placed into slavery without personal possessions, and forced to live in a new world which was unique and foreign. In this new strange land, African-Americans adapted their own African cultural traits to their environment. Drawing on documentations of slave experiences, this paper examines the uses and functions of slave apparel in the nineteenth century, an era which spans both slavery and freedom.

As the nineteenth century began, more than a million African-Americans lived in the United States, most of them were slaves. By the mid 1800s the United States government declared trade in slaves illegal. However, because the ban was not enforced, trade continued to prosper. Slaves were considered valuable because they were used largely to sustain the economy of the southern plantations. They were also hired out to other white families who needed work done .

Just as laws determined the slave or freed condition for African-Americans, both written and oral laws determined how African-Americans could be dressed or clothed by the masters of the plantation. An 1856 issue of *Harper's Weekly* illustrates contemporary perceptions of slave dress (Fig. 2). Actual dress could differ from plantation to plantation, or from town to town, based on available resources to supply clothing needs. Slave dress also differed because of the financial means and attitudes of those in control. There were, however, enough similarities as noted in slave narratives, plantation accounts, autobiographies and biographies to give credibility to the descriptions. By noting the likeness in the apparel described in these accounts, we are better able to make generalizations and gain an understanding of slave clothing worn during the era.

Clothing of the House Slave Versus the Field Slave

Records and reports tend to show that slaves assigned house responsibilities were better clothed than those working in the field. Louis Hughes, a house slave, had access to clothing that was distinctively different from the clothing of the field slaves. He only worked the farm during busy seasons and did not own the regular wear of the farm hands. In his autobiography he stated, "I wore pants made of Bosse' old ones, and all his old coats were utilized for me. They rounded them off at the tail just a little and called them jackets." He also noted "my shoes were not brogans, but made of lighter leather, and made suitable for in the house" (42). That house slaves wore

THE COOK.

Fig. 2. *Harper's Weekly* (1856).

cast off clothing was confirmed in another slave narrative: "master's children and his wife would have white cotton suits made, and after they got tired of them they would give them to us" (Rawick 2:131). It is clear that field hands fared less well than house slaves (Fig. 3).

Sources of plantation records indicate that an annual clothing allotment was routinely given to adults whether male or female (Starke 878). Each account of the clothing allowance given to slaves, whether from the early nineteenth century or after the mid-century, revealed very little individualization in style. This is not surprising since clothing and fabrics were ordered in lots with no special difference except for sizes. For the slaves, clothing was meant to serve only a protective function. For the most part, slaves grew accustomed to these meager provisions (Fig. 4).

Plantation records cited by Stampp relate that "four shirts, four pairs of pants (two cotton and two wool), and one or two pairs of shoes were the yearly issue for men. Women were issued four dresses, head kerchiefs, and material to make four more dresses" (116). However, Hughes observed in *Thirty Years a Slave* that the allotted clothing from his plantation was meager and of poor quality: "Each man was allowed for summer two pairs of pants and two shirts, but no coat. The women had two dresses and two chemises each for summer. For winter the men had each two pairs of pants, one coat, one hat and one pair of coarse shoes." According to Hughes, men were happy to receive their winter goods. The women's dresses for winter, he noted, were "made of the heavier wool-cloth used for the men. They also had one pair of shoes each and a turban." The women also cut up old clothes to make pantalets which were their only undergarments. "The pantalets were made like a pant leg, came just above the knee, and were caught and tied.... The men's old pant-legs were sometimes used" (41-42).

Frederick Douglas in his *Life and Times of Frederick Douglas* observed that for the slaves the "yearly allowance of clothing was not more ample than the supply of food." For summer it consisted of two tow-linen shirts, one pair of trousers of the same coarse material. For winter they were allotted "a woolen pair of trousers and a woolen jacket, with one pair of yarn stockings and a pair of shoes of the coarsest description." He further added that "children under ten years old had neither shoes, stockings, jackets, nor trousers," they had only two coarse tow-linen shirts per year, and when these were worn out they went naked until the next allotment day. This he observed was true for girls as well as boys (64). Indeed as Mundy Lewis of Marion County, Missouri recalled,

We never wanted for clothes very bad. We wore long shirts that reached to the knees

Fig. 3. *Harper's Weekly* (April 24, 1875).

Fig. 4. From *Harper's Weekly*—"Colored People Gathering Fire-Wood—A Winter Scene in Virginia"—(Sketched by W.L. Sheppard).

until we was twelve or fourteen years old. Them wool shirts was warm. We had one pair of shoes a year. Many times I went after the cows barefoot when there was over a foot of snow on the ground (Rawick 2: 205).

Further observation regarding children's clothing comes from General Lee Ballard who noted that "all the little boys wore long shirts, kinder-like dresses only about half way below the knees." They were called "shirt-tail boys" because they had no pants. "After the war," Ballard noted, "they had pants and waists all made together and fastened all way down the back. They usually wore the same clothes on Sunday too," Ballard recorded, but in "winter we had some wool and ... homespun (Rawick 2: 36-37).

From these slave accounts it is apparent that boys were frequently clothed only in long shirts until they reached puberty. They also often went barefoot in winter. For as one former slave observed: "I can remember how we went to Sunday school barefooted and in our cotton dresses. We young ones didn't have shoes, but the older ones did" (Rawick 2: 138). Shoes for the older child represented the next stage of development and level of responsibility. Children remembered their first pair of shoes.

Most narratives noted that African-Americans were not satisfied with clothes functioning solely as protective coverings. They were concerned about their clothing and wanted to look their best for special occasions. They may have worn homespun during the week, but Annie Davis recalled that calico dresses were the choice for church on Sundays (Rawick 1: 112). "Every Sunday morning," she noted, "we put on our best dress and all us children went barefooted up to the Master's house for church and Sunday school...." "My grandmother," she observed, "took white domestic [cloth] and dyed it blue and yellow for our Sunday dresses" (Rawick 2:132).

Dress for Parties, Marriage

A marriage provided slaves the opportunity to dress more individually. It did not necessarily require elaborate preparation since the intent and the selection of a partner was often determined by the master or mistress of the plantation. In a narrative by Aunt Sally she describes how her marriage was arranged when she was thirteen years old. Her mistress made the decision regarding the time and the appropriate spouse. The account reveals that on the day of the wedding work stopped early "so that the servants might participate in the festivities." Sally observed that in her mother's absence, her own clothing became quite scant, and hence "she had no decent dress for the occasion." Her mistress, Sally recorded, came to her rescue and "produced from her own stores and old white muslin frock, and added to it a bright ribbon for her waist, and a gauze handkerchief to tie around her head." Sally's husband to be, Adam, was "equally destitute, and his coarse field dress was exchanged ... for some cast off clothes of his master's, which made him look," Sally thought, "quite like a gentleman" (50-51).

Occasionally no mention of special clothing or preparation was made for a wedding and the ceremony was less than festive. Indeed, one slave noted that when a man wanted to marry, he would simply ask the master if he could have "sich and sich a gal, and Ol'Marster would make them jump over a broom stick, and then they would be married" (Rawick 1:138).

Another very special occasion for self expression through dress occurred when the master of the plantation gave the slaves permission to have a dance or party. This was a rare and appreciated opportunity for the slaves to demonstrate skill and individuality with clothing. The dress for a party or dance differentiated between the classes of slaves. The house slaves or "aristocratic slaves" donned better quality clothing because, as noted previously, they often received cast offs from their masters and mistresses. As the ex-slave Austin Stewart noted, "the road leading to Col. Alexander's plantation presented a gay spectacle." The women's heads were adorned with "gaudy bandanna turbans and [they wore] new calico dresses, of the gayest colors—their whole attire decked over with bits of gauze ribbon and other fantastic finery." It was not until about ten o'clock that the "aristocratic slaves began to assemble dressed in the cast-off finery of their masters and mistresses, swelling out and putting on airs in imitation of those they were forced to obey from day to day" (Stewart 30).

Slave Attitudes About Their Clothing

The plantation owners often ordered fabrics in bulk and determined what would be made from the material, who could wear it, and when and where it could be worn. Hughes recalls that his master went to Memphis to purchase a bolt of gingham for turbans for the female slaves. The red and yellow check fabric was to be worn only on Sundays. During the week, the customary white turbans were appropriate for female attire and white wool caps were worn by the male field hands (42-43).

Former slaves told many stories about how they thought their clothing looked and how they felt when wearing the clothing. Cynthia Erwing of Alabama described plantation slave apparel. She noted that both "women and men's clothes were made of striped cotton. Women's clothes consisted of a dress, chemise and head rags; men wore plain cotton pants and shirts (Rawick

1:138). Emma Knight, a slave in Missouri, recalled her humiliation because she was forced to wear rags, cast offs and inadequate foot coverings. "We didn't have hardly any clothes," she lamented, "and most of the time they was just rags. We went barefoot until it got real cold. Our feet would crack open from the cold and bleed. We would sit down and bawl and cry because it hurt so." Her resourceful mother made moccasins for their feet from old pants. However, she noted, "late in the fall master would go to Hannibal or Palmyra and bring us shoes and clothes. We got those things only once a year." Clothing was scarce for she revealed, "I had to wear the young master's overalls for underwear and linseys for a dress" (Rawick 2: 202). Carrie Davis of Lee County Alabama remembers wearing rough homespun even though she was a house slave. "Us wore mostly slips woven in homemade looms and hit wus orsanberg and homespun, Sunday and Monday de same, our shoes wus made at er tan yard" (Rawick 1: 117).

Slave Produced Clothing: Homespun

African-Americans often were responsible for each step in the process of producing clothing. They raised sheep for wool and planted and harvested cotton. They also carded wool and cotton fibers, planted indigo for dyes, wove the yarns into fabrics and constructed garments. Aunt Sally reported that "every moment that [her mother] could gain from labor was spent in spinning, knitting, and sewing to keep them decently clothed" (47). Laura Thompson likewise noted, "My old grandmother would spin all day making goods and threads" (Rawick 2: 131). As Marie Askin Simpson stated, "We had our own wool. Raised our own sheep, carded and spun, wove and knit. The yarn was dyed all sorts of pretty colors, red, black, yellow, blue, brown, and purple" (Rawick 2: 232-33). She describes their use of dyes to obtain the various colors of yarns:

For brown dye, we used walnut hulls. If we wanted black dye, we used the ripe black hulls and for all shades of brown we used young green hulls. We boiled them good, then strained it. The yarn was laid in the cold juice of the walnut, until it 'took' on the shade we wanted. Then it was hung to dry without squeezing. Elder and Poke berries made red dyes. We would gather them ripe and squeeze the juice. Yellow dye was made of some kind of 'Yellow Root'—I don't remember the real name of the plant. Indigo made blues and purples. Just according to how long or how strong the dye was used. The indigo was bought at the drugstore (Rawick 2: 232-33).

Cynthia Erwing of Mobile, Alabama recalls that the men planted indigo and dried the seed and the women used that for dying their hats and dresses. She noted that as slaves, the women made fans and hats from palmetto. Erwing said that sometimes the hats were trimmed with ribbons to be worn on Sundays (Rawick 1: 137). Annie Davis, a slave from Mobile, Alabama, recalled that as a little girl she planted palmetto to make hats, and she saw women making fans from the palmetto (Rawick 1:113).

Clothing needed special care so certain days of the week were slated for making soap, washing and ironing. On Saturday afternoons and evenings the slaves were busy in the cabins "washing and fixing garments for Sunday" (Hughes 52). Also on Saturdays, they washed their clothes in a convenient branch and hung them to dry on the bushes (Rawick 1:114). Marie Askin Simpson makes the laundry process come alive as she recounts the tasks performed by her mother. She observed that "in those days they did the washing with battlin' sticks and boards. They layed the clothes on this board and battled with them battlin' sticks." She admired the pretty little buckets they used to carry water called little "piggins." The piggins were small enough to be carried anywhere, easily. Simpson observed that they did not wash clothes in a stream, rather they boiled their clothes in big iron kettles over a fire in the yard.

She went on to describe how they made their own lye and soap. The wood ashes from the fireplace were dumped into a wooden hopper set over a big iron kettle. "Hot water was poured over the ashes and they drained down into the kettle. She noted they used a "turkey feather (a chicken feather won't do, 'cause it would eat up too quick)" to determine "if the lye from the hopper was strong enough." When it was, they started a fire under the kettle. "Into this big kettle of boiling ash-lye," Simpson recorded, "we stirred in cracklin,"—fried out fats left over from hog killing. Old meat rinds, and any kind of fat that was not used to eat, were thrown into this hot boiling lye. She noted that "when the meat did not melt anymore we knew that there was enough fat in the lye to make soap" (Rawick 2: 231-33). The mixture was boiled down until it got "ropey." Next day, it was cut into chunks, placed on boards and put in the smoke house or attic to dry. If anybody wanted soft soap, they just didn't let it "cook" so long. Soft soap was jelly-like and looked like molasses. Simpson observed that "nobody had any other soap but home made soap, to wash, scrub or use on their bodies.... The soft soap was a little handier to use to boil the clothes with."

Simpson went on to record that "the ironing was done with hand-wrought flat irons" which were kept hot by setting them in front of the fireplace and heaping clean hot coals onto them (Rawick 2: 231-32). Before ironing, starch was applied to keep the fabrics stiff, fresh and smooth. According to Cynthia Erwing, slaves made the starch from dry peaches and roasted ears of corn which were scraped and then dried (Rawick 2:137).

Clothing in Freedom

Generally the tasks of producing and maintaining clothing were delegated to the female slave. Even after slavery, the African-American woman continued to make and maintain family clothing. Accounts show that obtaining sufficient clothing was considered more of a problem than having enough food to eat. Many ex-slaves stayed on the plantation for years after they were freed simply because freedom's uncertainties and insecurities were overwhelming. In the late nineteenth century many successful free slaves were employed in jobs which centered around clothing. They worked primarily as domestics, laundresses, dressmakers, or as seamstresses using skills they had learned in slavery. Many slaves and later freed African-American women became accomplished seamstresses. Some slaves had been able to obtain enough sewing work outside the plantation to allow them to save money to purchase their freedom. Elizabeth Keckley was one former slave who took advantage of her exceptional dressmaking and tailoring skills to obtain freedom for herself and her son. She set up shop in Washington, D.C. and had clients such as Mrs. Jefferson Davis and Mrs. Stephen Douglas. Keckley became very well known among the elite of Washington and subsequently she met Mary Todd Lincoln. Keckley became the personal modiste for Mrs. Lincoln. She designed and constructed gowns especially to flatter Mrs. Lincoln. Keckley's story is recorded in her autobiography, *Behind the Scenes*.

The assimilation into the American way of life continued to progress as African-Americans gained more self-confidence and improved their social and economic conditions. Their clothing behavior began to reveal these improvements and to reflect some of the seemingly lost African style. It is obvious that even without outward, visible support for the African cultural values, traditions and clothing styles, apparel designs emerged that were characteristically African. The African influence on style can only be explained by the assumption that slaves passed on their African culture from generation to generation through stories and music. In more recent years, knowledge of African cultural heritage has become readily available to guide African-Americans in making decisions about dress and individual style which reflects this heritage.[2]

Conclusion

The struggle for clothing identity actually began at the point where African-Americans were transported to America as involuntary immigrants. They were not allowed to bring with them their clothing or other important symbols of

African culture. They became immersed in slavery without the comfort of personal possessions from their homelands.

Although it has been left out of most textbooks, it is important to be knowledgeable about the history of slaves, for it is a part of the total picture of the history of the United States. To locate valid information, one must seek out primary sources such as slave narratives and official records and documents. The slave narratives, biographies and autobiographies provide commentary on the desperate marginality of life experienced by slaves during the nineteenth century. "The slave narratives are the Blues in prose. They are the honest records of the slave experience written by those who suffered under the system" (Bayliss 9).

Work is being carried out to fill the gap in our knowledge of the history of African-American dress. Mrs. Lois K. Alexander has been a pioneer in the effort to identify and save the fashion and apparel which was worn, designed, or made by African-Americans. She is the founder of the Harlem Institute of Fashion and the Black Fashion Museum in Harlem, New York. She received a grant from the National Endowment of the Arts to establish this museum as a monument to African-American fashion and apparel and has taken steps to establish a branch of the museum in Washington, D.C. In a personal interview, Mrs. Alexander stated that her efforts to locate and retrieve nineteenth century and early twentieth century articles of value has been a longstanding effort. There are very few known extant nineteenth-century items of apparel designed and made by African Americans.

Notes

[1]While the literature on slave dress is sparse, recent works are enlightening. See Kidwell, Starke, Tandberg, and Wares.

[2]Afro-centric products are becoming more readily available as individuals, like entrepreneur Barry Austin, open stores selling African products (Hunter-Gadsen).

Works Cited

Alexander, Lois. Personal Interview. *The Black Fashion Museum*. New York City, 1981.

Aunt Sally. *Aunt Sally or The Cross the Way to Freedom*. Cincinnati: American Reform Tract and Book Society, 1858.

Ball, Charles. Slavery in the United States. New York: Negro UP, 1849.

Bayliss, John F., ed. *Black Slave Narratives*. New York: The Macmillan Company, 1970.

Botkin, Benjamin A. *Lay My Burden Down:* A Folk History of Slavery. Chicago: The U of Chicago P, 1954.

Douglas, Frederick. *Life and Times of Frederick Douglas*. New York: Pathway Press, 1941.

Hughes, Louis. *Thirty Years a Slave*. Milwaukee: Southside Printing Co., 1897.

Hunter-Gadsen, Leslie. "Marketing the Motherland." *Black Enterprise*, 21. 5 (1990): 76-82.

Keckley, Elizabeth H. *Behind the Scenes or Thirty Years a Slave and Four Years in the White House*. New York: G. W. Carleton & Co., 1868.

Kidwell, Claudia. "Short Gowns." *Dress The Journal of the Costume Society of America*, 4 (1978): 30-58.

Ordonez, Margaret Thompson. "A Frontier Reflected in Costume, Tallahassee, Leon County, Florida: 1824-1861." Diss. Kansas State U, 1978. Ann Arbor: UMI, 1978. 78-15474.

Parks, Lillian Rogers. Personal Interview. Washington, D.C., 1989.

Rawick, George, ed. *The American Slave: A Composite Autobiography*. Supplement Series. Westport, Connecticut: Greenwood Publishing Company, 1972, 1977.

Stampp, Kenneth M. *The Peculiar Institution: Slavery in the Antebellum South*. New York: Alfred A, Knopf, 1956.

Starke, Barbara M. "A Mini View of the Microenvironment of Slaves and Freed Blacks Living in the Virginia and Maryland Areas from the 17th through the 19th Centuries." *Negro History Bulletin*, 41. 5 (1987): 878.

Starke, Barbara M., Lillian Holloman and Barbara Nordquist. *African American Dress and Adornment: A Cultural Perspective*. Dubuque, Iowa: Kendall Hunt Publishing Co., 1990.

Stewart, Austin. *Twenty-two Years a Slave and Forty Years a Freeman*. Reading, Mass.: Addison-Wesley Publishing Co., 1969.

Tandberg, Gerilyn G. "Field Hand Clothing in Louisiana and Mississippi During the Ante Bellum Period." *Dress The Journal of Costume Society of American* 6 (1980): 89-103.

Wares, Lydia Jean. "Dress of the African American Woman in Slavery and in Freedom: 1500 to 1935." Diss. Purdue U, 1981. Ann Arbor: UMI, 1981. 8210269.

The American Cowboy:
Development of the Mythic Image

Laurel Wilson

No segment of the landscape has captured the imagination of artists and writers as much as the American West or one of its principal characters, the cowboy. We all recognize this heroic figure by his dress: chaps, boots with spurs, wide-brimmed hat, bandanna, and the revolver in the holster at his hip. Today this dress is central to the characterization of cowboys on screen, in plays, and to many practicing cowboys. Although the image is clear to us, it bears only a little resemblance to the original working dress of cowboys in the American west. Clothing recognized as cowboy dress today is much more "showy" than that worn by the cowboys portrayed in photographs taken during the open-range eras of the late nineteenth century (Wilson 57-58). This stereotypical image is a composite which owes its form to the nature of the work, the environment in which the work was done, and to tradition. Changing attitudes toward the west and changing settlement patterns during the 1880s and 1890s also contributed to the changing image of the American cowboy as he was depicted on stage, in literature, and in art. It was during this time that the Wild West shows were most active in displaying the dominant players in the development of the west to eastern and European audiences; and it was when the stereotypical image of cowboy dress emerged. A newspaper reporter wrote in May 1892, "in presenting their rough picture of `a history almost passed away, they [those in the wild west show] have done some moiety of good in simplifying the work of the historian, the romancer, the painter, and the student of the future, and in exemplifying in themselves and their experiences..." (Buffalo Bill Scrapbooks n.pag.). As can be seen by this quote, Buffalo Bill's Wild West[1] captured the imagination of the public and the images the show presented became what the public expected as the "true" images of the participants in the development of the west.

Source of Cowboy Dress

As early as 1521, the Spanish brought cattle and the horses needed to herd them to the North American west (Dobie 3). Their descendants practiced large scale cattle ranching in the American southwest and California. It was not until the late 1840s that Anglo-Texans began cattle raising in the Mexican ranchero style (Dobie 80). There appears to be little doubt that some of the more stereotypical garments worn by American cowboys had their origins in Spanish North America as many of the names of these items are of Spanish derivation (Bishko 507). Garments which originated in Spain or Hispanic America were adopted and adapted to suit different climates and cultural needs determined in part by the nature of the work and by tradition.

The most visible of what became stereotypical cowboy garb were the shotgun chaps which were based on the chaparejos worn by the Mexican vaqueros (Dary 45). The shotgun chaps were leather leggings that usually fastened at the sides. Boots and spurs were a necessary part of the costume of both the vaquero and the cowboy. Mexican spurs used by vaqueros were also available to Montana cowboys by 1882 (*Yellowstone Journal,* Advertisement n.pag.).

Differences between the dress of the vaquero and the American cowboy were evident in their hats. The hats worn by the Vaqueros tended to have very wide brims which were decorated with braid trims while those of their Anglo counterparts had narrower brims and were plain. Another aspect of dress which distinguished the vaquero from the Anglo cowboy was in the wearing of a sash which originated in Spanish dress (Bishko 507). While the sash was originally part of the American cowboy image, most Anglo cowboys abandoned it by 1900.[2] Another distinguishing feature of American cowboy dress was the bandanna, which was not included in vaquero dress. In America, a bandanna worn at the neck had long been part of working men's dress.

The Changing Opinions About the West

The changes in cowboy dress from that exhibiting Spanish characteristics to that which was perceived as being purely Anglo reflected more than a simple reaction to change in environmental conditions. These changes were also affected by the attitudes of eastern Americans toward the west and those who inhabited it. Early opinions of the west were negative. Unfavorable views were based on prejudices of easterners who had been there, or heard about it. Many easterners believed that the "great plains," a major cattle raising region, was nothing but "the great American desert," and, as such, was a barrier to more desirable lands farther west. Government sponsored expeditions like that of Stephen Long in 1819 did little to dispel that image (Rotella 20-35). The inhabitants of much of the west during this period were American Indians and people of Spanish descent, also considered if not dangerous, of little worth. The opinion of easterners toward Indians is reflected in the diary entry of Adam Mercer Brown who crossed the great plains in 1850. He wrote "These Indians are decidedly a dissipated and debased people, having acquired all of the vices and none of the virtues of the whites" (Kiefer 18). Francis Parkman wrote in 1849 that "the human race in this part of the world [the west] is separated into three divisions, arranged in the order of their merits: white men, Indians, and Mexicans; to the latter of who the honorable title of 'whites' is by no means conceded" (deBuys 101). Both of these groups were seen as benign until they were viewed as obstacles to the manifest destiny of a United States that stretched from sea to sea.[3]

While Anglo cowboys were not an ethnic minority, early opinion of them was that they, too, had little merit. Indeed, the cattle herders who trailed the cattle from Texas to the railheads were considered ruffians rather than the heros they later portrayed (Taylor 64). Often this reputation was well deserved for, after the cattle were delivered to their destination, the cowboys had a "little fun" by drinking until they were nearly insensible and then shooting up the town. A Fort Benton, Montana newspaper of 1880 reported, "For some time the herders on the Snake River, commonly known as cow-boys, have been emulating the deeds of their kind in Texas and have established a reign of terror in the towns where they meet or pass through on their drives and are as desperate and reckless marauders as ever infested any country" (*River Press* n.pag.). Understandably, townspeople were very glad to see them leave. The view of cowboys as ruffians or villains was also apparent in the early dime novels (Taylor 66).

It was Richard Henry Dana (1840), in his book *Two Years Before the Mast*, who helped to dispel the idea of the west as being a worthless place by describing California as a fruitful land which needed only an industrious population to show its worth (72-73, 79-87). Once these western lands were seen as a useful means to expand political and economic influence of the United States, a concerted effort was made to bring them under the direct control of white Americans with very little concern about what happened to those who already lived there.

Attitudes toward the southern plains were also changing as Americans began to establish settlements in Texas during the 1820s and 1830s (Richardson et al. 54, 153). The admission of the Republic of Texas as the 28th State in 1846 began the push toward bringing the entire west, desert and all, into the union. The discovery of gold in California,[4] then subsequent gold strikes in other western territories, brought floods of gold seekers from the east. While a great number of those who rushed to the west to seek their fortunes returned to the east, many also stayed on to pursue other professions. Cattle raising, however, remained a small scale operation until after the Civil War when it expanded northward reaching Montana in the 1870s. For ranching to expand, railroads first had to be built to the Midwest, then to the far west, so cattle could be transported to markets in the eastern United States (Dary 168-97; Fletcher 45).

The creation of a mythic west was aided in part by artists whose paintings presented a splendid, awesome vision, in which nature appeared to overpower human efforts toward control (Anderson 237-284). Such a landscape would surely require superhuman effort to tame it. Popular journalism of the late 19th century portrayed the west as "a mythic region whose wildness made it at once a region of darkness and an earthly paradise...whose hidden magic was to be tapped only by self-reliant individualists, capable of enduring the lonesome reach..." (Slotkin 11).

When easterners viewed these works of art and read the accounts of journalists, they could easily envision the cowboy as a stalwart hero who had the power to tame this great landscape. Easterners undoubtedly imagined the people who worked the land to be as heroic as the land was tough. This vision was shared by Frederick Jackson Turner who said in 1893 that the frontier was important for "keeping alive the power of resistance to aggression, and developing the stalwart and rugged qualities of the frontiersman" (15). The idea that taming the west required extraordinary abilities was perpetuated by novelists and those who produced the melodramas. Their cowboys were the Turner frontiersmen for they were both stalwart and rugged.

The first cowboy heros appeared in print in the early 1870s, two decades before Turner presented his frontier thesis to the American public (Taylor 66). The covers of these novels show cowboys whose clothing shows the Mexican vaquero influence by means of the sash, the style of pants, and the short jacket. It was about this time that the first cowboys appeared on stage in the Buntline melodrama "Scouts of the Prairie, or Red Deviltry As It Is" starring "Texas Jack" whose attire sometimes included buckskin trousers (Taylor 65-66). These melodramas spawned new dime novels making "Texas Jack" the hero, helping to change the disreputable image of the American cowboy.

While artists, writers, and journalists all had an impact on creating a mythic image of the American west and its principal figure, the cowboy, it was Buffalo Bill's Wild West that captured the imagination of the public. In the minds of the public, the images the show presented became the "true" picture of how the participants in the development of the American west looked. Indeed, in 1883, Buffalo Bill Cody brought actual westerners, including cowboys, to public view with his show (Amon Carter Museum of Western Art 7). A London reporter for *Eve* wrote in June 1892, "These Wild West people are no mimics—they represent no one but themselves. They are the very people who have helped to make history—the very pioneers of civilization..." (Buffalo Bill Scrapbooks n.pag.). This show consisted of a series of events, presented in no particular order, which had dramatic impact but no particular plot. Buffalo Bill's Wild West included characters and events he considered emblematic of the west. As a program from 1885 stated:

Hon. William F. Cody ('Buffalo Bill'), in conjunction with Mr. Nate Salsbury, the eminent American actor (a ranch owner), has organized a large encampment; the cowboys and vaqueros; the herds of buffalo and elk; the lassoing of animals; the manner of robbing mail coaches; feats of agility, horsemanship, marksmanship, archery, and the kindred scenes and events that are characteristic of the border (n.pag.).

Of course among the central figures were cowboys. A photograph (Fig. 1), taken in 1884, shows a group of men who were the cowboys who participated in the first shows. As can be seen in the photograph, there was a wide variety in the form of dress worn by the cowboys. The two men with Spanish surnames were from San Antonio and of Spanish descent but were American cowboys. Yet, Antonio Esquival, second from the right, was wearing a serape showing a Spanish influence. While his brother, Joe Esquival, standing at the far left, was wearing what is now considered more typical American cowboy dress. Johnny Baker, left front, wore clothing which is very different from what we would describe as typical cowboy clothing. By 1885, when Mexican vaqueros were added to the show, at least some differentiation was made between the dress of American "cow-boys" and the Mexicans. The show program explained:

In their work, the methods of the two are similar; and to a certain extent, the same is true of their associations. Your genuine vaquero, however, is generally, when off duty, more of a dandy in the style and get-up of his attire than his careless and impetuous compeer. He is fond of gaudy clothes, and when you see him riding well mounted into a frontier town, the first thought of an Eastern man is that a circus has broken loose in the neighborhood, and this is one of the performers. The familiar broad-brimmed sombrero covers his head; a rich jacket, embroidered by his sweetheart perhaps, envelopes his

Johnny Baker.

Fig. 1. Group of Cowboys with Buffalo Bill's Wild West, 1884. Standing left to right: Joe Esquival, Jim Kid, Jim Mitchell, Dick Johnson, Billy Bullock, Antonio Esquival, Tom Duffy. Lying in front, left to right: Johnny Baker and Billy Johnson. Courtesy, Buffalo Bill Memorial Museum, Denver Parks and Recreation Department, Denver, Colorado.

shapely shoulders; a sash of blue or red silk is wrapped around his waist, from which protrudes a pair of revolvers; and buckskin trowsers, slit from the knee to the foot and ornamented with rows of brass or silver buttons, complete his attire, save that enormous spurs, with jingling pendants, are fastened to the boots, and announce in no uncertain sound the presence of the beau-ideal vaquero in full dress. (*Buffalo Bill's Wild West Program* n.pag.).

The clothing of the Anglo-cowboys pictured in the program, however, continued to exhibit some Spanish characteristics. In one illustration, a cowboy, dressed in full-legged trousers which were tucked into the knee-high boots, was pictured wearing a sash around his waist. All three cowboys in the illustration were dressed in short jackets typical of Mexican dress. A Wyoming cowboy, Jim Kid, pictured in the same program, was wearing "woolies" and thus comes closer to resembling what the cowboy image came to be (*Buffalo Bill's Wild West Program* n.pag.). Inconsistencies in the Anglo cowboy images indicate that, at this time (1884-1885), the image of how the cowboy should appear was still developing.

It is significant that during this period cattle ranches were only beginning to become established on the northern plains, once considered the great American desert. The weather and terrain of the northern plains required changes in traditional cowboy dress. The vaquero and the cowboy of southern Texas needed leather chaparejos to protect themselves from the thorny brush of the southwest. Although in the treeless southern plains chaps were not needed, the tradition of cowboy dress was firmly established and most cowboys owned chaps even if worn only for the photographer (Erickson, K. C. 3). Cowboys in the northern plains did not require protection from vegetation but they did need to shield themselves from the wind. While shotgun chaps served as fine windbreaks during the summer, they were inadequate for braving fierce winters. For warmth, then, cowboys adopted "woolies," which were chaps usually made of the hide of angora goats with the hair left on. The bandannas which became an expected part of cowboy costume were not only a traditional part of workmen's dress, but a necessity during the trail drives when the thousands of cattle crushed vegetation and raised huge clouds of dust. A bandanna worn over the mouth and nose would have afforded at least some protection. Even though revolvers are considered a traditional part of cowboy costume, there is little evidence that they were part of the working cowboys' gear (Taylor 22).[5] The most common use for guns appears to have been in terrorizing the citizens at trail's end. However, nearly every photographed cowboy posed for posterity with at least some form of firearm, preferably a revolver (Wilson 52-53, 56).

The decorative elements which appeared on dress worn by the acting cowboys of the Wild West show of 1884 did not appear in the dress of the working cowboys. It is not surprising that an encounter between an easterner and an actual working cowboy was a disappointing experience on the part of the easterner, who expected to see the version he had read about or seen on stage. Edwin Trafton, reporting on a trip he made to Wyoming in 1885 for *Frank Leslie's Popular Monthly*, wrote:

A grotesque result of every man being his own tailor, I saw illustrated at Durbin's horse ranch, on the Poison Spider Creek, where one of the cowboys wore a pair of black doeskin trowsers, the worn-out seat of which was covered with a generous expanse of white bagging with the trade mark of the mill standing out distinct and clear (427).

The cowboys themselves helped to create the image which eventually appeared on stage. Rather than posing for photographs in clothing they actually wore while doing their work, they dressed in garb they knew would be recognized as cowboy dress, that is large hats, bandannas, revolvers in holsters, chaps, boots, and spurs (Wilson 56-57). While many of these articles of clothing were used on the job part of the time, the photographic evidence indicates that the revolvers, bandannas, and chaps were used only occasionally. Yet it was these very items that made the cowboys distinct from other men who also did their work outdoors. The importance of these cowboy trappings can be illustrated by a quote that D.J. O'Malley wrote on the back of a studio photograph of himself, "I was a pretty proud kid when I had this picture taken. I had just begun with the N-N [N bar N ranch] as a horse wrangler, and was wearing my first pair of chaps and also my first six-shooter and it was a bone handled one too" (O'Malley Collection). O'Malley, like most of the cowboys pictured in studio photographs, was young. Older cowboys, seemingly, did not have studio photographs taken of themselves dressed in cowboy gear (*United States Population Census Schedule of Montana*).

As stated previously, the image of the "old" west was romanticized by artists who painted pictures of cowboy, soldier and Indian battles (Nemerov 285-339). Cowboy heros in the paintings, completed in the late 19th and early 20th centuries by artists such as Russell and Remington were very definitely wearing clothing that could only be interpreted as American dress rather than as Mexican dress. The American dress form also reflected the popular images of cowboys including bandannas, leather and "woolie" chaps, and buckskin jackets with fringed sleeves.

Buffalo Bill's Wild West probably would not have sold as many tickets if cowboys were portrayed in the dress they actually wore while working on the range. In the early years cowboys in Cody's show wore clothing that could be identified as cowboy or vaquero dress but which showed no unified theme. Items of dress were taken from vaquero costume and by the 1890s other elements were added, forming an image that reflected changes made by the northern plains cowboy, differentiating him very clearly from the Mexican vaquero who also appeared in the shows. By the turn of the century when the free-range cowboy had all but disappeared, the Wild West cowboy looked distinctly Anglo by wearing the clothing used on the northern plains (Fig. 2). Few of the characteristics seen in the Wild West of 1884 were retained to make up this new image.

This real difference between the dress of the performing cowboy and working cowboy was quite apparent, especially to the celebrated cowboy artist, Charlie Russell. In 1915, Russell illustrated a letter with pictures of two cowboys. One image was of a man on horseback, clad in a flat brimmed hat, drab bandanna, white shirt, pants with rolled pant-legs, boots, and spurs. He was pictured wearing a pistol, but it was in a holster. The saddle he was riding was plain and the bridle on the ambling horse was strictly utilitarian. Over this illustration Russell wrote:

> This species is almost extinct but he once ranged from the timber river in the east to shores of the Pacific from Mexico north to snow bound lands. He knew horses and could tell you what a cow said to her calf. The floor of his home was the prairie the sky his roof which often leaked. His gift of God was health and he generly [sic] chashed [sic] in with his boots as he was only part human but always liked animals (Foxley 135).

The other image was of a cowboy wearing a broad-brimmed hat with a rolled brim, a very large, bright red bandanna, and very wooly "woolies." He also carried a pistol but was pictured firing it into the air. His boots and spurs cannot be seen because of the extremely large tapajeros on the stirrups. The running horse was wearing a breast strap decked in silver and the bridle was decorated similarly. The notation over this drawing said, "This kind I don't know. He's not down in natural history." (Foxley 135).

Charlie Russell himself was photographed (Fig. 3) in a cowboy costume that resembled clothing worn by Buffalo Bill, Wild West hero (Fig. 4). Charlie's coat was a buckskin leather jacket, decorated with fringes at the sleeve and with beaded flowers decorating the front. Russell arrived in Montana in 1880, but having grown up in St. Louis he certainly could have seen some of the

Fig. 2. Group of Buffalo Bill's Wild West Cowboys, Paris, France, 1905. Courtesy of the State Historical Society of Colorado, Denver, Colorado.

Buntline stage productions. One biographer wrote that he read the Buntline dime novels, which could have possibly formed an idea of appropriate dress to be worn by a person who lived in the wild west (Adams & Britzman 18). Russell was also an admirer of the Indians and trappers of the west. For his rendition of appropriate dress, Charlie combined elements from several of these groups. His sash was Canadian French in origin but was similar to those worn by Mexican vaqueros. His jacket was a "scout" type like that worn by Buffalo Bill. His leather chaps were acquired from the Carr estate after his cowboy friend Childs Carr died in an accident in 1882 (Adams & Britzman 70). In an earlier picture taken shortly after he began the cowboy life, he was wearing a pair of dark "woolies" (Adams & Britzman 32).⁶

Charlie Russell took part in the creation of the "unnatural" cowboy he described. The image had been created in part by cowboys themselves and was successfully promoted by Buffalo Bill's Wild West. It has been this image we have come to recognize as the "real" cowboy, and we are disappointed when the men who still work cattle in the west do not bear this likeness.

Notes

¹While Buffalo Bill's Wild West was a wild west show, it was simply called Buffalo Bill's Wild West by the participants and front men who advertised the show.

²One notable exception was C.M. Russell, Montana cowboy artist. He wrote of his sashes, "I have all ways worn one and like them better than a belt. I believe they keep me from having a big belly all breeds usto ware them Mex french lots of people in Quebeck ware them. I saw men in france waring them all that I saw [were] all silk Italians ware" (Dear n.pag.).

³For a complete explanation of manifest destiny see: Merk, Frederick. *Manifest Destiny and Mission in American History: A Reinterpretation.* New York: Vintage Books, 1963.

⁴California was declared a portion of the United States on July 7, 1849 and then became a State in 1850 as part of the compromise of 1850 (Bean 102, 125).

⁵Webb wrote that the six-shooter was a necessary part of the equipment of cowboys who worked very wild longhorns. He recounted an incident in which a cowboy, pinned under his fallen horse, pulled his revolver and shot the charging steer before it could reach him with its lethal horns (298). Once more docile breeds dominated cattle herds, guns were no longer needed for protection.

⁶None of the sources consulted knew of the source of these chaps. It is probable they were borrowed from another cowboy or were the photographer's property (Dear, telephone interview; Adam & Britzman).

Fig. 3. Charles M. Russell and his horse "Monte," early 1880s, Towner and Runsten, Photographer. Courtesy of Montana Historical Society, Helena, Montana.

Fig. 4. Flamboyant Fraternity, c. 1873. Left to right: Elisha Greene, Wild Bill Hickok, Buffalo Bill Cody, Texas Jack Omohundro, Eugene Overton. Courtesy Buffalo Bill Historical Center, Cody, Wyoming.

Works Cited

Adams, Ramon and Homer E. Britzman. *Charles M. Russell: The Cowboy Artist.* Pasadena, CA: Trail's End Publishing Co., Inc., 1948.

Advertisements. *Yellowstone Journal.* Miles City, Montana, January-May 1882.

Anderson, Nancy. " 'The Kiss of Enterprise': The Western Landscape as Symbol and Resource." *West as America.* Ed. William H. Truettner. Washington: Smithsonian Institution Press. 1991. 237-283.

Bean, Walton. *California: An Interpretive History.* New York: McGraw-Hill Book Company, 1968.

Bishko, Charles Julian. "The Peninsular Background of Latin American Cattle Ranching." *The Hispanic American Historical Review,* 32.4 (1952): 491-515.

Buffalo Bill Wild West Collection. Buffalo Bill Historical Center, Cody, Wyoming.

Buffalo Bill's Wild West Program. Hartford, CT: The Calhoun Printing Company, 1885.

Cody Scrapbooks, Buffalo Bill Historical Center, Cody, Wyoming.

Dana, Richard Henry. *Two Years Before the Mast.* 1840. New York: Scott, Foresman and Company, 1914.

Dary, David. *Cowboy Culture: A Saga of Five Centuries.* Lawrence, KA: University Press of Kansas, 1989.

Dear, Elizabeth A. "I Can Tell by Your Outfit...CMR's Sashes." Unpublished essay, n.d.
_____ Telephone interview. 18 June 1992.

deBuys, William. *The Life and Hard Times of a New Mexico Mountain Range.* Albuquerque: University of New Mexico Press, 1985.

Dobie, J. Frank. *The Longhorns.* Austin: University of Texas Press, 1987.

Erickson, J.R. *The Modern Cowboy.* Lincoln: University of Nebraska Press, 1981.

Erickson, Kenneth C. "Hats and Boots: Some Regional and Temporal Aspects of the Cowboy Complex as Seen in the Photographic Record." *Wyoming Contributions to Anthropology.* Laramie: University of Wyoming, 1978.

Fletcher, Robert H. *Free Grass to Fences.* New York: University Publishers Incorporated, 1960.

Foxley, William C. *Frontier Spirit.* Denver, CO: Museum of Western Art, 1983.

Kiefer, David M. "Over Barren Plains and Rock-Bound Mountains." *Montana the Magazine of Western History* 12.4 (1972): 16-29.

Merk, Frederick. *Manifest Destiny and Mission in American History: A Reinterpretation.* New York: Vintage Books, 1963.

Nemerov, Alex. "Doing the 'Old America': The Image of the American West, 1880-1920." *West as America.* Ed. William H. Truettner. Washington: Smithsonian Institution Press, 1991. 285-343.

O'Malley Collection. Montana State Historical Society Manuscript Collection, Helena, Montana, n.d.

Richardson, Rupert, Ernest Wallace, and Adrian Anderson. *Texas: The Lone Star State.* Englewood Cliffs, NJ: Prentice Hall, 1988.

94 Dress in American Culture

River Press. Fort Benton, Montana, 17 November 1880.

Rotella, Carlo. "Travels in a Subjective West." *Montana*, 41.4 (1991): 20-34.

Slotkin, Richard. *The Fatal Environment*. Middletown, CT: Wesleyan University Press, 1985.

Taylor, Lonn. "The Open-Range Cowboy of the Nineteenth Century." *The American Cowboy*. Eds. Taylor, Lonn & Marr, Ingrid. Washington, DC: Library of Congress, 1983, 16-28.

_____. "The Cowboy Hero: An American Myth Examined." *The American Cowboy*. Ed. Lonn Taylor & Ingrid Marr. Washington, DC: Library of Congress, 1983, 62-80.

Trafton, Edwin. "Wyoming on Broncho-Back." *Frank Leslie's Popular Monthly*, 20.4 (October 1885): 423-431.

Turner, Frederick J. "Significance of the Frontier in American History." *Annual Report of the American Historical Association for the Year 1893*, 1-38.

Tyler, Ronnie C., ed. *The Wild West*. Fort Worth: Amon Carter Museum of Western Art, 1970.

United States. Bureau of Statistics. *United States Census of Population*. Washington: United States Printing Office, 1880.

Webb, Walter Prescott. "The Cattle Kingdom." *The Cowboy Reader*. Eds. Lon Tinkle and Allen Maxwell. New York: Longmans, Green and Company, 1959. 293-307.

Wilson, Laurel. " 'I was a pretty proud kid': An interpretation of differences in posed and unposed photographs of Montana cowboys." *Clothing and Textiles Research Journal*, 9.3 (1991): 49-58.

From Folk To Fashion:
Dress Adaptations of Norwegian
Immigrant Women in the Midwest

Patricia Williams

Introduction

An outward sign of an immigrant's desire to belong to America may be seen in the rapid transition which was made from folk costume to American fashions. Although they preserved their heritage in language, traditional holiday foods and the Lutheran religion, rural Norwegian immigrants quickly adopted American clothing styles for all occasions. From the middle nineteenth to early twentieth centuries, this clothing transition was often eased by incorporating subtle characteristics of Norwegian national dress into current American fashion. Social factors involving clothing choices among the immigrants, the demise of Norwegian details after the turn of the twentieth century, and the renewed interest in wearing folk costume among the descendants of the immigrants will be examined in this essay.

Nineteenth Century Norwegians in America

A. P. Dennis, in his 1930 report on the history of the Norwegian people, noted that it was their fate to conquer and be absorbed by alien peoples (31). Scandinavians have been invading and settling diverse areas of Europe since Viking times, giving one of their tribal names, Rus, to the country of Russia. Throughout history, Scandinavians could be found serving as palace guards in the Byzantine Empire, ruling Kiev, and conquering Sicily. In France they became Normans, in England, Saxons; they became Scotsmen in the Orkney Islands and Tuscans in Northern Italy. In America, Norwegians successfully assimilated into all levels of society but preserved a strong cultural identity for over 150 years while contributing fully to the general culture of America.

In 1825, a group of Norwegians sailed to the United States aboard a small vessel called *The Resurrection*. The three-month journey was the beginning of a flow of emigration which would bring 2 1/2 million Norwegians to America.

95

During the period 1861-1890, one-fifth of the population of Norway left for the United States. In proportion to its population, no other country except Ireland gave America more citizens. Between 1838 and 1865, Wisconsin was the major focus of settlement. Olaf Norlie, in his *History of the Norwegian People in America*, states that by 1890 every state in the union had Norwegian immigrants, Minnesota leading the top four which included Wisconsin, Illinois and Iowa.

In areas of heavy Nordic settlement, early arrivals continued to live as they had in Norway, regarding English as a foreign language. However, they soon learned that communication with Yankee neighbors was the essential key to economic survival. The Germanic roots of English and the Scandinavian languages gave them an advantage of similarity in vocabulary and word structure, making the linguistic transition easier for them than for immigrants from eastern or southern Europe.

Clothing on the Frontier

After language, the greatest immediate cultural barrier to assimilation was dress. Letters offering advice to those about to leave Norway frequently mention the need to conform to American standards: "A newcomer can immediately be detected by his garb and since newcomers are regarded with very little esteem, all of them proceed at once to buy clothes of an American cut"(Fapso 30). An 1884 diarist in Illinois reports that clothing was also sold by the immigrants, who had plenty of land but often lacked basic necessities: "Some of the finest (ethnic) clothes were sold for the money ... to buy necessities like beef and pork, since such fine clothes were of no use to people of the working class; they need things that are more durable" (Blegen 177). Sturdy work wear, like sheepskin coats and heavy woolen pants, were brought from Norway since such items were necessary for cold northern winters and were unavailable on the frontier. Most colorful festive dress was left behind: "The women had better take as few of their clothes with them as possible, since they won't do here in America at all. Women's clothes are entirely different here" (Blegen 176). The advice was followed almost without exception; what was viewed as an anomaly was noted sometime between 1853-1857: "Ingrid, a pretty, brisk peasant woman, has continued to wear a part of her national costume" (Blegen 180).

As time went on, Blegen states that the tone of American letters changed with reference to Norwegian clothing. Lack of quality goods and limited choices in rural areas contributed to the feeling that American-made clothing was inferior. Wool and linen were the preferred fabrics but American wool was regarded as low grade and linen seldom available. Claims that American clothes wore out in a single summer were followed by the statement, "Ragged Yankees are therefore a very common sight." In 1863, a farmer's wife passed along the following advice to her family in Norway:

> No one emigrating from Norway ought to sell everything he has, the way the majority do because everything that is useful in Norway is also useful here. Women could well bring their clothes with them, with the exception of their headdress, bodices, jackets and kerchiefs—those they might as well sell—but their other clothes can be made over and used here, for Norwegian things are much better than anything you can buy here (Blegen 177-78).

Except in larger cities, most women's clothing continued to be drab and utilitarian. Manufactured cotton gradually replaced homespun and immigrants purchased sewing machines shortly after they came on the market. "Mother Hubbard" wrappers of gingham, calico, and percale, using ready-made patterns, were the usual daily wear.

Economic factors and the physical isolation of rural dwellers played a part in the continuing lack of stylish American clothing. Equally responsible for the restraint in fashion was the deep strain of puritanism which characterized much of immigrant religious belief. Those who were influenced by pietist preachers believed that the plainer the costume, the more pleasing to the Almighty.

Conflicting Impulses

Hans Nielsen Hauge was a late eighteenth to early nineteenth century Lutheran reformer who had awakened interest in a low-church movement in Norway. Hauge espoused ideals of pietism and the rightness of lay preaching which caused a religious revival among the common people. His disciple, Elling Eielsen, a lay preacher, traveled and evangelized incessantly throughout the country. Emigration was frowned upon by the Norwegian church which refused at first to send ordained state ministers to the new world. Eielsen, filled with missionary zeal and in search of new frontiers, left Norway in 1839 to evangelize the Norwegian immigrants in America.

After he arrived, Eielsen charged that Norwegian immigrants were the most indifferent to religion of all immigrants, and blamed it on drinking and dancing. Those who shared Eielsen's viewpoint supported temperance, disapproved of the theater, dances, card-playing and display in dress. Such practices, springing as they did from cultural conditioning, were not disapproved in Norway where weddings, baptisms, and even funerals were occasions for elaborate costume, dancing and moderate drinking by all, including the clergy. There, the pietist movement was primarily one of the common people against the aristocracy and did not challenge the church's tolerant attitude toward popular culture. In contrast, the acceptance of evangelical religion on the frontier was a response to the insecurity and loneliness of frontier life. The conversion experience enabled people to go back to their farms and focus on a future life rather than on the physical conditions which surrounded life on earth (Hague 109).

In America, church discipline continued to become more strict and social pleasures brought from the Old World fell under the ban. Ultimately, the immigrant churches adopted much of the New England atmosphere. In some settlements older women wore Shaker bonnets which had no "sinful taint," while younger women wanted something different, which proved their "sinful inclinations." They had "outpuritaned the puritanism of New Englanders." Recollections by an Iowa pioneer included comments about women's appearance:

Our women were rarely beautiful. What they might have been, with greater care given to the needs of the body and the selection of clothing, cannot be known; but economic and religious ideals forbade much attention to these matters.... We believed with the preacher that all is vanity (Blegen 181).

Norway to America: The Changing Wedding Tradition

The Norwegian pioneers and their children faced a confusing breakdown of traditional ways in the transition from Norway's settled valleys to frontier conditions in America. One of the changes involved marriage celebrations. To understand how they adapted to the differences, it is necessary to briefly explore the traditions they left behind.

Weddings in rural Norway could last many days, accompanied by feasting, music, dancing and the use of intricately embroidered folk costume. Accessories for the bride included an elaborate crown or *kranse* symbolizing virginity, a belt with streamers indicating married status and many silver brooches or *solje*, covered with spoon-like dangles. These items appeared in a variety of forms depending on the local style, but were worn by all classes. When the family was unable to provide jewelry and a crown, they could be rented from a local silversmith or the church.

Bridal accessories are included in European traditions which reach back to antiquity and were widespread among both Nordic and Slavic people. Virgin brides, thought to be particularly vulnerable to the workings of harmful spirits, were protected by reflective objects like the silver dangles on Norwegian jewelry. Shiny metal or mirror-like surfaces were believed to cause confusion among evil forces (Hammerton 354). The crown has roots in neolithic times and was connected with goddess worship (Gimbutus 275). After Christianity was introduced, pagan customs were adapted to the new religion. The crown became associated with the Virgin Mary as Queen of Heaven and symbolized chastity. The earliest extant bridal crowns in Norway are thought to have once been used in the practice of adorning the image of the Madonna with an actual crown during the pre-Reformation Period (Nelson 21).

At the time of the emigrations to America, bridal customs were still prevalent among rural people in Norway, but the original meanings had been forgotten. A family biographer relates that her grandmother, before emigrating to America, sold two bridal crowns, one a precious old heirloom of silver and the other beaded (Blegen 187n.). An exquisite gold and silver crown, hung with dangles, was brought to America by an immigrant family and is now on display at Vesterheim Norwegian-American Museum in Decorah, Iowa.

Although their heritage included colorful weddings, Norwegian pioneer couples in America often had no accompanying festivities. Marriage was performed by a lay preacher or Justice of the Peace, with official church sanction occurring at a later date when clergymen arrived from Norway. Frontier settlements did not always have musicians, traditional foods were not available and festive costume had been left behind. Many immigrants had also fallen under the influence of the pietist movement in America which frowned upon festivity. Elizabeth Koren, a Norwegian minister's wife, after her husband had performed a wedding ceremony unaccompanied by any special celebrations, was said to have exclaimed, "Ugh! What a terrible way to be married!" (Blegen 220). Another Norwegian pastor's wife, in Scandinavia, Wisconsin, also responded to the difference. In June of 1857, Sophie Duus, who had been married in Norway three years earlier, "made a wreath of flowers and placed it over the bride's brow to represent the crown, or kranse, that was worn at weddings in Norway" (Rosholt 79).

A Return to Festivity

After the difficulties of pioneering had passed, special wedding celebrations returned, but folk costume was seldom worn. One exception can be noted in Odd S. Lovoll's book, *The Promise of America*, in which a North Dakota bridal couple appear in Hallingdal costume. However, it would be incorrect to conclude, on the basis of one photograph, that it was customary for immigrants to wear traditional dress in America for festive occasions. Many wedding photographs of immigrants exist but they show almost exclusive use of fashionable American dress.

Wedding celebrations never took on the flavor of the old Norwegian festivities, and they varied in degree of celebration. Letters to Norway from Wisconsin dated 1889 to 1904 relate, "They didn't have any wedding, as is the custom here, unless one absolutely wants to," "We had a nice little wedding," "We have been to three weddings this summer, big weddings." In a 1903 letter, the writer responds to a letter and photographs which she has received from Norway, "I see you had an old-style wedding .... the old ways are the best" (Zempel 111-24).

Black and white photographs cannot provide evidence of color, but green appears frequently in written references to wedding wear and in surviving examples worn by Norwegian-Americans. Green is considered unlucky as a wedding color in most countries, but there was no proscription in Norway (Hammerton 254). As a color with traditional backing, sentiment may have outweighed the popular American bias stated in the Victorian jingle: "Married in green, ashamed to be seen." Two dark green wool wedding bodices, dated 1895 and 1898, in the collection of the University of Wisconsin-Stevens Point, were worn by brides of Norwegian descent.

In 1854, Miss Ingeborg Listul charged the family account in the general store at Scandinavia, Wisconsin, $5.50 for a green Orleans dress. This represents a considerable expense, indicating a special occasion, likely her wedding (Rosholt 21). In comparison, the same store was selling whiskey for 13 cents a quart and linen for 10 cents a yard. (The account states that a dress was purchased but more probably she purchased the material for a dress.) Wearing an exceptional dress on the frontier was an event not soon forgotten, as a descendant of an early settler recalls: "The women never tired of describing mother's beautiful wedding dress of green and white striped delaine with garlands of roses" (Blegen 182).

Blegen states that in some pioneer groups it became the custom for the prospective bridegroom to buy material for the bride's dress and for the bride to make the groom's wedding shirt (220). Rather than originating in America, this custom is more likely traceable to Europe. Similar customs survived there well into the twentieth century.

In photographs from the 1870's onward, bodice details and belt streamers reminiscent of Norwegian folk wedding accessories appear. Floral crowns or wreaths were popular with and without veils. Many dress colors were used with light-colored ones frequently mistaken for white in old photographs. Before 1900, only the wealthy were able to afford an impractical white dress to be worn once. The flowing white veil and dark or middle-toned "best dress" became a practical compromise. One possible influence for the choice of wearing a veil and dark colored dress may be Queen Victoria, who by this time was never out of black widow's weeds worn with her magnificent white lace bridal veil. Photographs of the Queen in similar attire appeared in publications throughout the world on the occasion of her Golden Jubilee in 1887 and again for her Diamond Jubilee in 1897.

White wedding gowns were so uncommon in midwestern small towns that when the first one was worn in Stevens Point, Wisconsin, in 1883, the entire town came out to see the bride. The event was reported in full detail in the local newspaper, including a list of all gifts received. The bride was the daughter of Norwegian immigrants and she married an immigrant from Norway who had become a successful businessman.

Norwegian-Americans may have had a tradition-based reluctance to wear all-white for weddings. Just as green was acceptable in Norway for weddings, white carried an association with death. In some Norwegian districts women in mourning were enveloped from head to foot in white cloth, a custom still in use during the latter nineteenth century (Traetteberg 166).

After the turn of the century, changes in fashion simplified the construction and alteration of women's clothing. Home sewing became easier and was less expensive than employing a seamstress for fashionable wear, making a white wedding dress affordable for middle and working class brides. Many white wedding gowns exist in both museum and family collections from this period. In Norwegian-American writings and photographs, distinctive details setting them apart from mainstream fashion are no longer detectable.

The practical rural midwesterners found ways to wear white bridal gowns more than once. The family album of Inga and Morgan Torbenson yields a fascinating record of extended use. Married in 1914 in Iola, Wisconsin, their wedding photograph seems typical of the period: a seated bridal pair are surrounded by three couples, the women attendants all wearing different styles, not an uncommon occurrence at the time. Further inspection of the album revealed wedding photographs of the other three couples, two dated 1910 and one from 1913. The brides' dresses are those used in the 1914 Torbenson wedding party as bridesmaids gowns. Anna Fiane, one of the 1910 brides, is also photographed wearing her wedding gown on the occasion of her golden anniversary.

Issues of Assimilation

During the last quarter of the nineteenth century, early immigrants became concerned with the speed of acculturation and assimilation occurring among the newer arrivals (Figs. 1 and 2). Family groups had comprised the majority of immigrants during the pioneer period, but mass migrations in the 1870's to 1900 were composed of many young, often unmarried men and women. These later immigrants along with second and third generation Norwegian-Americans were under strong pressure to adopt Yankee American ways, often anglicizing their names and dropping cultural traits. In 1878, a Norwegian immigrant school teacher wrote to his friend in Norway:

Here in America it is very difficult to find a girl who ... would not be considered a clothes horse .... I have often been irritated by all the vanity and pomp which the girls here are loaded down with. And yet the girl I love is ... also a clothes horse. It's just that each one of these poor people wants to be like all the others and I can only hope that under the fine clothing beats a humble heart (Zempel 15).

Servant girls and seamstresses were the first to adopt American fashion dress. Advice to prospective emigrants who intended to go into domestic service in the cities was to bring no extra clothes; American clothes would be required immediately. Norwegian girls were considered clean and industrious and always in demand in American households. They became the despair of Norwegian bachelors who resented the independence their wages gave them. The one to one and a half dollars a week they earned was considered fabulous. In a mocking letter to Norway, a young man describes peasant girls in the homeland as flat-heeled, round-shouldered and clumsy, but:

You should see our Norwegian peasant and serving girls here! You wouldn't recognize them or believe your own eyes—that these lovely creatures have been transplanted from Norway's mountain crags! ... [They] trip about, their backs arched, with their parasols and their fans and their heads all enveloped in veils. Aase, Birthe and Siri ... are converted to Aline, Betsy and Sara [with] a little "Miss" before their names (Blegen 184).

Another bachelor wrote home wishing for a pretty, unspoiled Norwegian girl:

I am sure you will laugh but, believe it or not, the servant girls have certainly come into their own here. The first Sunday after their arrival in America they still wear their usual old Norwegian clothes; the next Sunday, it's a new dress; the third, a hat, a parasol, a silk shawl, new clothes from top to toe (Blegen 184).

Fig. 1. The Boe Family in East Telemark, Norway, c. 1897. This photograph was sent to the four oldest children who had left for America. *Collection of the author.*

Fig. 2. The Boe Family in Wisconsin, c. 1902. The four oldest children are pictured with their parents and younger siblings. The youngest child had died in Norway before the family emigrated. No trace of the folk costume so recently worn remains. *Collection of the author.*

He expresses further despair by admitting that there was "an avalanche of boys" visiting them "nearly every evening." However, not every Norwegian woman rid herself completely of her national dress. Photographic evidence portrays a combination of Norwegian details with fashionable American dress. Wearing part of the national dress kept her in touch with the homeland and was a source of ethnic pride.

Norwegian Details

After they arrived in America, Norwegian women, who were unaccustomed to changes in fashion, wore their best dress even when it became outdated by American standards. To it they often added details which had a Norwegian folk flavor. Most frequently found are small details, like collars and bonnet lappets embellished with patterned needlework in traditional designs. A photograph in the collection of the Wisconsin Historical Society records not only a Norwegian collar but be-dangled silver closures placed like buttons on the front of the bodice. No doubt this was heirloom silver brought from Norway. Silver breastpins or brooches are frequently mentioned and photographed throughout the immigrant period. In her memoires, Elizabeth Koren noted that her silver breastpin was admired by the ladies of the congregation. Pastor Duus, in letters to his family in Norway, requests they send a solid good brooch for his wife Sophie, since American jewelry is "mere trash."

Silver played an important part in folk life, not only for its monetary value but also for its spiritual characteristics. In rural Norway, men, women, and children wore silver ornaments, not only with festive costume, but also as part of everyday wear. Silver objects were used as a protective device and a curative for both people and animals. Superstition, while seeming inconsistent with a belief in Christianity, continued to be an influence even in the nineteenth century (Stewart 123). Women who wore silver brooches only with their best dress in America seem to have done so more for sentimental rather than mystical reasons.

At the turn of the twentieth century, white cotton lingerie dresses composed of lace insertion, tiny tucks and white embroidery became fashionable for summer wear. Lingerie dresses were the ideal fashion in which to incorporate Norwegian handwork. White-on-white geometric drawn work and embroidery used on folk costume of many districts was substituted for the lace and eyelet on lingerie dresses. The most popular embroidery was Hardanger style found on aprons and blouses of that district. Examples of this adaptation can be found in photographs and museum collections in the midwest. Most notable are the pieces in Vesterheim Norwegian-American Museum which date from around 1905. Clothing details with a distinct Norwegian character no longer appear after 1910 although silver brooches are occasionally seen in family albums.

Folk Costume: A Second Chance for Life

The abandonment of Norwegian details in American dress did not signal the end of cultural identity. The Lutheran Church and a strong Norwegian-American press were cohesive forces which helped preserve the language and reminded Norwegian-Americans to appreciate their heritage. The improvement of frontier conditions and strong ethnic neighborhoods in urban areas led to the proliferation of local and national societies composed of Norwegian-Americans. In addition to ethnic insurance programs, which encouraged preservation of the culture, larger societies, like the Sons of Norway, founded in 1895, had cultural activities which outlasted the assimilation process.

The nineteenth-century European romantic movement which captured the imagination of urban intellectuals reawakened interest in folk culture in Norway. Romanticism was a change in emphasis from the noble and elevated classicism of the Enlightenment to an appreciation for the realism and simplicity of the popular culture of the rural classes. Norwegian nationalists who initiated the change, collected the literary products of peasant origin: folk tales, poetry and song. Prior to the romantic movement, the pursuit of folk culture was thought too simple and common for educated people.

In Norway, Hulda Garborg (1862-1934), an ardent supporter of folk traditions, worked to preserve national dances, for which suitable costumes were needed. A simplified version of the Hardanger costume had become the national symbol of dress, but Garborg worked to raise awareness of the range of style originally used in the numerous districts of Norway. Over time, each isolated valley had developed its own style of dress with many variations.

In some districts, traditional styles had not died out; other districts experienced changes as a result of increased outside communications (Bosworth 637). Garborg introduced the term *bunad*, meaning clothes, to indicate the conscious effort to reconstruct a traditional style or to create new apparel designs based on old traditions. During the 1920s the desire for local bunads (traditional clothes), along with an increasing distance from authenticity, produced bunads with little resemblance to the original folk dress. A city girl, Klara Semb (1884-1970) became a bunad reformer and insisted on faithful copies of the old clothes, ultimately resulting in the formation of The National Bunad Committee (Skavhaug 10).

The bunad activities in Norway renewed ethnic pride among Norwegian-Americans. When in 1925 a parade was organized in Minneapolis to honor the centennial of Norwegian immigration, American women of Norwegian descent paraded in folk costumes which their families had originally brought from Norway. Kits with the materials necessary for constructing authentic bunads became available and silver and gold ornaments needed to complete the ensemble could be ordered from Norway. Dance groups, Nordic choirs, folk festivals and meetings of ethnic groups, like The Sons of Norway, have given American women the continuing opportunity to wear and cherish the costumes of their Norwegian ancestors.

Costume's Full Circle

In summary, national dress was left behind by most Norwegian immigrant women in an effort to quickly assimilate into the society of their new land. A changed religious climate in America also contributed to the abandonment of the elaborate clothing worn for festive occasions in Norway. Some traces of traditional design were incorporated into fashionable American dress by those whose emotional needs were better met with a gradual transition.

Issues concerning Norwegian nationalism, reported by the Norwegian-American Press, kept ethnic pride alive among the immigrants and their descendants. Beginning in the 1920's, wearing the dress of their ancestors in Norway became a source of pride for American women. Folk festivals, lodge meetings and other special occasions have provided the descendants of the immigrants with increasing opportunities to express their ethnicity through the use of traditional dress.

Works Cited

Blegen, Theodore C. *Norwegian Migration to America: The American Transition.* Northfield, MN: Norwegian-American Historical Association, 1940.

Bosworth, Abbie L. "Life in a Norway Valley." *National Geographic* May 1935: 627-637.

Dennis, Alfred Pearce. "Norway, A Land of Stern Reality." *National Geographic* July 1930: 1-44.

Fapso, Richard J. *Norwegians in Wisconsin.* Madison: The State Historical Society of Wisconsin, 1982.

Gimbutas, Marija. *The Civilization of the Goddess.* San Francisco: Harper, 1991.

Hague, John A. "The Romantic Heritage and American Culture." *American Personality and the Creative Arts*. Joel Mickelson, ed. Minneapolis: Burgess, 1969.

Hammerton, J. A., ed. *Manners and Customs of Mankind*. London: Amalgamated Press, ND.

Haugen, Einar. *The Norwegians in America 1825-1975*. Oslo: Royal Ministry of Foreign Affairs, 1975.

Lovoll, Odd S. *The Promise of America, A History of the Norwegian-American People*. Minneapolis; University of Minnesota Press, 1984.

Nelson, Marion. *Vesterheim: Samplings from the Collection*. Decorah, Iowa: Museum Catalog, 1975.

Norlie, Olaf Morgan. *History of the Norwegian People in America*. Minneapolis: Augsburg, 1925.

Rosholt, Malcolm. *From the Indian Land*. Iola, WI: Krause Publishing, 1985.

Skavhaug, Kjersti. *Norwegian Bunads*. Trans. Bent Vanberg. Oslo: Hjemmenes Forlag, ND.

Stewart, Janice S. *The Folk Arts of Norway*. New York: Dover, 1972.

Thallaug, Jon & Rolf Erickson, eds. *Our Norwegian Immigrants*. Oslo: Dreyers Forlag, 1975.

Traetteberg, Gunver Ingstad. "Folk Costumes." *Native Art of Norway*. Roar Hauglid, ed. New York: Praeger, 1967 (139-176).

Zempel, Solveig, ed. & trans. *In Their Own Words*. Minneapolis: University of Minnesota Press, 1991. In cooperation with the Norwegian-American Historical Association.

Dressing the Colonial Past: Nineteenth Century New Englanders Look Back

Beverly Gordon

One of the interesting issues in the study of dress is the subject of purposeful "dress up" or costuming. The very act of putting on clothing and affecting mannerisms of other times and places allows individuals to project themselves elsewhere and imagine themselves differently. Costuming was particularly popular in this country in the middle of the nineteenth century, when Americans were swept up in a new passion for theatrical entertainment. A variety of allegorical and fanciful subjects were portrayed, but historical characterizations were especially well-loved. These were often based on American prototypes, and Americans who "enacted" their own history through costumed activities were able to imagine the past in an intimate and immediate way.

Dressing the part of the colonial past was popular, especially in the New England region, and served both as a source of amusement or entertainment, and as a vehicle through which people could measure or assess where and who they were and how far they had come. They saw colonial dress, and in particular the image of the New England Pilgrim farmer, as a symbol of American identity and a representation of democratic values and principles. They did not want to return to the past, however, and costuming was often used to highlight class distinctions and strengthen the hold of the Yankee elite. While individuals were able to identify with the past by putting on or surrounding themselves with old-fashioned garments, their actions served to reinforce feelings of distance from it. Costuming enabled mid-nineteenth century Americans to contrast their lives with lives of the past and to feel satisfaction with their modernity. Dressing the part of the colonial past reinforced their own values and assumptions, including such precepts as separate spheres for men and women. They felt pleased and secure in their wholly "modern" era.

109

Theatricality at Mid Century

Theatricality of all kinds caught the American imagination in the middle of the nineteenth century. As early as the 1830s, Bostonian Fanny Appleton was noting in her diary that the Tremont Theater was "turning away thousands" (Wagenknecht 15) and, by the 1850s, theater attendance had reached unprecedented numbers. Americans also embraced the recently developed theatrical parlor games such as charades, *tableaux vivants*, short staged farces and burlesques. According to historian Karen Halttunen, guides with titles like *The Sociable; or One Thousand and One Home Amusements* and *Hudson's Private Theatricals for Home Performances* began to "pour off the American press" in the 1850s. These works not only suggested actual scripts or tableaux scenes and characters, but also advised the middle class citizen how to construct stages, create appropriate lighting effects, and fashion believable props and costumes from everyday home accouterments (Chap. 6, esp. 174-82). Halttunen argues that theatricality was embraced at this time because Americans were beginning to see their lives and social relationships in dramatic terms, and to think in terms of roles and role-playing.

The Sanitary Fairs: Costuming in the Civil War Era

The predilection for costume, posing and melodramatic impersonation was also manifested in community get-togethers and entertainments, and served as the basis for innumerable successful fundraising efforts from the 1860s until well after the turn of the century. Among the most important of these fundraisers were the "sanitary fairs" of the Civil War. These were a series of large-scale events held in the 1860s in over fifteen northern cities to raise money for the Sanitary Commission, the government agency responsible for supplies, transport and hospitals for the soldiers of the Union army. Hundreds of thousands of people attended the bazaar-like fairs, each of which ran for several weeks. In total, the fairs raised over five million dollars for the Commission coffers[1] (see Goodrich, Gordon [a] and [b]).

The women who organized one of the earliest fairs, held in Rochester, New York in December, 1863, pioneered a type of theatrical marketing that became standard at subsequent events. The main hall was arranged with a series of thematic, tableaux-like booths with costumed salespeople set against scenic backdrops and appropriate sales goods. Visitors encountered some characters like the "Turks" or "Russians" who were leaning on hangings of thick, icicle-surrounded furs and selling items like skates and sleds,[2] but the largest of the thematic areas was devoted to the United States. The United States area included a Yankee booth with a family of satirical characters, "Mr. and Mrs. Jonathan Slick" and their children "Sophronia, Jerusha and Jonathan," a national booth featuring a "Goddess of Liberty," "General and Mrs. Washington," and a corps of salesgirls in military-style red, white and blue outfits (Goodrich 172-78, *Report of Christmas Bazaar* 14-17).

This kind of display caught on with New Englanders. There was extensive networking among the women who managed these fundraising fairs, and individuals travelled to other cities to "take lessons" about successful attractions from their local counterparts ("Bazaar and Its Arrangements" 1). Only two months after the Rochester event, "Brother Jonathan" and his wife were present at the sanitary fair in Albany (Figs. 1-2), and a full-blown theatrical presentation, the "New England Kitchen," was set up by New Englanders at the Brooklyn and Long Island Fair. Mrs. Ray Potter and a group of transplanted Bostonians turned a 40 x 100 foot space into a theme-room restaurant with actual antique furniture and a huge fireplace with swinging pots. Potter's committee stated that it was intending to revive the revolutionary spirit through the reproduction of New England-farmhouse life, drawn out through "the manners, customs, dress, and if possible, the idiom of the [last century]" (*History of The Brooklyn Fair*).

It is significant that it was the farmhouse, and most particularly the kitchen, that was chosen to represent the national past. As indicated, these fairs were conceived, organized and staffed by women who were not only comfortable with the idea of running a good service area and cognizant of its money-making potential, but who naturally thought in terms of what in nineteenth century ideology was identified as the woman's domain—the domestic environment. They presented a sort of distaff view of colonial American history. Such a gender-identified history was also indicated in contemporary written sources. In 1851 Elizabeth Ellery published the second of two major studies of women in the Revolutionary era. Her *Domestic History of the Revolution* was written to "portray the social and domestic conditions of the times...and experiences of a class not usually noticed" (39-42). It focused on women's activities such as making stockings, boycotting tea, soliciting contributions and donating property.

The New England Kitchen at the Brooklyn fair featured long tables laden with pork and beans, cider and other regional specialties, and mood-setting interior details like dried apples hanging from exposed rafters, but what made it come alive were the costumed characters that animated it (Figs. 3-4). There were well-dressed "dames" spinning before the fire and knitting in the corner of

Fig. 1. Costumed participants at the "Yankee" booth, Albany Sanitary Fair, 1863. Bunker Hill Monument in background. Courtesy New York State Library, Manuscripts and Special Collections.

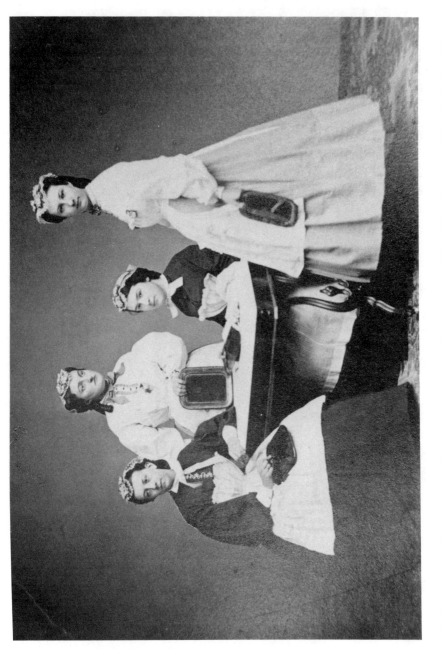

Fig. 2. Costumed participants at the "Yankee" booth at the Albany Sanitary Fair, 1863. Courtesy of New York State Library, Manuscripts and Special Collections.

Fig. 3. Costumed participants at the "Knickerbocker Kitchen," Metropolitan (NYC) Sanitary Fair, 1864.

the room and "damsels with curious names and quaint attire" serving as waitresses. An "Indian," "hideous in horns and paint," periodically stalked the crowd (E.C. 3; *History of the Brooklyn Fair* 72-73; *Record of Metropolitan Fair* 182).

Actual staged entertainments also took place in the Kitchen and were said to be the most talked-about feature of the entire sanitary fair. Included were a series of "old folks concerts," with century-old musical numbers and costumed chanteuses; a "donation visit," recreating the colonial New England practice of contributing goods to the local minister; a quilting party (Fig. 5), which concluded with a young people's festival; an "apple paring," which included storytelling and riddles (Fig. 4) and as a finale, a staged wedding, where an already-married older couple humorously reenacted their nuptial ceremony in colonial attire in front of the 250 people who had purchased tickets. The minister officiated in "laced cocked hat and black knee breeches" (*History of the Brooklyn Fair* 73; *Northampton Free Press*, 11 March 1864). The Kitchen was such an unmitigated success that those who chronicled the fair noted the room was always crowded and more money would have been raised if it had been held in a larger space (*History of the Brooklyn Fair* 77). Such Kitchens were emulated at numerous subsequent fairs (see Table I), even until the end of the century. They provided participatory amusement, where visitors could step into the drama and affectively experience the projected reality that was suggested. Costuming was always a critical part of the illusion. The organizers of the New England Kitchen at the second sanitary fair held in Chicago in 1865 even improved on the Brooklyn version of the reenacted wedding by requiring that all wedding "guests" also appear in colonial attire. They also choreographed participatory parlor games to take place after the ceremony, including Blind Man's Bluff and Thread The Needle (*Chicago Evening Journal*; *Voice of the Fair*, 17 June 1865:4). Even where there was no actual Kitchen exhibit, colonial dramatization was incorporated. At the National Sailor's Fair held in Boston in 1864, a farce entitled "Modern Antiques" was performed to the accompaniment of "Yankee Doodle" (*Boatswain's Whistle* 21).

Fairs, Parties and Balls: Costuming in the Centennial Era
Some of the historic Kitchens at the sanitary fairs varied the Yankee theme by changing to a local emphasis—in New York City and Poughkeepsie, it was the Dutch colonial heritage that was stressed; in Philadelphia, Germanic traditions were highlighted (Roth 159-183, esp. 173; Gordon [b] Chap. 2)—but

Fig. 4. Costumed participants at the "Apple Paring," reenactment at the Brooklyn and Long Island Sanitary Fair, 1864.

Fig. 5. Costumed participants at the "Quilting Bee" reenactment at the New England Kitchen, Brooklyn and Long Island Sanitary Fair, 1864.

it was the New England focus that persisted in other fundraising events after the war. The Ladies Benevolent Society of Northampton, Massachusetts staged a New England Kitchen at their 1871 fair held to benefit the Springfield Home for

Table 1:

Colonial Kitchens and Thematic Displays
At Civil War Sanitary Fairs

Location	Date	Feature
Rochester, N.Y.	December, 1863	Yankee and U.S.A. booths
Albany, N.Y.	February, 1864	Colonial theme booths
Brooklyn, N.Y.	February, 1864	New England Kitchen
Cleveland, Ohio	February, 1864	Colonial theme booths
Poughkeepsie, N.Y.	March, 1864	Dutchess County Homestead
New York, N.Y.	April, 1864	Knickerbocker Kitchen
Baltimore, Md.	April, 1864	New England Kitchen
St. Louis, Mo.	May, 1864	New England and Holland Kitchen
Philadelphia, Pa.	June, 1864	Pennsylvania Kitchen
Indianapolis, Ind.	October, 1864	Yankee Kitchen
Boston, Mass.	November, 1864	Colonial theme drama
Chicago, Ill.	May, 1865	New England Farmhouse
Milwaukee, Wis.	June, 1865	Holland Kitchen

Friendless Women and Children and an Old Folks' Kitchen was incorporated into the Good Templar's [temperance] Festival and the Methodist Church fair in the same town within a few years' time (*Northampton Free Press*, 28 December 1866, 21 April 1871, January 1872). A similar Kitchen was featured at a fair held in the nation's capital to raise funds for an Aged Women's Home in 1868 (Roth 159-83). Even simple fairs often included a dramatic presentation featuring costumed salespeople or tableaux which required a separate admission ticket. "When the sanitary fairs sprang up all over the country, the drama was one of the most successful means employed to raise money," recalled the author of the 1875 guide *Parlour Amusements for the Young Folks* (Bartlett 9), which offered many new dramatic presentations to continue the tradition. Some of the offerings in guides like this referred distinctly to historical events such as "Penn's Treaty With the Indians" (Mayne), but most were more vaguely historical with the past being indicated by male characters in knee breeches, white stockings, and powdered hair; and female characters in calico dresses and white aprons.

Throughout the country, there were also independent Old Folks' Concerts and other community entertainments or benefits. Such colonially-oriented events took on even more importance as the centennial year approached. The Centennial Exhibition was seen as a way of bringing the war-divided nation back together, and New Englanders in particular threw themselves into its preparation with an almost missionary zeal. When the Women's Centennial Executive Committee held a "Centennial Tea Party" in Philadelphia in December, 1873, for example, participation from Massachusetts was second only to that from Philadelphia. The event, which was intended to raise funds for the upcoming Exhibition, was in fact a fair, with patriotic programs, a display of "relics," and sale goods arranged on state-identified tables. Sale tables were "presided over by ladies arrayed in full 'Martha Washington' costume," and the evening program was preceded by a procession of 500 such "Marthas" ("Centennial Tea Party" 189-90).

In the next few years, New Englanders attended a rash of Old Folks Concerts, Centennial Tea Parties, Centennial Balls, Martha Washington Parties, Calico Parties, and similar events that involved colonial costume (Figs. 6-7). Fancy-dress balls were particularly popular on Washington's birthday, and other events were coordinated with the fourth of July or the centennial celebration of June 1875 commemorating the battle of Bunker Hill, but specific holidays were not prerequisites. In November, a "grand quilting party" was held to benefit the centennial in Waltham, Massachusetts, while groups in Cambridge, East Boston, and Boston Highlands sponsored tea parties. The next March the ladies of the Baptist church in Northampton held a fair and supper to pay for repairs on their church vestry and featured "old time waiters," singers in "ancient costume," and the presence of "George and Martha Washington" (*Hampshire Gazette* 29 February 1876:2-3).[3]

Similar characters and amusing activities were seen throughout New England. At a Centennial Tea held in Sunderland, Massachusetts, relics were brought out, and "Lawyer Beals" made an appearance "in a queue *a la* Centennial." Amherst held a mock court, "presided over by Judge Biging, who sat on Mr. Naugherty, the accused. Lawyers [were] G.W. Cloak and H.D.

Fig. 6. Mrs. Samuel Colt dressed as Mrs. James Madison for the Martha Washington Reception and Tea Party. Courtesy the Wadsworth Atheneum Hartford. From the Elizabeth Hart Jarvis Colt Collection.

Fig. 7. Miss Ellen Gray posed in costume she wore to the Centennial Ball, Boston, 1876. Reported with the permission of the National Society of the colonial Dames of America in the Commonwealth of Massachusetts.

Maxon, of the classes of '76 and '77" (*Hampshire Gazette* 29 February 1876:3). In Woonsocket, Rhode Island, a "Martha Washington reception" held on Washington's birthday drew over 2,000 participants and, according to a report by the *Boston Evening Traveller* (24 February 1876), 1,000 more tried to get in. On that same day there were balls in Newport, Boston, and Manchester, New Hampshire; a centennial parade in Keene, New Hampshire; and an entertainment and "antiquarian supper" at the First Methodist Episcopal Church in Somerville, Massachusetts. Children's pageants were also popular (*Boston Daily Traveller* 10, 11, 15 November 1875; 22, 23 February 1876).[4]

It is clear from these varied examples that a wide spectrum of the population took part in activities that involved dressing in colonial attire. Balls, as might be expected, were functions for the established social elite. Organizers of fairs and other large public events were typically drawn from the same group, or in smaller or more rural communities, from the pool of leading local families. Less privileged individuals were encouraged to participate but more often followed in the role of spectator. At least some of the time, part of the attraction of the event was the opportunity for ordinary people to observe and literally rub shoulders with members of society.[5]

Men's Events: Pageantry and Parades

Large numbers of men also appeared in colonial costumes in the centennial era, but only at two types of events: military processions and historical reeanactments. A reenactment of the battle of Bunker Hill in Allentown, Pennsylvania, for example, involved 12,000 costumed "troops" and lasted for two hours. Twenty five thousand people came to watch (*Hampshire Gazette and Northampton Courier* 22 June 1875:2). Military outfits were sometimes incorporated into fairs—flag and shawl dances and "gavotters in appropriate costume" were included in the annual fair at Boston's Warren Street Chapel in 1876, for example—but were more typically seen in independent, non-pecuniary celebrations.

Some independent celebrations were serious military revues, but apparently more common were satirical pageants, akin to the humorous weddings and other dramatizations of the New England Kitchens. "Antiques and Horribles" parades "have [recently] come to be considered a necessary adjunct to a Fourth of July celebration," noted a spokesman for the city council of Newton, Massachusetts in 1876 (*Hampshire Gazette and Northampton Courier* 22 June 1875:24), and his statement is well borne out by reports of actual events. Three hundred people marched in the Newton parade that year, and two hundred marched in the south shore community of Mattapan. The *Evening Traveller* (3 July 1875:2, 6 July 1875:2) proclaimed the Mattapan celebration a "most grotesque⁶ impersonation" which sent shouts of laughter resounding through the Village. It also referred to "masqueraders" who went to a party after their "dress parade." In Newburyport, the "Horribles" procession was said to be two miles long, and "full of the most ludicrous presentations."

"Horribles" processions and similar activities had existed for some time. In the early part of the century burlesque street parades had taken place in many communities, often as a kind of grass roots mockery of the class-based militia system. Mock militias were staged with exaggerated and incongruous costumes, including oversized hats, whiskers, particolored pantaloons, and the like. The military parodies were immensely popular and well attended but sprang from serious political dissatisfaction (Davis 196-202). The defiant tone of the activities seems to have softened, however, by the mid-century. In 1870, Bostonian Sarah Putnam wrote in her diary about attending a number of satirical events at Papanti's dancing school. She not only mentioned an "Antiques and Horribles" event, but also a "Cheap and Hungries," an "Ancient and Honorables," and a "Married Sociable" (Putnam and Putnam 115-166). Putnam was a member of a leading Boston family, and the fact that these activities took place at an institution like a dancing school indicates they no longer had the same class association or biting edge. The street processions of the centennial year must still have involved participation from the rank and file, but their mockery was harmlessly aimed at people and events from a long-ago era.

The New England Kitchen at the Centennial Exhibition

Costuming was brought to the Centennial Exhibition itself, once again in the form of the New England Kitchen and once again under the auspices of wealthy New England women. Emma B. Southwick, a Bostonian, arranged for the construction not just of a kitchen facility but of a whole house, including a parlor and bedrooms. Dubbed the New England Farmer's Home (alternately, the New England Log Cabin), it was supposed to represent a "backwoodman's cot[tage] in Vermont or Connecticut 100 years ago" (Pennsylvania Board of Centennial Managers 146). It was built as a single-story, 49' x 39' structure (Fig. 8) and was juxtaposed against a fully-equipped modern kitchen. Like its Civil War predecessor, it featured a thematic restaurant and appropriately dressed characters (Fig. 9). Southwick brought a contingent of New Englanders with her to Philadelphia and installed them for the duration of the fair. These

Fig. 8. Exterior view, New England Kitchen (Farmhouse), Philadelphia Centennial Exhibition, 1876.

Fig. 9. Interior view, New England Kitchen, Philadelphia Centennial Exhibition, 1876.

individuals seem to have functioned as guides more than as waitresses, although the restaurant was fully operative and costumed servers must have been an integral part of it as well. About twenty young women led visitors through the rooms, describing the antique furniture and utensils that had been gathered from New England homesteads (Ingram 707-08; Norton 187). Dramatic enactments may also have taken place during the Centennial; Southwick and her assistants posed for photographs costumed as "Priscilla," "Mother," "Obadiah," and "Jerusha." Some extant photos were taken at the "Permanent Exhibition," which was set up in the main building after the official fair closed. Southwick rented space there to continue her New England display and presumably remained for the three years this auxiliary Exhibition remained open (Roth 177-78).

While it is beyond the primary time frame of this article, it is worth noting that colonial dramatizations did not end in the 1870s. Similar staging was used throughout the century whenever a Yankee theme seemed appropriate. Southwick again established a New England Kitchen and Log Cabin for the bazaar given for the Soldiers' Home in Chelsea, Massachusetts in 1881, and featured "Aunt Tabitha" singing Puritan songs and "Aunt Sally" spinning by the fire (*Sword and Pen* 3). A similar Kitchen included in an 1885 carnival for the same institution raised $2,000 (*Annual Report* 73). Southwick (then Brinton) was yet again present at the World's Columbian Exposition in 1893 with another "New England Log Cabin and Olden Time Restaurant," where costumed girls from Vassar and Wellsley served pork and beans and similar foodstuffs (Roth 178-81).

The fact that students from Seven Sisters colleges served as waitresses at the 1893 event indicates how consistently the New England Kitchen was reenacted by members of the upper class. This was somewhat ironic by the time of the Columbian Exposition, for although the farmhouse was selected to represent the United States in the international area of the fair, it was also considered an amusement. Costumed waitresses were included in a gallery of pictures of "Midway Types"—a gallery that also included exotic eastern dancers and other entertainers (Roth 178-81).

The Function of Colonial Impersonations

This dual identification of patriotic representation or even veneration on one hand and amusement or mockery on the other held true for almost all colonial impersonations. The New England Kitchens, mock courts and Horribles parades all served to recall and celebrate the colonial past, but their lighthearted tone helped keep that past distanced as a bygone era. The events functioned as public versions of the familiar parlor theatricals. In wartime, they provided an escape from the difficulties of the present, and their amusing quality was suitable to the morale-boosting purpose of the sanitary fairs. Morale-building was still appropriate at the time of the Centennial, for the nation was trying to pull itself together after the war and forge a coherent identity. In both periods the colonial experience could be contrasted against the present and could be used as a measure of how far society had progressed. This function was particularly explicit at the Centennial, where the "antiquated" kitchen was compared to its state-of-the-art counterpart and where the very setting was an industrial exposition celebrating the new technological world and the nation's place within it. Amusement was exaggerated because the customs of the past seemed old-fashioned, simple and consequently remote and distant.

The Nature of the Costume

Costuming in the domestic environments of the Kitchens reinforced the idea of the simple Yankee farmhouse. Waitresses and the impersonated characters generally appeared to be rural people with relatively unelaborate dress. Women, who were the dominant characters, almost invariably wore white caps (usually referred to at the time as mobcaps, which were associated with home and hearth[7]) or, occasionally, simple large-brimmed "pokebonnets." These were often accompanied by large neckerchiefs of the type worn fairly extensively in the colonies during the eighteenth century.[8] Long aprons were seen on waitresses, and many commentators remarked on their impressive whiteness. The significant symbolic elements of the costume were comprised of these accessories. All connoted the hard-working, virtuous, country citizen.

The exact nature of the actual dresses worn in these reenactments is more difficult to determine. Although they had little to do with true colonial wear, calico dresses were mentioned frequently, so much so that the aforementioned calico parties were synonymous with patriotic teas.[9] However, engravings and photographs of costumed individuals do not indicate that such fabric was always used. In fact, nineteenth century "colonialists" generally did not diverge from the silhouettes and mores of their own times. Those who appeared in the New England Kitchens of the Civil War often continued to wear dome-shaped petticoats or hoops, for example (Fig. 3), and those who were costumed for the Centennial sometimes sported bustles (Figs. 7,9). Hairstyles similarly followed contemporary norms, with center parts and low chignons typical in the 1860s and higher topknots and frizzed bangs in the 1870s; the eighteenth century style of brushing the hair straight back was little in evidence.

It was important to give a feeling for the past without getting too close to its reality; when historical accuracy was attempted, it was not always met with enthusiasm. Maria Lydig Daly, a New York judge's wife, wrote in her diary about being asked to impersonate the Washington Irving heroine Katrina Von Tassel at the Knickerbocker Kitchen at the Metropolitan Fair. She declined, indignantly exclaiming how unpleasant it would be in appear before crowds of people in a cap and shortgown (Hammond 280-81). The shortgown was a garment associated not only with working class women but also with slaves (Kidwell 30-65), and Daly was apparently uncomfortable with the idea of appearing too out of her own class. She and other mid-century women were so used to hoopskirts, center-parted hairstyles and similar details, furthermore, that they would have felt uncomfortable without them, and would not have noticed their historic anomaly. Moreover, since the root of the characterizations was the amateur theatrical, symbolic elements were what counted most. Calico dresses were as much a part of the popular mythology as the log cabin, and the veracity of either element was not an issue.[10]

Historical inaccuracy or blurring of periods in these mid-nineteenth century costumes is also related to both the idealization and the sense of progress alluded to earlier. The advanced state of contemporary society was taken as a given, and almost everything that was more than a generation or two removed from it was considered "antique" or "ancient"—at once rather primitive and laudatory. The pre-industrial past was seen almost as a continuous, single period. The furnishings of the New England Kitchens, which were supposed to represent a period one hundred years earlier, actually included two-hundred-year-old items such as the cradle used by Peregrine White who was said to have been born on the Mayflower, Governor Endicott's folding chair, and a two-hundred-year-old quilt (Ingram 707). Costume was generally reconstructed and did not date from the seventeenth century, but it too might look extremely old. Editorial commentary on the 1876 mock court in Amherst indicated that "costumes manufactured for the occasion were of more antique appearance than the genuine apparel." The same observation had been made about the Centennial party in nearby Northampton (*Hampshire Gazette and Northampton Courier* 29 February 1876:3). Ironically, early nineteenth century detailing was considered suitably old as well. Such blurring or running-together of historic periods was even seen in contemporary scholarly works. A possible source of information for mid-century individuals interested in learning about the New England past was *The Customs of New England* which was organized alphabetically like a dictionary. Detailed descriptions of particular items of dress were provided, but no distinctions were made among periods; for example the hundred pair of shoes provided for Plymouth settlers in 1629 was treated in almost the same context as the boots of 1840.

The Use of Actual Colonial Clothing: Relics and Ball Gowns

Although it was not prevalent in the New England Kitchens or most of the theatrical entertainments, there were some places where actual historic or antique costume was on view in the centennial period. Authentic eighteenth century garments were occasionally brought out for balls; for example, Mrs. Richardson, a descendant of the Hancock family, appeared at Boston's Centennial Ball "in a yellow brocade silk worn by Madame Hancock on receiving her wedding guests." Other historic garments worn on that occasion, according to a long description in the Boston paper ("Centennial Ball" 1), included an unidentified great-grandmother's wedding dress and a Watteau-style overdress with petticoat. A neckerchief of lace crossed over the bodice of the latter, and it was worn by a descendant of Elbridge Gerry, one of the signers of the Declaration of Independence. Mr. George Rivers wore an embroidered full dress suit worn by his ancestor Jonathan Russell when he was United States minister to France. These garments were freely intermingled on the dance floor with fancy-dress costume, and unrelated pieces were indiscriminately mixed together. Mr. D. Slade combined a waistcoat worn at the court of Louis XVI with a scarlet cloak worn by Bostonian Richard Broomfield; an unidentified woman wore a ninety year old dress with "large sleeves like inflated bags of the style popular in the 1830s" with turn of the century or Empire style slippers and a large, "very old handkerchief." The outfit was pronounced "unbecoming."[11]

Heirloom garments of this sort served the interests of the increasingly genealogy-minded New England elite, for they helped members of old and established families set themselves apart from ordinary workers and especially from recently arrived immigrants. The very existence of the garments indicated a kind of "pedigree" and served as evidence of the family's long presence on American soil. The garments had been passed on through the generations and were well cared for. They were treated reverently, as relics.

Heirloom garments were only worn on occasions where participation was limited to members of the elite, but they could be seen by people of all classes for they were also shown at actual relic displays. Such displays had been part of the Civil War fairs, but at that time they focused on souvenirs of the war itself, and most of the garments on display were part of battle uniforms. During the centennial era garments were brought out in a different context and were part of a more global patriotic fervor. Inspired perhaps by the relic display at Philadelphia's Centennial Tea Party in 1873, women's committees throughout the northeast set up "temporary museums" of eighteenth century items. A broadside distributed by the Ladies' Centennial Committee of Boston, for example, implored citizens to loan portraits, arms, clothing, furniture and other relics for the week-long Exhibition of Revolutionary Relics. The broadside noted the central women's Centennial committee advised the formation of similar organizations in all the villages, towns and states of the Union ("Appeal to Women"). The call was taken to heart in New England where groups in large cities like Boston and New Haven complied, as did groups in smaller towns like Salem and Northampton ("Centennial Tea Party" 190; *Handbook of the Centennial; Catalogue of Antique Articles; Catalogue of Revolutionary Relics; Hampshire Gazette and Northampton Courier* 21 December 1875:2).

Catalogues of centennial relic displays indicate that clothing accounted for a significant portion of the total items; between ten and twenty percent of the objects were garments or personal accessories. In most cases, the items were associated with particular individuals of the past. Sometimes the association was with the person who made the item, such as a "shawl wrought by the wife of Noah Cook—over 150 years old" in Northampton, or an "apron embroidered at a boarding school in Boston during the reign of Queen Anne by Mary Canee" in New Haven. More often the association was with a particular user or owner. This was most impressive when a famous person was involved. At the Boston display there was a baby cap said to have been worn by both John and John Quincy Adams; a pair of shoes worn by Major Baylie, aide to General Washington; a collar worn by the Washington himself; a chatelaine that had belonged to Elizabeth Almy, wife of one of the signers of the Declaration of Independence; and a pocketbook used by Major Lawrence at Bunker Hill. Salem similarly featured a slipper worn by Madame Crowninshield when she opened a ball with President Washington, and New Haven included knee and shoe buckles that had been used by John Hancock. Like the proverbial ubiquitous pieces of the true cross, pieces of Martha Washington's dresses were also plentiful: three were displayed in the New Haven exhibit alone. Either the story of their origin was totally apocryphal or Mrs. Washington's dresses had in fact been cut up into small pieces, for these stories abounded. At the Philadelphia Centennial Tea Party, a quilt said to be made of pieces of dresses that Mrs. Washington had worn at state receptions was suspended between two sales tables. The quilt attracted a "large number of reverent admirers" throughout the afternoon ("Centennial Tea Party" 190).

Pieces were all that remained of other treasured dresses as well. In New Haven, fragments outnumbered intact garments. Sometimes these had been made into new items such as thread cases; at other times they were framed. There were also fragments of men's breeches; waist coats which, like the treasured dresses, were typically made of silk and subject to disintegration.

Smaller, often sturdier items of dress were very plentiful in the displays. There were hats and bonnets, stomachers, shawls, and breeches, as well as infant's clothes, including christening gowns. Also on display were purses and other assorted accessories like fans, knee and shoe buckles, busks, and jewelry. An item that was most likely to survive was the shoe. There were wedding shoes and fancy silk slippers, but also wooden pattens and numerous unspecified types of presumably more practical shoes. The shoes, which were in most cases handmade, must have been likely candidates for safekeeping over the years because of their small size, their often sturdy material and their lack of suitability for reuse.

Portraits were another important relic category, and these too must have provided nineteenth century Americans with a reference point for historic clothing. Portraits of colonial ancestors were typical in the local displays and in at least one instance in Boston a displayed artifact was also represented in a painting. A gorget worn by (Revolutionary War) General Sullivan, which appeared as Number 165 in the catalogue of Boston relics, was cross referenced to a portrait on the wall. Both were donated by T.C. Armory. Portraits of George and Martha Washington were shown where possible. Three separate examples were mentioned in the *Godey's Lady's Book* report on the Centennial Tea Party in Philadelphia (190).

The Symbolic Meaning of Colonial Costuming

George and Martha Washington clearly symbolized the Revolutionary past and were treated as the larger-than-life hero and heroine that represented the new country. A centennial event was considered complete when characters representing the Washingtons were present; at a Northampton tea party, for example, it was a matter of some regret when only Martha and not the expected George and Martha pair made an appearance (*Hampshire Gazette and Northampton Courier* 4 January 1876:2). Important as they were, however, the Washingtons seem to have functioned for New Englanders as iconic figureheads more than as symbols of the deeper American character. That quality was seen to emanate from New England itself. When George and Martha made their appearance at the fair and supper sponsored by the Baptists in Northampton in 1876, they were accompanied by the familiar "Brother Jonathan" whose presence was a strong reminder of the importance of Yankee heritage (*Hampshire Gazette and Northampton Courier* 29 February 1876:2). It was no accident that the aristocratic garments brought to the balls and seen in the relic displays gave way for symbolic purposes to the mob caps and aprons of the farmwife. New England was not only the site of the Boston Tea Party and the beginnings of the war for independence, it was also the home of the Pilgrams who were appropriated as the symbol of the American experience and the repository of American virtue. While some of this appropriation may have been due to the discrediting of the south after the Union victory in the war, New Englanders were instrumental in building and maintaining the image on ideological grounds as well. The early New England settler was portrayed as a hard-working, non-aristocratic individualist who represented the republican ideal. It was not accidental that the Mayflower cradle and the two-hundred-year-old quilt were included in the New England Kitchen exhibits, for the independent small farmer was identified with the virtuous Pilgrim pioneer. They were blended or overlaid into a single idea about America and represented an emotional icon of the nation's past.

Class and Gender Distinctions

The contradictions between the ideological image and the realities of the present were many, and the image of modest or humble beginnings was perpetuated most vociferously by individuals who were themselves well-off. As indicated, it was the social elite who generally organized the colonial events. The "Appeal to Women" sent out by the Boston Women's Auxiliary Committee was signed by members of the city's most prominent and wealthy families; names like Adams, Amory, Hemenway, Lodge, Lowell, Quincy, Revere, Saltonstall and Winthrop read like a "who's who" of contemporary society. Centennial balls could also be among the most important social events of the year. In Newport, for example, invitations to a ball given by "railroad king" John Griswold were highly coveted (*Boston Evening Transcript* 23 February 1876). The ball sponsored by the Women's Committee was so important to the local social scene that it was granted first page coverage in the evening newspaper. The report discussed its brilliant display. "The dresses worn were many of them of the highest value," explained the reporter, "and it is probable that a dozen of them could have been selected the cost of which would far exceed the net profits of the evening" ("Centennial Ball" 1).[12] Elaborate dress was expected in that setting, and it followed an aristocratic model. Powdered hair, associated with fashionable individuals before the French Revolution, "was very prevalent" ("Centennial Ball" 1).

The presence of elite dress at exclusive events did not ameliorate the symbology of the more modest New England farmer. The farmer was presented as the model for everyone else and could be claimed as a long-ago ancestor. Farmers were virtuous, almost by definition, and helped establish a morally righteous pedigree, one which was unistakeably Yankee and untainted by the questionable qualities of more recent immigrants to the New World shores. The hard-working farmer who tamed the wildnerness was perceived as a different breed than the new urban worker. The farmer could also be embraced wholeheartedly because he or she was far in the past. The country as a whole, and well-off New England families in particular, had progressed beyond their beginning stages and had left such primitive simplicity behind. It was possible to simultaneously revere the image of the Yankee farmstead and, because it belonged to a less enlightened age, to gently poke fun at or mock it.

Just as colonial costuming was used to reinforce class distinctions, so too it was used to reinforce gender roles. We have established that women "dressed up" in more domestic contexts, usually in indoor settings, and that the predominant presence in the New England Kitchens was female because they were recreations of female-identified domestic environments. The mid-century parlor theatrical fad was essentially also domestic, emanating as it did from the household, relying on domestic props and costumes, and often focusing on domestic rituals (see Halttunen, 174-77, 181).

Women also used costuming to exert a positive, moral influence. Contemporary ideology considered moral guidance and leadership to be an integral part of women's role in the domestic sphere. The Kitchen displays and other costumed fundraising efforts were seen as morally laudable and were felt to further patriotic goals. In the Civil War era they were associated with the righteous cause of the Union. In the Centennial period they were an acceptable way of generating American pride. At the 1873 Centennial Tea Party, the Honorable William H. Armstrong addressed the assembled crowd, proclaiming that the American nation was in a dominant position in relation to public morality and the maintenance of personal liberty. The Centennial was to function as a "school" where American values and accomplishments could be exhibited, and it would have an important influence on the future of the nation. Women who were sponsoring fundraising events were "doing the work of the country." Their efforts would help highlight the "wonderful growth of the great Republic in the last one hundred years" ("Centennial Tea Party" 190).

Women were most likely to both attend these events and to appear in costume. When 500 people paraded at the Centennial Tea Party, all of them were women, and when "George" Washington did not make an appearance with "Martha" at the Northampton fair, people were disappointed but probably not too surprised. Even at the Centennial Ball where attendees were fairly evenly divided between men and women, far fewer of the men were costumed ("The Centennial Ball" 1).

Men liked to dress up, also, but we have seen that they did so in different, more public and male-defined settings. They were less drawn to domestic characterizations than to judicial or military ones, and they often appeared in outdoor settings. Their occasions were congratulatory rather than educational, and they tended to participate within the context of their ongoing organizations rather than as part of special short-term groups or committees. "Many thousands" of men marched with their civic and military organizations in the Boston Bunker Hill celebration in 1875, and hundreds marched in Portland, Maine on Independence Day in 1876. Cambridge town officers marched in their official capacity in that city's centennial celebration in 1875, as did the postmaster, Congressional representatives and other public figures (*Boston Daily Traveller* 15 June 1875:1, 18 June 1875:1, 3 July 1875:1). Men with official public roles were also well represented in local celebrations that included illuminated houses, ringing bells and huge bonfires in such cities as Worcester, Massachusetts, New Britain, Connecticut, and Rutland, Vermont ("The Centennial Year" 5). Both women and men associated colonial costuming with patriotism, but their definitions of patriotic activity were strongly affected by prevailing ideas of proper domain and spheres of interest.

Conclusions

In conclusion, New Englanders of the mid-nineteenth century found meaning in dressing the part of the colonial past. On one hand they approached colonial dress with veneration. They saw it as a symbol of American identity and used it to symbolize democratic values. At the same time they approached colonial dress with levity and both viewed and used it as entertainment. Clothing and costume provided an intimate, immediate, and affective experience. It allowed individuals to both identify with the people of the past and to feel "modern" and up-to-date. It was the costuming at the Centennial parties and balls and the New England Kitchen exhibits that most directly helped the public feel the past was far behind them. It highlighted how far they, as Americans, had come.

Costuming was used by both men and women in the mid-nineteenth century, but with different emphases that reflected their different social roles and positions. Whether they approached them as serious figures in historic reenactments or as amusing, almost stock characters in "Horribles" parades, men were most likely to dress as their military or political forebears. Women represented themselves in domestic settings and were responsible for the popular domestic reenactments of the era.

Costuming seems to have appealed to a wide cross section of the population, but it was the social leaders from well-established New England families who typically organized visible public events. Fine clothing of the wealthy people of the past was venerated, especially if it was associated with particular individuals who had come to take on almost heroic dimensions in the public mind, but it was presented only to members of the elite or in situations where it was perceived from a distance. It was a codified image of the New England farmer that held the most symbolic import. The Yankee pioneer stood for the kind of hard work, independence and morality that Americans identified with, and both farmers and their wives were seen to represent these qualities. Because it was the symbolic rather than the educational meaning of the clothing that was foremost, historical accuracy was not a serious concern or salient characteristic of Victorian colonial costuming.

The mid-century reenactments sowed the seeds of the colonial revival movement that took hold at the turn of the twentieth century and shared with that revival an interest in colonial artifacts. Events of both eras were organized to a great extent by individuals of the same Yankee elite, but the events elicited different feelings. At a time when massive immigration had not yet become overwhelming and modern technologies such as telephones and electricity had not yet transformed everyday life, mid-century colonial events did not express an antimodernist attitude or a yearning for an earlier golden age.[13] Mid-century Americans used colonial garments to reaffirm and reinforce who they were and to express satisfaction with the present day. When the mid-nineteenth century New Englanders looked back, furthermore, they were able to do so with amusement and humor because they perceived both present and past as a kind of dramatic play and were convinced that the present was superior. The past could be incorporated into the present and add to its general belief in progress and confidence in the rightness of the modern world.

Notes

[1]This figure is an approximate one, based on proceeds reported by individual

sanitary fair committees and reports. The numbers are not always consistent and it is difficult to ascertain in some cases whether a net or gross figure is given.

[2]Both foreign and allegorical subjects were represented in theatrical performances and tableaux; almost anything that was different from the norm was considered exotic and seemed to feed the Victorian imagination. The one exception to this is that Africans, other than the relatively light-skinned Moors, were essentially ignored. Racist assumptions were so ingrained in this period that white Americans could not project themselves into dark-skinned people's lives.

[3]An amused or droll tone was taken toward this event in the local press. The newspaper "reported" that "the ladies [had] sent to Boston and had the harbor dragged for tea chests," which were now selling for $20 apiece. "They were found to be in an excellent state of preservation...and little did those who threw that tea overboard think they were simply coining it for future generations." A working spinning wheel was also seen at this event.

[4]It is important to point out that such celebrations were not limited to New England, although they may have been particularly spirited there. Similar events were taking place in most areas, with the possible exception of the deep south. For an example of pageants, see *The Centennial Celebration of the City of Newton* 132.

[5]This assertion is based on the author's encountering numerous instances of this phenomenon in the process of researching *Bazaars and Fair Ladies*.

[6]In nineteenth century usage, "grotesque" meant exotic and fanciful. The term was closer to its original meaning of "grotto-esque" and did not necessarily have a horrific connotation.

[7]"Mobcap" was a term used to describe a variety of soft informal caps worn at home by women in the eighteenth and early nineteenth centuries. The cap was originally a "morning" cap, and the prefix "mob" was derived from "mop" or "mab", originally associated with morning and with the concepts of untidiness, "negligee" or "undress." It was not related to the mobs of the French revolution, although women of that time did wear such headcoverings; the strongest association was with the home, and by extension, with domesticity and goodness. Eventually the garment became identified with older, more conservative women (*Encyclopedia Britannica* 635).

[8]In Europe, this sort of neckerchief was associated with peasants or modest, conservative or religious individuals, including Quakers. It was not highly fashionable. There are numerous American portraits that illustrate fairly well-off, well-dressed individuals wearing kerchiefs, however, and it is the author's belief that there was a distinctly different norm in the colonies and the early days of the republic. See Gordon [d] 49-60.

[9]"Calico" originally meant any cotton fabric from India. Over time, it became associated with cottons embellished with small-scale floral printed designs. Such fabric was not on the market until about 1825, after the advent of the cotton gin and roller printing. It was not a part of colonial dress.

[10]Some of these same symbolic elements of dress were also used in actual parlor

theatricals. Calico dresses and white aprons were listed as appropriate costumes for characters, for example, in Bartlett's *Parlour Amusements for Young Folks*. In "Love in Ambush," a farce with a sweet innocent maiden who cannot find her lover, the heroine is to dress this way. In "Sleeping Beauty," the maids are to wear these items, and the fairies are to wear thin white aprons and kerchiefs.

[11]Costumes worn at the ball may have been taken out on several occasions. Sarah Putnam went to a reception at Mrs. Winthrop's house several days after the ball where guests were asked to wear their costumes again (Putnam and Putnam 210).

[12]Colonial costume and even fancy dress was not required. Several individuals came as non-American exotic characters—Mr. Abbot Lawrence was dressed as Mephistopheles, for example, Mr. Iasigi appeared in Greek costume, Mrs. T.E. Richardson wore a sixteenth century velvet outfit, and two unidentified women came in red silk Spanish dresses with black veiled headdresses.

[13]The idea that the mid-century interest in the colonial past represented a different sensitivity than that of the Colonial Revival was previously developed by Maas (89-90).

Works Cited

*Albany Relief Bazaar.*Photograph album, 1863. Archives of the New York State Library, New York Cultural Center, Albany, New York.

Annual Report. Chelsea, Massachusetts Soldier's Home, 1885.

"Appeal to Women," *Exhibition of Revolutionary Relics in Boston, 1875* (broadside).

Bartlett, G.B. *Parlour Amusements for the Young Folks*. Boston: James R. Osgood and Co., 1875.

"The Bazaar and Its Arrangements," *The Canteen*, Albany Sanitary Fair (February, 1864): 1.

Boatswain's Whistle, National Sailor's Fair newspaper, Boston], November, 1864.

Boston Daily Evening Traveller, various issues.

Boston Evening Transcript, various issues.

Catalogue of Antique Articles Exhibited at Plummer Hall. Salem: Press of the *Salem Gazette*, 1875.

Catalogue of the Revolutionary Relics Exhibited at 56 Beacon Street. Boston: Ladies' Centennial Committee, 1875.

"The Centennial Ball," *Boston Evening Transcript*, February 25, 1876: 1.

Centennial Celebration of the City of Newton. Newton, MA: Order of the City Council, 1876.

"Centennial Tea Party," *Godey's Lady's Book* 88 (February 1874): 189-190.

"The Centennial Year: Welcoming the Advent of 1876," *New York Times* 1 January, 1876:5.

Chicago Evening Journal, 24 April, 1865 (clipping in library of the Chicago Historical Society, n.p.)

Davis, Susan. "The Career of Colonel Pluck: Folk Drama and Popular Protest in Early Nineteenth Century Philadelphia," *Pennsylvania Magazine of History and Biography* 109, no.2 (1985): 179-202.

E.C. "A Letter from Brooklyn—The Brooklyn Fair, 25 February 1864," *The Canteen* (Albany, N.Y.), 1 March 1864.

Ellery, Elizabeth Fries. *Domestic History of the Revolution.* New York: Baker and Scribner, 1851.

Encyclopedia Brittanica. 11:17 New York: Encyclopedia Brittanica, 1911.

Felt, Joseph B. *The Customs of New England.* Boston: Press of T.R. Marvin, 1853.

Gillespie, Mrs. E.D. Letter to the Editor [regarding Centennial Tea Party in Washington], *New York Times,* 10 January 1875: 6.

Goodrich, Frank B. *The Tribute Book: A Record of the Munificence, Self-Sacrifice and Patriotism of the American People During the War for the Union.* New York: Derby and Miller, 1865.

Gordon, Beverly [a]. "A Furor of Benevolence!" *Chicago History* 14 (Winter 1986-1987): 48-69.

_____. [b]. *Bazaars and Fair Ladies: A History of the American Fundraising Fair.* In production.

_____. [c]. "Dress and Dress-up at the Fundraising Fair," *Dress* 12 (1986): 61-72.

_____. [d]. "Fossilized Fashion: 'Old Fashioned' Dress as a Symbol of a Separate, Work-Oriented Identity," *Dress* 13 (1987): 49-60.

Halttunen, Karen. *Confidence Men and Painted Women: A Study of Middle Class Culture in America, 1830-1870.* New Haven: Yale UP, 1982.

Hammond, Harold Earl, ed. *Diary of a Union Lady, 1861-1865.* New York: Funk and Wagnalls, 1962.

Hampshire Gazette and Northamption [Massachusetts] Courier, various issues.

Handbook of the Centennial and Antiquarian Exhibition. New Haven: Punderson and Crisand, 1875.

History of the Brooklyn and Long Island Fair. Brooklyn: The Union, 1864.

Ingram, J.S. *The Centennial Exposition Described and Illustrated.* Philadelphia: Hubbard Brothers, 1876. Reprint ed. New York: Arno P, 1976.

Kidwell, Claudia. "Short Gowns," *Dress* 4 (1978): 30-65.

Maas, John. *The Glorious Enterprise: The Centennial Exhibition of 1876 and H.J. Schwarsmann, Architect-in Chief.* Watkins Glen, New York: American Life Foundation, 1973.

Mayne, Leger D. *What Shall We Do Tonight—Or Social Amusements for Evening Parties.* New York: Dick and Fitzgerald, 1873.

Northampton [Massachusetts] Free Press, various issues.

Norton, Frank, ed. *Frank Leslie's Historical Register of the United States Centennial Exposition, 1876.* New York: Frank Leslie, 1877.

Our Daily Fare, [Philadelphia Sanitary Fair newspaper], June, 1864.

Pennsylvania Board of Centennial Managers. *Pennsylvania and the Centennial*

Exposition: Comprising the Preliminary and Final Reports. 2 vols. Philadelphia: Gillin and Nagle, 1878.

Putnam, Elizabeth Cabot and Sarah Putam, eds. *The Hon. Samuel Putnam and Sarah Putnam. With a Genealogical Record of Their Descendants.* 10 vols. Danvers: Danvers Historical Society Collections, 1922.

Record of the Metropolitan Fair in Aid of the United States Sanitary Commission Held in New York in April 1864. New York: 1864.

Report of the Christmas Bazaar, December 14-22. Rochester, N.Y.: Benton and Andrews, 1864.

Roth, Rodris. "The New England, or 'Old Tyme' Kitchen Exhibits at Nineteenth Century Fairs." In *The Colonial Revival in America,* ed. Alan Axelrod. New York: W.W. Norton, 1985.

The Sword and the Pen [Soldiers Home Bazaar newspaper, Chelsea, Massachusetts], December 17, 1881.

The Voice of the Fair [Second Northwest Sanitary Fair newspaper, Chicago], June 1865.

Wagenknecht, Edward, ed. *Mrs. Longfellow: Selected Letters and Journals of Fanny Appleton Longfellow.* London: Peter Owen, 1959.

The Gym Suit:
Freedom at Last

Patricia Campbell Warner

Introduction

The term "gym suit" brings frissons of distaste to any woman over the age of forty. We remember with misery every detail. Mine was a shapeless, blue cotton bag buttoned down the front and drawn in at the waist with a belt that had two white buttons. In my high school, athletic girls preferred to demonstrate their independence by doubling the belt around at the back through the belt keepers, and buttoning it there. It looked even worse this way than with the belt defining the waist. White, splotchy winter legs emerged from the romper legs whose elastic got looser as the years wore on. Goose-bump arms, with each hair standing straight on end in the cold gym at the beginning of every class, dangled from depressing, styleless short sleeves. Each limp, dull, unironed suit was adorned with the wearer's name, painstakingly embroidered in white on the back. The application of our name was a task we were all assigned as we entered high school—if we were handy with a needle, we did it ourselves; if not, our mothers came to our rescue. At the end of each class, we'd roll it up and stuff it into our lockers, wrapped around our gym shoes, to forget about it until the next gym class; rarely did we take it home for washing unless we were scheduled for inspection.

We remember its color, its style, its smell. We suffered mortification if the boys saw us in it because it made even the best of us look so awful. The gym suit for North American women remains indelibly etched in our group memory. We all wore it; we all hated it.

But the lowly gym suit, so despised in our youth, played a major role in our collective history as educated women; one generally unrecognized. It is tied, from the very earliest days, to the history of women's higher education in the United States. Its role was to free women's bodies for one reason: to participate in active exercise and sport. And it was the first widely accepted garment not

140

only to encourage but to insist on no inner support in the form of corsetry for the female body. To discuss the American women's gym suit is to discuss the painfully long, slow process of the successful adoption of a trouser form for women. I believe the clothing for physical education has wider influence on women's clothing in the twentieth century than any other, except perhaps dance.

The earliest formal version of the garment we call a gym suit, or gymnastic costume as it was referred to then, dates from the early 1890s and the invention of team sports for women, notably basketball. The image of the daring young women in their gymnastic suits from that period is a familiar one. Yet in costume history lore, in the rare references to the gym suit, it is usually tied to the bicycle bloomer, suggesting they both were updated revivals of the Bloomer dress some forty years after it had suffered its ignominious sartorial death in the 1850s. It is simplistic, if not wrong altogether, to suggest that after a forty-year hiatus the gym and bicycle bloomers emerged fully formed, rather like Venus rising from the head of Zeus. The emergence of the bloomers of the 1890s came as a step, and only a step, in a long development that lasted throughout the nineteenth century and continued into the twentieth. Indeed, to be correct, the gymnastic dress was a forerunner of the Bloomer dress, rather than the opposite, which is generally claimed.

Four Factors Influencing Women's Gymnastic Costumes

The case of the gymnasium costume represents a good example of how a particular form of clothing comes into acceptance. Rarely can a student of clothing make a simple declaration of lineal ancestry behind any fashion development; many factors influence the emerging look of clothing in each generation. In this particular case, at least four major historic movements occurring simultaneously over time had impact on the bifurcated gym dress that emerged in the last decade of the nineteenth century.

The earliest origins of a garment for gymnastic wear actually lay in the late eighteenth century and the adoption of the trouser form into male fashionable dress. Straight-legged trousers were humble in origin, worn by peasants for centuries before they were adopted around 1770 by European aristocrats for their little sons to wear.[1] The lavish but fundamentally sensible trouser suits, called "skeleton suits," represented the first time in history that an outfit was designed specifically for children. Sometime around 1803, with the general acceptance of sheer, lightweight muslin fashions for woman, mothers concerned about modesty borrowed the trouser idea from their sons for their daughters to wear underneath the simple, shorter little dresses. Even at that time, and even with small children, a display of leg was determined unacceptable by society. The trousers for females were called pantaloons after the earlier straight-legged trousers of the same name that men had worn, or pantalets. By definition, they hung free, with no gathered hem. They also represented a first "in near history," this time for girls.[2] About the same time, fathers gave up knee breeches for the long, tubular trousers, and eventually even adult women adopted pantaloons from their little daughters. This represented the first time in well over a hundred years that fashionable women wore a bifurcated garment as part of their underclothes. Until then, women had worn only shifts, stays and petticoats, believing that fresh air needed to circulate freely around the body. The exception to this, as Boucher points out, was in the theater where drawers had been "obligatory...since 1760"; another was found in common costume in the eighteenth century (Boucher 304). It is very likely that the dubious reputation of women in the theatre at that time affected the slow speed of adoption of trousers as underwear for other women.

At first the trousers remained hidden, but as skirt lengths rose the pantaloons stayed ankle-length and therefore visible. A 1906 French publication, *Le Pantalon Feminin*, also credited the origin of this garment in women's dress to English children but added that it was worn for exercise:

En 1897 nous arrive de Londres la mode des pantalons pour les petites filles. Les exercises du saut se pratiquent en Angleterre dans les écoles de jeunes filles: c'est pour cela qu'on leur a donné des pantalons.[3]

By the 1830s, clothing for little girls had given up the freedom of the previous generation, losing out to the elaborateness of the early ornate and restricting Romanticism. But by that time, the pantaloon had become more or less a permanent article of female clothing.

A second factor influencing the development of the gym suit was the great interest in things "Oriental," including what now would be referred to as Middle Eastern but which then included anything east of Europe. Many things had conspired to encourage this trend, but mainly a combination of burgeoning trade and the British and French imperial expansion into India, Persia and Turkey. The interest in the exotic increased with these great forays of empire building, and expressions of it entered the popular culture from the mid-1770s on; in fine art, interior design, even opera. The fascination with the mid-Eastern way of life, particularly with the custom of isolating women in a harem, captivated Europe in the later eighteenth century, and is reflected, for example, in Mozart's

Abduction from the Seraglio of 1782.

For our purposes, the adoption of Eastern clothing played an important role. It was loose, much more functional than contemporary European dress, and was either borrowed directly or adapted to European fashion, mostly for private leisure wear or costume balls. Both men and women wore it. Many aristocrats had their portraits painted wearing Eastern dress; even Mme de Pompadour was portrayed by Carle van Loos wearing filmy Turkish trousers and being served by a similarly clad black woman (Mitford 145). By the turn of the nineteenth century, Napoleon's incursions into North Africa renewed the Eastern, exotic influence, and the continuing French involvement with Morocco played its role in influencing fashion.

By the 1810s through the 1830s, popular painters like Ingres and Delacroix reflected the taste in orientalism. Delacroix, one of the first French artists to espouse the Romantic, visited Spain, Morocco and Turkey in 1832. He returned to France with a portfolio of watercolors and drawings that he used as the basis for some one hundred paintings later. He documented in romantic and imaginative works the dress of both men and women, rich in color and exotic detail. Some representations were of the harem, and many women were shown wearing Turkish trousers, that Eastern form with its long, baggy, full pants, gathered at the ankle and worn beneath a tunic or bolero. It is that trouser which provided the generic term, used throughout the century, to describe any gathered trouser form. From these two examples, it is clear that the model of trouser forms for women was well established before the middle of the nineteenth century, well before the Bloomer dress, even if it was virtually hidden as underwear or worn as exotic fancy dress.

A third phenomenon creating its impact was the health movement in Europe and America, taking roots just about the same time. Physical training was a new concept and very much part of this movement.[4] Early European proponents developed entire systems of gymnastics. The German, Friedrich Ludwig Jahn, wrote his famous *Die Deutsche Turnkunst* in 1816, and in Sweden the influential Per Ling established the Royal Gymnastics Central Institute in Stockholm in 1814. His son Hjalmar turned the emphasis of gymnastics towards education. It must be pointed out that both countries at this time concentrated their efforts on educating boys only (Gerber 126-33, 155-62). However, the growing interest for both sexes was apparent in the mid-century commentary given at Mount Holyoke Seminary: "Miss Catherine Beecher glowingly describes the Russian Seminary she visited, where more than 900 girls from noble families were being trained in Ling's calisthenics."

In the United States, *Godey's* editor, Sarah J. Hale, in the July 1841 issue of *Godey's Lady's Book*, wrote extolling the merits of "Physical education...for the constitution." The need for an article on exercise arose because, as Mrs. Hale stated, "We think that this department of training children is, in our country, more neglected than any other." In her article, she quoted a "physician of Glasgow, Scotland" at some length giving among other details, his idea of appropriate clothing for girls:

> The most suitable dress is unquestionably that which is called Turkish, consisting of pantalettes or trowsers, and a short frock (the latter to be brought up sufficiently high on the bosom to prevent the exposure of the shoulders) and the covering of the head should be light and cool—a straw hat answers the purposes very well. (GLB, "How to Begin" 41)

An 1832 illustration in *Atkinson's Casket* (Fig. 1) showed what the agile woman wore to do her exercises—clearly a cross between the Turkish trouser and the pantalette (Murray 115). Throughout the next couple of decades, there were occasional references about this kind of outfit being worn in spas, asylums, or sanitoria, which, with their water cures, were very much a part of the health movement.

It is this latter dress and trouser combination, copied by Elizabeth Smith Miller who brought it to Seneca Falls on a visit to her cousin, Elizabeth Cady Stanton, that influenced the mid-century outfit that came to be known as the Bloomer dress. Named after the intrepid Amelia, a friend and neighbor of Elizabeth Cady Stanton's, it was introduced to a wide audience on both sides of the Atlantic through Mrs. Bloomer's temperance newspaper, *The Lily*. (Fig. 2) Elizabeth Cady Stanton in her old age recalled that the Bloomer costume was worn by "Many patients in sanitariums, whose names I cannot recall," and also by "farmer's [*sic*] wives, skaters, gymnasts, tourists and in sanitariums" (Murray 114). Although it was regarded as daring, even ludicrous, in its day, it seems rather surprising that it was so reviled when, in fact, it had already existed for some thirty years previously as an exercise dress.

After the Bloomer's ignominious banishment, what happened to it? Did it vanish, as costume historians have always suggested, only to reappear as a bicycle suit in the 1890s? The answer, of course, is no.

At about the same time the Bloomer was facing its social Waterloo, the exercise movement was just beginning to gain momentum. Schools of gymnastics sprang up, particularly in Massachusetts, centered in Boston,

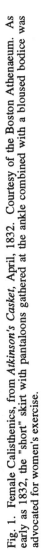

Fig. 1. Female Calisthenics, from *Atkinson's Casket*, April, 1832. Courtesy of the Boston Athenaeum. As early as 1832, the "short" skirt with pantaloons gathered at the ankle combined with a bloused bodice was advocated for women's exercise.

Amelia Bloomer in 1851. Daguerreotype by T. W. Brown.

Fig. 2. Amelia Bloomer, Engraving from a Daguerreotype, 1851. Courtesy of the Library of Congress. This outfit, later dubbed the "Bloomer costume," was advocated by Mrs. Bloomer in her Seneca Falls publication *The Lily*. It consisted of a top in contemporary fashion but shortened to the knee without petticoats and Turkish trousers gathered at the ankle.

Cambridge and Springfield. The most famous, the Normal Institute for Physical Education in Boston, was founded in 1860 and run by Diocletian (Dio) Lewis. By 1862, with the publication of his book, *The New Gymnastics for Men, Women and Children*, the interest in gymnastics had become something of a craze. His book became a best seller of the time, going into dozens of editions. Dio Lewis illustrated this book with etchings of men and women doing his exercises, (Figs. 3 and 4) and stated that the most suitable clothing for women was the Turkish trouser outfit. The outfit featured two skirts covering the trousers, an outer and an underskirt. The underskirt was thin and slip-like, worn in place of a hoop, just stiff enough to keep the outer skirt away from the legs. The design's chief asset was that it allowed "perfect liberty about the waist and shoulders" since, if they were "trammeled, the exertions will serve no purpose" (16-18).

Even *Godey's Lady's Book*, that arbiter of American taste, approved the fad, and in January, 1864, cast light as it so often did on contemporary customs and usage. Calling them "light parlour gymnastics," (Fig. 5) *Godey's* made it clear that the exercises were intended to be done at home since few had access to one of the rare, new, and usually predominantly male gymnasia. The article went on to describe in minute detail the "very attractive costumes for the always healthful, now popular...gymnastics." *Godey's* suggested that an eight-inch velvet border and trim, with jet and "the tiniest gold braid," was very tasteful, and rounded off the whole outfit with "wide Turkish pants of the same." It's notable that neither Godey's nor anyone else used the term "Bloomer" in describing these outfits at the time, probably avoiding it because of the disastrous connotations the term had come to suggest.

The fourth and most important factor influencing the gym suit's development was the rise of the colleges for women that were also being founded in these same years. The earliest still in existence today was Mount Holyoke College, opened as a seminary for woman in 1837. Mary Lyon, its founder, was regarded as something of an eccentric for insisting on exercise for her young ladies, but other seminaries or colleges for women followed her lead: Rockford Seminary (later College) offered some form of exercise by 1849, Vassar by 1868, and Smith and Wellesley by 1875, the year of their opening. The earliest formal exercise was calisthenics, listed in the curriculum in a preliminary pamphlet Mary Lyon issued in 1835, before Mount Holyoke Seminary opened. Actually more like the quadrille dances of the day, they required no change in clothing, not even "concerning the removal of 'stays' "(McCurdy 144).

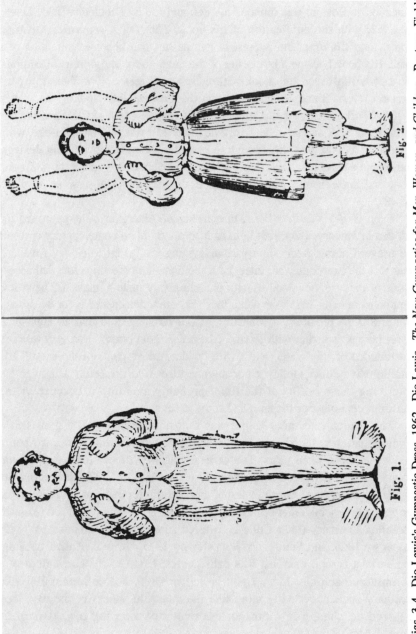

Figs. 3-4. Dio Lewis's Gymnastic Dress, 1862. Dio Lewis. *The New Gymnastics for Men, Women, and Children.* Boston: Fields, Osgood & Co., tenth edition, 1869. The relation between Lewis's dress and the exercise dress of thirty years before is evident.

Fig. 5. "Home Exercises," *Harper's Weekly,* July 11, 1857. *Harper's Weekly* referred to them as home exercises, *Godey's* as "light parlour gymnastics," but both sets of exercises were clearly intended to be done in the home with existing furniture while wearing a Turkish-trousered outfit.

The first accepted outfit for gymnastic activity in a collegiate setting occurred when Mount Holyoke adopted the Dio Lewis costume in 1863 after substituting his "new gymnastics" for the older calisthenics. It was "a very short skirt with 'zouave' trousers drawn up just below the knee and falling over nearly to the ankle" (McCurdy 146). (Fig. 6) The style wasn't uniform, and it is clear that as late as the 1890s the dresses were homemade. In a Manual of Gymnastics from 1883, an instructor at Mount Holyoke gave clear directions to any dressmaker what the appropriate gymnasium dress should be (Fig. 7):

The dress may be of flannel [which was wool] (dark blue preferred), made with blouse-waist, loose belt, sleeves moderately full, good length and closed at the wrist.

It requires about 8 yards of flannel, single width, or four and a half double width, for the dress, including drawers, which may be pieced at the top with cambric.

The dress should not be trimmed heavily; a flounce about six inches deep should be stitched on to the lower edge of the skirt, not put on the skirt, and a band of trimming to match collar and cuffs, or rows of braid, may be placed above the flounce.

Width of skirt about two and one fourths yards, and seven inches from the floor.

The waist should be made long enough under the arms to allow the arms to be stretched upward to their utmost extent without drawing upon the belt at all. Shoulder seam should be short, and armholes large.

Corsets and high-heeled boots are out of place in the gymnasium. (Clapp 33)

The adoption of Dio Lewis's gymnastics system provided the necessary impetus to build a gymnasium at Mount Holyoke—no small feat in wartime— and, after a fund drive led by the governor of Massachusetts who visited the school and was impressed by the gymnastic display put on by the students, it opened in 1865.

Vassar College was slightly different in its approach, as it was to much else in establishing private women's degree-granting education in the United States. The first catalogue (1865-66) pointed out that the building housing the riding hall and gymnasium was still being built but that "Classes for Physical Training were organized and instructed in the corridors on the college by Elizabeth M. Powell." These corridors were "Beautifully lighted, aired and warmed...[to] afford ample means of indoor exercise in inclement weather (Ballintine 6). Other "feminine sports and games" would diversify the physical exercises," including "boating in the summer and skating in the winter, without danger of outside intrusion...archery, croquet (or Ladies' cricket), graces, shuttlecock, etc" (Ballintine 6-7). A suitable dress was deemed "indispensable"; accordingly,

Fig. 6. Mount Holyoke Gymnastic Team, 1865. Courtesy of Mount Holyoke College Archives. Note the general bagginess of the outfits, both in the blouson top and the trousers. The variety of styles indicates the home-made nature of the gymnasium dresses.

Fig. 7. Calesthenic Class, Mount Holyoke Seminary, late 1870s. Courtesy of Mount Holyoke College Archives. Under each shortened dress was a pair of "Turkish trousers," albeit hidden from the camera's view.

a uniform [was] adopted for the calisthenics classes in College, the material for which can be procured and made up on arrival.... Every student will be required to provide herself with a light and easy-fitting dress, to be worn during these athletic exercises. It will be left optional with her, whether to wear it or not at other times.... (Ballintine 7)

The suit was referred to as a "simple uniform of gray and red sash." Judging from illustrations, it too was based on Dio Lewis's gymnastic dress. But because it was mandated that all wear the same dress, made from the same material, it is the first uniform for women's athletic activity in a collegiate setting, or almost certainly any other, in the United States. Incidentally, Vassar, by suggesting that students might wear their gym dresses elsewhere than for physical training, was unique. Generally, such freedom was prohibited. Perhaps the physical isolation of the college and its buildings from the town of Poughkeepsie had something to do with leniency.

It is doubtful that the Vassar suit lasted long. Dr. Eliza M. Moser, who went to Vassar as resident physician in 1883, recalled in an afterdinner speech given in 1920 that she had presented a request the year she had arrived on behalf of the director of the gymnasium to replace "the monotonous calisthenics exercises in very proper ankle-length skirts [clearly not the gray and red turkish trouser outfits of the 1860s] by the newly developed Sargent system of gymnastics, physical measurements and divided skirts." She further reported that "an old faculty member" declared that, "The girls will not stand for it," while another flatly stated, "They will not wear divided skirts" (Hazard). Both proved to be wrong, or course; the girls did wear the new outfits, and willingly.[5]

The women's colleges led the way in advocating exercise for women, but, as noted earlier, the entire health-exercise movement was at its peak in the years during which the women's colleges were being founded. So strong was the demand for gymnastic dresses generally that popular magazines like *Godey's, Peterson's* and *The Delineator* all had articles on them, with pictures, telling how to make them from the 1860s into the 80s.

By the late 1880s, outfits consisting of full Turkish trousers and a "blouse" (the late nineteenth century term for a blouson bodice) had taken precedence over skirted gymnastic dresses. One writer referred to "the fluffy little skirt" that

turned out to be no skirt at all. It is two skirts, a divided skirt, it clothes each leg separately. It makes a pretty drapery while the gymnast was motionless, but it does not interfere with the perfect freedom of the limbs. She is wearing Turkish trousers, after a model of the gymnasts' own.[6]

In 1888, the dress reformer, Annie Jenness Miller, referred in an article, "Exercise for Women," to "a regular costume...which will not impede or interfere with the free movements of any member of the body...." It should, she continued,

properly consist of a pair of full Turkish trousers with a jersey underwaist or blouse, which can be worn with an abbreviated tunic drapery, [hard to visualize from a late twentieth century perspective] if one be supersensitive to appearing in the simple trousers and blouse, which are now worn as the regulation costume in all of the popular gymnasiums patronized by both sexes.[7]

Finally, by 1893, Butterick came out with a pattern for the gymnasium bloomer, (*Arena* 7:24). This coincided with the earliest manufacturing of the garments by commercial companies which heralded a new uniformity.

The question arises, then: Why was there a need for uniformity?

The Beginnings of the Gym Uniform

With the single exception of Vassar College, the gym bloomer as a uniform emerged because women began to participate in team sports, indoors, in the gymnasium. Basketball was the first. It had been devised as a game for men at Springfield Training School (later College), in 1891. The next year, after its rules had been published in the *Journal of Physical Education*, Smith College's gymnastics instructor, Senda Berenson, adapted it for women. Until this time, exercise had meant calisthenics: Indian club swinging, wand waving, even Dio Lewis's "new gymnastics" which were a form of calisthenics. It was frankly boring, so this new, energetic game put vigor into the physical education program. It was adopted by schools everywhere in an amazingly brief period of time: by 1894 or 1895, most schools with female students had basketball for women. In many cases it was not part of any regular education curriculum; often it was introduced through Women's Athletic Associations or through the interest of the girls themselves.[8] Whatever its auspices, this game spelled the end of the old skirted gymnastic dress in the schools—it was simply too bulky. Thus, the skirt was finally banished from the gymnasium, bringing a simplification to the outfit. The bloomers shortened and widened to give the appearance of a short skirt, and the separate blouse buttoned onto the bloomer waistband. That much, women gained. What they sacrificed was the ability to wear this new garment out of doors where someone—men—might see them.

At first there was a variety of gym suit styles even on the same team.

(Fig. 8) But by the mid-1890s, uniformity in design began to appear. By the early years of the new century, a uniform as we think of it had taken shape. This suit, with slight variations, was worn by all girls participating in all indoor athletic endeavors. For outdoor activities, it was only when the field was remote and hidden from the public that the girls could wear gym suits, and even then, they had to cover their legs with skirts to get to the playing fields. Trousered legs for women simply were not accepted—not even when the trousers looked like skirts.

A notable, and for the time shocking, exception to this was in California. In his history of Stanford University, Orrin Leslie Elliott wrote:

> Basketball, a very recent sport, was taken up with enthusiasm and in 1894 an off-campus game was played with the Castilleja School in Palo Alto, Stanford losing 13 to 14.
>
> This was going about as far as the mores of the time would stand for. "This is the initiation of public athletics for the girls here", one of the juniors wrote. "They played in their gym suits on the grounds by Castilleja Hall. They rode to the game in a bus in their suits just as the men do. While some are quite opposed to such doings, there seems to be very little said in the matter. I don't feel in the least like entering into any such thing, nor do I feel like criticizing the girls who do, if they keep on their own ground or play with the prep school girls. (Elliott 197-98)

However, two years later, a sensational game between Stanford and the University of California girls (basketball at this time was only a women's sport in the West) was played in the Armory in San Francisco. At California's insistence, and much to Stanford's scorn, only women were permitted in as spectators (Elliott 197-98). In this, the girls from Berkeley followed the tradition of modesty already established at Smith College in Massachusetts (Warner, "Public" 51). Stanford won, by a score of 2 to 1. It should be noted that these two games were intercollegiate, which was another major innovation. The Eastern schools categorically refused any such recognition of competitive spirit.

Another factor emerging at this time that required new clothing choices was the invention of other team sports for women. Within eight years of basketball's appearance, the game of field hockey was imported from England by Constance Applebee, a visiting scholar at a Harvard Summer School program in athletic training, first opened to women in 1896 (Ballintine 15). Applebee traveled to New England in the summer of 1901 bearing her hockey sticks, eager to teach the new game to collegiate women.[9] Since this sport had to

Fig. 8. Smith College Basketball Team, Class of 1895. Courtesy Smith College Archives, Smith College. Note how the numbers have been sewn on sometimes with little regard for the design of the gymnasium suit underneath.

be played out of doors, what to wear became a pressing question. The Boston *Sunday Herald* later reported,

> When hockey was first introduced to Smith...the question of the proper costume immediately arose. Many of the girls thought they must wear bloomers, instead of skirts, in order to play well, but Miss Berenson said:
> Well, girls, since we have to do all our running after we leave college in skirts, isn't it wise to learn to do it gracefully?
> That settled it, and now the girls think that skirts are best, after all, because they often catch the ball when it would otherwise go out of bounds. Besides, they do not want to ape their brothers, or to be athletic in any sense such as men give the word. (7)

Whatever Miss Berenson's reasons, the truth behind the choice lay more in the conventions of the day. Since the sport was played out of doors in view of the public, skirts had to be worn. It was as simple as that. The players all wore roughly the same long skirts and tops, but differentiated teams through hats; half wore tams, the rest sailors. The one concession to the physical activity of the game was that the skirts were "short," that is, four to six inches off the ground. It is interesting to note that this tradition was maintained when the game was revived as an intercollegiate sport for women in the late 1970s. The correct uniform remains the skirt in the form of a short kilt, still worn today. But the seeds of that kilt lie in the prudishness of turn-of-the-century America. From the beginning, outdoor team sports for women, whether crew at Wellesley from the 1870s, baseball at Mount Holyoke in the 1880s, or field hockey at Smith, devised different styles of uniforms from those worn indoors in the gymnasium. This dichotomy continued until the 1970s.

The Gym Suit

The gym suit that emerged with basketball was a two-piece, inky navy blue (almost black) serge, which was a tightly-woven, rather harsh and hard-wearing wool fabric, not too thick but dense and scratchy.[10] The entire suit was made out of this material. (Fig. 9) The trousers, usually called "divided skirts," were really almost two full skirts , pleated to confine the amounts of material and gathered at the knee. The crotch rested at knee height, often cut in a single large gusset, up to 18" square, and set in on a diamond pattern. It was not until after 1900 that journalists and authors began to refer to them as "bloomers". The "blouse" or "waist" of the gym suit allowed the arms to move freely in all directions, and buttoned onto the bloomer's waistband. The women wore long black cotton stockings, held under the bloomer with garters, and flat, rubber-

Fig. 9. Gym-suited student with Class mascot, 1902. Courtesy Smith College Archives, Smith College. Should any doubt remain about the difference between the general silhouette of the clothing worn in the gymnasium and the fashionwear of the day, note the spectators in the background. They were there to see the Smith College basketball match between the Freshmen and the Sophs. Each team had its own mascot; that particular team dressed a tiny sibling in her own miniature gymnasium outfit, complete in every detail.

soled shoes. The whole outfit in the mid 1890s cost under $6.00, including the shoes.[11] Interestingly, almost everyone, no matter where they lived, wore this same outfit, even in the humid warm South. No regional differences in climate had any bearing on the approved garment.

I believe the reasons for the universality of the suit style and fabrication were two-fold. First, all the early instructors of gymnastics were trained in only a handful of schools, mainly in Massachusetts and New York. These women carried their programs far and wide throughout the country, primarily into the Midwest and the South, even into Canada, and as they went they took their regulation gym costume with them. Second, when manufacturers began to supply the gym suit for physical education programs, they produced only a limited number of styles. Many of the manufacturers were located in the Boston area. Of the institutions I visited, California schools (University of California, Stanford) used suppliers located in the West.[12]

A few gymnastic directors attempted to design alternate styles of costumes, notably at the University of Michigan and Stanford. Dr. Eliza M. Mosher, a medical doctor (Michigan, '75), returned to Michigan in 1896 as dean of women and professor of hygiene, (not an unusual combination of credentials at that time). She graduated from the Anderson Normal School of physical education in New Haven, Connecticut and studied at the Sargent School of gymnastics in Cambridge, Massachusetts. It was she who had gone to Vassar as physician in residence in 1883, and who wanted to change the program and consequently the gymnasium dress. When Dr. Mosher went to Michigan she designed a uniform which the *Detroit Free Press* (2 November 1896) called "the most novel thing about the whole programme." The costume consisted of the typical serge bloomer, but rather than having it button onto a blouse top, it attached instead to a

low-cut bodice of the German peasant pattern with narrow bands passing over the shoulders. This bodice buttons under the left arm and fits the figure closely, giving the exact lines of the body from the arm pit to hip. It never pulls or shifts with any motion of the body, the arms and shoulders being left perfectly free. Under the bodice will be worn a sweater or jersey of peculiar design with full sleeves to the elbow leaving the forearm uncovered. This suit leaves the outlines of the neck, shoulders and back fully revealed to the instructor who can thus catch at a glance any defects in the pupil of figure movement. The usual gymnasium stockings and shoes complete the outfit. The skirt and bodice will be dark blue, and the sweater or jersey yellow, making the suit a veritable university uniform. (Fig. 10)

Fig. 10. The Moser suit at the University of Michigan, The Basketball Team, 1901. Courtesy of the Bentley Historical Library, University of Michigan. (MU Dept. of Physical Education, Women, Box 9, Basketball.)

It remained in use at Michigan for at least a decade. Photographs indicate a new model replaced it by about 1905.

Stanford too attempted a different design, but it did not have even the small success the Michigan suit enjoyed. It appeared in photographs labeled "The Stanford Gymnasium Suit" sometime about 1896.[13] It is the only suit for women prior to the 1920s which had narrow, unpleated knicker bottoms similar to those worn by men. Another startling departure from the norm was the waistline, which sat at the small of the back but dropped in front to curve beneath the belly. It appeared to button up the front, and probably buttoned onto the knickers. The high-cut funnel neckline was set in a yoke that attached in a curve into the bloused bodice. Apparently it was too avant garde for even the daring Californians to wear; it appeared nowhere else, vanishing completely, to be superceded by standard gymnasium suits.

If the search for the ideal gymnasium suit presented something of a problem, so did the underwear to wear with it. Few sources refer to it at all. However, we get a glimmer of what was expected in the Third Annual Catalogue (1894-95) from the State Normal and Industrial School (later renamed the Women's College of the University of North Carolina, still later, the University of North Carolina at Greensboro). It stated that the "gymnasium outfit, including a pair of gymnasium shoes, *a union undersuit* [my emphasis] and an over suit of blue serge, is required to be of uniform material and make, and cannot be made at home" (522-23). This represents one of the few references to appropriate underclothing to wear with the gymnasium dress, and one of the few directives that indicated how a uniform style for the gymnasium suited emerged.

Not everyone believed the standard gymnasium suit was appropriate for exercise. In 1910 and 1911 a series of articles under the general title "gymnastic costume for women" by Leonhard Felix Fuld appeared in the *American Physical Education Review*. In 1910 Fuld discussed the need for reform in exercise clothing, noting among other aspects of the gym suit the underwear worn with it—"if the student wears underwear, as should always be insisted upon...." (574). It is clear he was addressing his remarks to teachers of physical exercise at the high school level; nevertheless, many of his comments are universal. Fuld ridiculed the physical education programs and the clothing girls and women wore. He was not alone for this time but was the most outspoken in attacking the "physical torture of a waistband cutting into her abdominal walls" caused by multitudes of layers of cloth found in the many overlapping waistbands. Fuld kept up the attack in 1911:

By actual count it has been found that this costume has nine thicknesses of material at the waist. The serge bloomers have three thicknesses of material, lining and stiffening; there is a separate belt of two thicknesses of lining to button the blouse to the bloomers; there is a belt on the blouse consisting of two thicknesses of lining and the blouse itself with its folds of material adds to the thickness of this mass of material at the waist. In addition the underclothing worn by the student may add three additional thicknesses of material to the waist line and in some cases even more. The student accordingly wears twelve thicknesses of material at the waist. (522-23)

He was also the only writer who expressed concern about the various gapings of the parts of the gymnasium suit; at the waist where it buttoned, at the side where the bloomers fastened and at the knee, commenting on "the mental disquietude resulting from the fact that the wearer is 'always coming apart at the belt' when engaged in vigorous exercise. No refined woman", Fuld observed in 1910, "can enjoy herself in the gymnasium when this nagging consciousness is constantly present...."(574). He also was the only one who addressed "mental discomforts" and "the injurious effects of round garters

—little bands of torture worn around the knee as bracelets worn around the wrist—they permit their pupils to wear them in the gymnasium because they are the most convenient. It is true that when removed at the end of the gymnasium lesson they leave deep-cut furrows, but it is claimed that when they are worn the stockings present a prettier because more taut appearance....

The mental torture which the student suffers from the existing conditions at her knee results from the fact that with the activity in the gymnasium there seems to be constant danger of exposure at the knee. Much of this danger is fancied rather than real. Yet to a sensitive girl or woman this consciousness is a perfectly real discomfort. Ordinary thrift and tidiness on the part of the student would seem to be able to remedy this condition by the renewal of the elastic band at the knee of the bloomers as frequently as may be necessary...[if it isn't renewed] there is always a likelihood that during exercise the leg of the bloomers will ride upwards and leave a portion of the leg exposed (573).

Instead of the round garters ("an instrument of torture worthy of the Middle Ages") Fuld recommended "a stocking or garter girdle with garters at the sides which do not exert any pressure over the bladder", one that crossed "the sacrum in the back and slants down just on top of the trochanter, buckling over the pubic bones." He warned that the novice at first will fear the girdle will slip down, but assured them that this will not be the case, and they will be "delighted" with its lack of interference (578).

In the same article, Fuld blasted the "present day gymnastic costume for women" not only because it caused physical discomfort owing to the fullness and weight, and "unnecessary disquietude because of existing conditions at the knee and at the waist", but primarily because "the costume is outrageously unhygienic."

In explanation of this statement it should be borne in mind that gymnasium costumes are almost invariably made of non-washable material,—usually of coarse, scratchy serge, or heating, moisture-absorbing flannel. Furthermore, the students seldom wear any underwear while exercising. In this way all of the perspiration and other skin exudations from the surface of the body are absorbed by the gymnasium suit which itself is never washed.[14]

By "underwear", one might assume he was speaking of a union suit, rather than a chemise and/or drawers—but perhaps not.

The general unwashability of the gym suit created universal problems. By the time Fuld was writing his diatribes, a movement was afoot to find a solution to his objections and other difficulties identified by wearers. Florence Bolton, director of the women's gymnasium at Stanford, published an article in the *American Physical Education Review* earlier the same year. In it, she too tells us that a suit may be worn for "years without cleansing; the blouse especially is charged with oil and perspiration. Where a sweater replaces the blouse, its name is fully suggestive of its condition" (338-41).

She also criticized the existing suit for its mass of cloth binding the waist— up to four bands—but unlike Fuld, she lay the blame in a particularly feminist fashion:

It produces what someone has spoken of as the "over-sexed" figure with abnormal protuberances above and below. These belts, usually fairly snug to begin with, are actually tight in many positions.... Men are undoubtedly somewhat responsible, directly or indirectly, for many of the absurdities in women's dress. Necessarily without experience in the matters upon which they pass judgment, often without any physiological, economic, artistic or other basis, their dictates are entirely arbitrary, but they dictate nonetheless. They love a certain tailor-made conformity. They allow women to go into gymnastics with the understanding that they should not make themselves look too dreadful and unfeminine. (338-41).

Bolton's solution was to design a suit that had no waist at all. Based on the English gymnasium slip—a knee-length, sleeveless, square-necked tunic with a straight yoke holding box pleats front and back—Bolton's incorporated the English top with the American bottom or bloomer. It fell loose from the high yoke, and was lightly "girdled" rather then belted. Underneath, the gymnast wore a "washable guimpe" or shirt, adding to its hygienic appeal. In 1910 Fuld commented on this new outfit, singing its praises: (Fig. 11):

Her costume consists of a one-piece slip which has no belt and no waist. A girdle loose enough to rise and fall and to return to place in the various positions assumed by the student in the gymnasium, is fastened firmly across the back and drops low in front, fastening with a snap. There is no pressure and as the suit is in one piece there is no danger of exposure or of coming apart at the waist. There is no sailor collar to flap in a most disconcerting manner about the head and ears of the student while she is in an inverted or semi-inverted position. The gymnasium suit is a one-piece slip which comes over the shoulders with two shoulder straps. At the neck a guimpe of some thin, soft, washable material is worn in place of the heating and irritating flannel, or the hard, scratchy serge." (576)

The problem with this suit, as Fuld saw it the following year, was the reluctance of students to wear an outfit with no waistline in that very waist-conscious period (521). For whatever reason, this outfit too found little outside acceptance, although it was adopted by the University of Wisconsin and used to some extent into the 1920s. It remained in use at Stanford throughout the 1920s.

Possibly the major reason the Bolton suit failed to capture a greater audience was the introduction, as early as 1908, of the middy. (Fig. 12) Made of white cotton duck, the sailor blouse had the benefit of being not only cooler but washable. Fuld tells us in 1910 that it had "come into use and into great popular favor" during the previous year; indeed, when there were no facilities to change clothes, girls were encouraged to wear the top and a skirt over their bloomers so they might remove the skirt and be ready for exercise in little time (573-75). Since the same voluminous serge bloomer was worn with it, one wonders at the bulk it must have produced under the skirts. Sometimes, for outdoor sports (where the players might be seen in public), it was worn with a "shortened" skirt. (Fig. 13) Another variation appearing in the early 1890s with the bloomer and used primarily for outdoor activities was the turtle-necked pullover, borrowed from the men's schools. But basically, the middy-and-bloomer was the gym suit worn in high schools and colleges for the next 25 years, until it was finally abandoned about 1930.

Even the middy was not without its drawbacks. Once again, the critical eye of L.F. Fuld draws them to our attention in his 1910 article. He was ever alert to the "sensitive" nature of the students, so pointed to the low V neckline as a possible source of chill, although he admitted that "the danger of catching cold

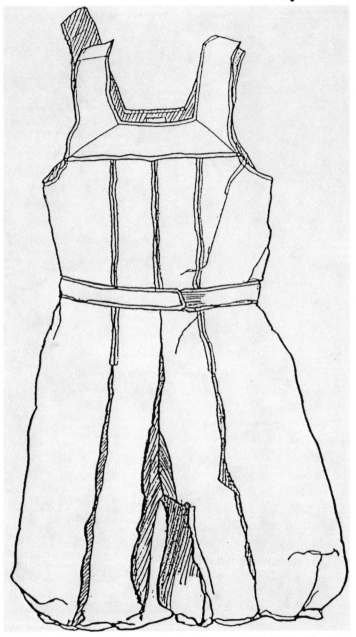

Fig. 11. The Bolton Gymsuit worn at Stanford from c. 1910-1930. The illustration, drawn by the author, was taken from a suit in the Stanford Archives (AM-79-12.13), donated by an alumna, Class of '29.

Fig. 12.   The Middy Blouse and Bloomer, University of North Carolina Women's College, 1913.   Courtesy University of North Carolina at Greensboro.

Fig. 13. The Middy and Shortened Skirt, 1911. Courtesy University Archives, University of North Carolina at Greensboro. Tennis champions at the UNC Women's College enjoyed greater freedom with middies and skirts that no longer trailed on the ground. Yearbooks from the University of Wisconsin show skirts almost as long were worn through 1921 for women's tennis. Tennis was an outdoor sport, so skirts were worn rather than bloomers.

because of the low-cut neck [was] more apparent than real." His solution was to insist that a "chest guard provided with the blouse be worn." His second objection had much the same importance:

When engaged in work on the heavy apparatus, the blouse frequently becomes disarranged [at the neckline] so as to expose the student's chest and breasts. This objection is also not entitled to much weight, since such exposure is not considered improper at a ball, or at the opera, and furthermore men are very seldom present in a gymnasium class.(575-76)

Far worse, in Fuld's opinion, was what happened when "the student is in an inverted or semi-inverted position." This not only caused the "sailor collar to flap in a most disconcerting manner about the head and ears of the student," but brought even greater misery to the wearer because the blouse,

which has no waist, frequently rides up and in such cases exposes the trunk of the student in a manner which is likely to cause serious embarrassment to the student and places her in a condition in which she lacks that mental quietude so much to be desired in gymnasium work.(575-76)

Nevertheless, it was worn universally. A few minor changes were made by the 1920s. The bloomer became a slimmer knicker and the sleeves of the middy were sometimes short. All our grandmothers or mothers wore this outfit, in high schools and in colleges. In fact, it became synonymous with "schoolgirl" in those decades. And it permitted them to do things they had never been able to do before as girls. They could run, play, leap, dive, hurdle, and exert themselves. It cannot be stated too strongly that before gymnasium suits were devised, women were not permitted any of this activity, mainly because they were not permitted to wear clothing that was suitable for it.

Perhaps to cast a different light on the gym suit at this time we should look at the clothing male athletes were wearing. The late nineteenth century male gymnast wore an outfit not unlike the figure-revealing tights and tops or leotards that Americans wear today, only usually all black. Annette Kellerman, famous as the Australian swimmer who in 1910 "designed her own swimming suit" (without giving any credit to her inspiration), creating almost a scandal in the process, borrowed directly the outfit men had worn for gymnastics for at least a quarter of a century. It consisted of a form-fitting body covering with very short sleeves and a scooped neckline and black tights.[15] And while the girls were modestly encased in yards of navy serge, the boys were wearing knickers and short-sleeved pullover shirts. Even earlier than the middy blouse was introduced, as early as 1900, men were wearing primitive versions of tank tops and shorts; all brief, all washable.

Many twentieth-century developments in gym suit designs relate to clothing design in general. It is not coincidental that streetwear took on the waistless line and the V-neck of the middy after 1910. In fact, styles worn for college athletic wear predated fashion by as much as 15 years. (Fig. 14) The outdoor basketball uniform worn at Mount Holyoke College, with its knee-skimming pleated skirt, dates from 1910. The line of the early waistless gym suit, reinforced by the middy, and the rubber garter both became symbols of the flapper in the 1920s. The gymnastic outfit had heralded an unconstrained kind of clothing for women long before the leading designers of the time, like Paul Poiret, boasted of "abandoning the corset".

One might argue that the lowly gym suit, worn in the United States by what amounted to a handful of privileged young women, would never make any kind of impact on fashion—indeed, would never be seen at all in those circles—were it not for the following factors. Gymnastics and the accompanying clothing became fashionable in their own right and were written up in every major magazine for women and in some others, like *Harper's Weekly*. And they were illustrated. The proliferation of the image of the young, athletic, American woman, so popular in the Gibson version, was a phenomenon of the period, making her a sort of "pin-up girl" of the time. Popular illustrators such as Harrison Fisher projected her as an ideal, and often portrayed her wearing, if not a gym suit *per se,* then a variation of it, with the turtlenecked sweater and daring knee-length skirt that she wore for outdoor sports during the 1910s, long before knee-length skirts were seen anywhere else. I believe that the phenomenon of athleticism and American beauty, tied to the new ideal of "the college girl", had influence on the fashions of the day—perhaps if not immediately, then subtly and over time.

By the 1920s, the gym suit seemed to flounder, trying to find a new form. The Stanford bloomer-jumper, of very lightweight wool worn with a cotton blouse underneath, provided one variation. Team uniforms took other directions: short tunics worn over shirts with knickers and skirts were one, shirts and shorts were another, appearing as early as 1929 at Rockford College. But the jumper idea seemed sensible, and in 1931 the bloomer shrank into a romper style, with baggy, elastic legs that fell low on the thigh, generally just above the knee. It was worn either with or without a blouse. It seems almost unbelievable, but this was the first completely washable gym suit ever designed for women

Fig. 14. Mount Holyoke outdoor basketball team, 1910. Courtesy Mount Holyoke College Archives. The knee-skimming skirts predated fashion by some fifteen years.

and girls.[16] It prevailed in many schools throughout the 1930s.

In 1933, however, Mildred Howard at Mount Holyoke College, working with the sporting goods company, Wright and Ditson, started on the path to design the gym suit that most of us remember with something between affection and horror. Her first attempt was a shirt-and-box-pleated-short combination. The shorts hung straight, looked like a short skirt when worn, and were flattering to most figures. These were soon discarded at Mount Holyoke when Miss Howard realized that the girls preferred wearing the outfit with the shirt-tail out, hanging so low that the shorts vanished entirely. Her final design, then, was based on the tennis dress. It had a romper as the base and a separate skirt that could be removed if one wished. For certain activities such as gymnastics, the skirt generally was left off; for sports it was generally worn. (Fig. 15)

In a letter written to Mildred Howard in 1947, Eleanor Edwards of Wright and Ditson, who had worked closely with Howard in creating the new style, credited her with the innovation.

You were definitely responsible for the adaptation for gymnasium costumes, of the tennis dress which we are now using for the majority of the colleges we outfit.... And there is no reason in the world why you shouldn't claim that distinction!

And Mount Holyoke was the first college in the East to adopt, for Physical Education classes, the *cotton* wash suit which is now so universally worn for gymnastic activities. And certainly no one can deny that for this purpose cotton is a great improvement over the wool materials! It was an important step forward—not only from the point of view of hygiene, but also from the standpoint of style—the bright colors of the cotton are so much more attractive than the drab navy and black of the wool material.

It is our sincere belief that these changes in gymnasium outfits must have done a great deal for Physical Education as a whole. Certainly they were bound to increase its popularity with the students, since they meant a girl could wear an attractive outfit that she liked—instead of a dreary (and often dirty!) suit she loathed, and hated to wear.

With certain modifications, the gym suit designed by Howard became the symbol of physical education for girls from the 1940s through the 1960s, just as the middy and bloomer had been earlier in the century. My own high school gym suit, in Toronto, Canada, was an ugly variation of the Howard suit. (Fig. 16) Based on the romper idea, it had a camp shirt-styled top, an elastic-legged short bloomer bottom, a belt with two buttons at the front, and no skirt. It was a blue that can only described as unforgettable. Another variation was the skirted jumper with matching bloomers underneath. Although the move was slowly and inexorably toward a solely bifurcated garment, it is interesting to see how long it took to get rid of the skirt altogether.

Fig. 15. The tennis dress gymsuit, all one piece with bloomers underneath. Courtesy University Archives, University of North Carolina at Greensboro. This gymnastic demonstration from UNC Women's College in 1950 illustrates how wearers tucked their skirts into the bloomers to hold the gymsuit in place when they were in "an inverted position" while, at the same time, preserving their modesty.

Although the romper/tennis suit provided the model in mid-century America, once again, one must note the exceptions. Schools in at least two states, California and Texas, chose to dress high school physical education classes in shirts and shorts as early as the 1940s. The shorts were navy blue cotton twill, the shirts either camp-style or T. Once again, the wearer's name had to be embroidered (in navy) on the shirt pocket and down the white stripe of the shorts.[17]

One other new clothing feature accepted by around 1930 or 1931 was short socks. Up until this time in America, bare legs simply were never seen in public, not even, up until the mid-1920s, for swimming and bathing. Not until then did women dare to venture onto a public beach without stockings—indeed, in many cities, they risked arrest for indecent exposure.[18] So the ankle socks worn with the romper-and-shirt gym suit of 1931 completed the revolutionary look and allowed even greater freedom of movement and comfort.

As noted in Miss Edwards' letter, the tennis-style gym suit came in many colors. Blue was a preferred color, but others were an odd sort of sage green, while still others were yellow and lavender. Often, especially in private schools, different colors of gym suits signified different classes, first year students, sophomores, and so on, recalling a tradition that went back to the earliest days of team sports at Smith and elsewhere. At that time, the numbers and trim on the navy serge collars and cuffs were done in class colors.

Miss Edwards' comments about attractiveness notwithstanding, part of the trouble with gym suits, beside the self-image of their wearers, was the question of modesty. This had been an issue since the very beginning, as could be seen in the furor about wearing gym suits in public. Trousers and visible legs were not proper for genteel young ladies. The skirted gym suits of the 1940s, 1950s and 1960s also presented problems of modesty. Even though the bloomers matched, or were attached in some cases, women did not feel respectable having them show. After all, if they were under the skirt, they were underwear. This problem led to some interesting solutions (Fig. 16) in an attempt to "keep things decently covered." Girls tucked the skirts up into the bloomers to create, in effect, a second layering of bloomer. It has been suggested that this was to keep the skirts out of the girls' faces as they did acrobatics. Possibly so, but having undergarments show those years, in any form at all, was simply no more acceptable than bare legs had been a generation earlier.

The gym suit persevered into the 1960s, but died of natural causes some time at the end of that decade. In colleges, it vanished entirely at this time, to be taken over by non-regulation shorts and t-shirts. In certain private and parochial

Fig. 16.   Basketball, UNCWC, 1938.   Courtesy University Archives, University of North Carolina at Greensboro.
By the late 1930s, the romper had shortened considerably and offered an optional top styled like a campshirt that
buttoned to the waist.   By this time it was evolving into roughly the same suit the author wore in the early 1950s.

high schools, following the classic style developed in the 1930s, the gym suit lingered on into the 1970s. It is interesting to ponder in this century of rapid change in women's dress that not once but twice has a simple, functional and contemporary style been found for the gym suit, one that endured over time. The middy-and-bloomer suit lasted unchanged well over twenty years, the tennis dress/romper endured for forty. Such longevity in nineteenth or twentieth century fashionwear would be unthinkable.[19]

It is a paradox that in the years of turmoil of the 1970s when women were beginning to come into their own in so many ways, in public universities visible attention to women's athletics dwindled to little more than was offered through general physical education classes. Intercollegiate sports did exist under the aegis of the Association of Intercollegiate Athletics for Women, established to give women championship opportunities in national competition at the same time that NCAA oversaw men's athletics, but it struggled in a system of powerful men's Varsity athletics that gave scant financial support. Intramural and club teams carried on sport activities, as they had from the very beginning, and professional preparation for physical education teachers continued through those years, but little outside attention was given to them. Evidence of this can be seen by the total absence of any mention of women's athletics over the 10-year period between 1965 and 1974 in the year books of the Big Ten universities I visited.[20] The only women's athletic activity they reported that even remotely resembled sports in those years was cheerleading. One can't help recalling that the big business of college sports for men really took off at the same time, and indeed continues, through TV exposure, to the present time.

Clearly, Title IX, the 1972 law forbidding sex discrimination in federally-funded schools, responded to these inequalities. Even so, it took another couple of years for it to be implemented and set in place. But beginning in 1975, the results were clear. That year, new intercollegiate Varsity teams for women—basketball, soccer and field hockey—all appeared in the pages of the Big Ten year books. And each sport had its own new uniform. Basketball adapted the t-shirt and shorts, soccer much the same, and field hockey maintained the kilt, usually tartan.

Since the 1970s, no one gym suit remains.[21] Uniforms for various activities have taken over. Specialization has found its way even into the gym. But the gym suit remains bound in memory, hated and loved, and little understood as to its significant role in our collective growing up.

Notes

[1]Citations pertaining to children's clothing are from Elizabeth Ewing, *History of Children's Costume* (New York: Charles Scribner's Sons, 1977), 48-51; and Diana De Marly, Fashion for Men (London: B. T. Batsford, Ltd., 1985), 72.

[2]Ewing quotes Doris Langley Moore in saying this development of clothing for children, quite unaffected by their parents' dress fashions for the first time in near history, was "the greatest sartorial event of the eighteenth century." She further points out that "it was the first time comfort and convenience had been the basis of any fashion, at least in the present cycle of history." pg. 46. It should be noted, however, that sixteenth and early seventeenth women wore passementerie-trimmed drawers with pockets to hold their stockings up in combinations with a chemise as underwear. (Boucher, 255.)

[3]*Anne Wood Murray. "The Bloomer Costume and Exercise Suits." Waffen-und Kostumekunde*, Munchen (Berlin: Deutscher Kunstverlag, 1982), 113. A loose translation is, "In 1807 the fashion of pantaloons for young girls arrived from London. Leaping exercises are practised in English girls' schools: for these they wear pantaloons."

[4]The term "physical education" in the nineteenth century referred to education about the physical characteristics of the body and its parts. Only around the turn of the twentieth century did it become synonymous for exercise and sport.

[5]Unfortunately, no photographs or illustrations of Moser's suggested new outfit survive. Indeed, no other references to a divided skirt costume as early as the 1880s exist, either at Vassar or anywhere else, leading me to wonder whether Dr. Moser, some 40 years later, had confused the year of her suggestion. I have no doubt that the occurrence she described took place; I do doubt the year. In every instance, women wore skirts over trousers in college exercise programs in the 1880s.

[6]University of California-Berkeley University Archives. Mr. McGee's Scrap Books, "Muscular Maids," late 1880s. This little tale continues with a conversation between two of the gymnasts,

"Yes, if one could only be as free as this all the time." "Well," the other answers, "and why can't we, you and I?" They look at each other, the horror of a short-skirted promenade down Broadway making mischief in their eyes... And still the question is unanswered, why."

It is obvious that it was unthinkable for a woman to wear the daring, new, unskirted gymnastic dress anywhere except the gymnasium itself.

[7]All the information not otherwise cited has come from the archives of selected private and public colleges and universities throughout the United States. Bulletins, calendars, published and unpublished histories, letters, photographs, scrap books, year books and garments themselves provided the necessary information synthesized in this article. Schools included Mount Holyoke College, Rockford College, Smith College,

Wellesley College, Vassar College, the University of California-Berkeley and-Los Angeles, Iowa State University, the University of Michigan, the University of Minnesota, the University of North Carolina at Greensboro, Stanford University, the University of Wisconsin.

[8]The University of Michigan is a good example. Women's physical education officially began there in 1905, but a basketball club was organized by women students as early as 1893, the year after the game was introduced. *The University of Michigan An Encyclopedic Survey*. Vol. IX, Part IX (Ann Arbor: University of Michigan Press, 19580, 1994-2004.

[9]Various schools mention her visit in their archives, but reports vary as to which she visited first. It is certain she gave demonstrations at Wellesley, and gave instruction at Vassar, Smith, Mount Holyoke, Byrn Mawr and Radcliffe. Ballintine, 18.

[10]Almost invariably the color was navy/black. However, the Valentine Museum has a maroon serge two-piece gymnasium suit, c. 1905-1910 in its collection (v.72.351.5.a,b).

[11]*Second Annual Catalogue of the State Normal and Industrial School*, Greensboro, N.C., 1893-94, 33. The actual cost that year was listed as $5.75; by 1895-96, the Catalogue claimed the total "not more than $5.00."

[12]Further research into the companies who manufactured and supplied gym suits to the schools is yet to be done. Research so far bears the statement above out. Wright and Ditson and Spalding are two companies who manufactured garments for P E in the 1920s through the 1940s; earliest extant garments had no labels in them at all, or if any, that of a store, e.g. Stearn's in Boston.

[13]Department of Special Collections, Stanford University Libraries, photographs 1208, 1209 and 1219.

[14]"Flannel" here is woollen fabric. By 1910, many high schools throughout the country had physical education programs. Of these, many required only loose street clothing, since there were few facilities for changing in any of the schools. However, some with gymnasiums did demand appropriate gymnasium dress.

[15]Annette Kellerman. "Why and How Girls Should Swim," *The Ladies' Home Journal*, August, 1910. It took a century after it was devised for male gymnasts for a similar outfit to be generally accepted for women - only now, in the 1990s do we see women outdoors running in such apparel. As recently as 1985, Anne White scandalized Wimbledon by appearing in a white bodysuit, and was castigated for it in the international press.

[16]The wool suits, though in theory washable, were not. Indeed, as we have seen from the Fuld and Bolton articles, and from several references in letters and journals, it is clear that they lasted through the two years they were needed by the girls at school, uncleaned in any way.

[17]Letter to the author from Claire Masters, Waco TX, Sept. 18, 1990, and conversations with other Texans. Ms. Masters recalled her years at North Hollywood Junior High School, Los Angeles, California, and North Junior High School, Waco TX.

The shorts, she reported, "were cut straight and brief" and "were every bit as brief as those worn today."

[18]The author remembers, as recently as the 1960s when the question of topless bathing suits was being raised, several cities in the United States, among them Minneapolis, found to their embarrassment that they were still legally bound by statutes prohibiting bare legs on public beaches. Needless to say, they were laws that had been happily ignored for decades.

[19]The only other clothing to remain so remarkably unchanged over time is the menswear-based jodhpur and jacket riding habit of the twentieth century. Its tenaciousness has outlasted even the gym suit's, lasting from the first decade of the century into the last. One cannot avoid wondering that if such classic styles can endure in one area of women's dress, could they not in others?

[20]The Big Ten schools were: Iowa State University, the University of Minnesota, the University of Wisconsin and the University of Michigan. My thanks to Patricia Griffin and Larry Locke of the University of Massachusetts for their help in this area.

[21]Certain schools eliminated a mandatory gym suit even before that because of its general unpopularity; others, often parochial, maintained it even later. The author remembers in the 1950s that many women in high school and college were reluctant to participate in athletics because of the "ugly" suit, and found it a personal interview that at least one (male) athletic director of a small private college in Connecticut removed the gym suit requirement from his female students as early as 1952-55.

Works Cited

"1863 Oration at Seminary Anniversary," author unknown. Unpublished. MHC Archives.

The Arena, Volume 7, 1893.

Ballintine, Harriet Isabel. *The History of Physical Training at Vassar College*, Poughkeepsie, N.Y.: Lansing & Broas, Printers, 1915.

Bolton, Florence. "Women's Dress in Exercise." *American Physical Education Review*, Vol. XV, 1910. 338-341.

Boston *Sunday Herald* Magazine Section, February 10, 1907.

Boucher, Francois. *20,000 Years of Fashion*. New York, Harry N. Abrams, Inc., Publishers, 1987.

Clapp, Cornelia M. *Manual of Gymnastics*. (Mount Holyoke College), 1883.

De Marly, Diana. *Fashion for Men* London: B.T. Batsford, Ltd., 1985.

Detroit Free Press 2 November 1896.

Edwards, Eleanor. Letter to Mildred Howard. 6 November 1947. Mount Holyoke College Archives. Mt. Holyoke, MA.

Elliott, Orrin Leslie. *Stanford University: The First Twenty-five Years*. Stanford University: Stanford University Press, 1937.

Ewing, Elizabeth. *History of Children's Costume*. New York: Charles Scribner's Sons, 1977.

Fuld, Leonhard Felix. "Gymnastic Costume for Women." *American Physical Education Review*, Vol. 15, (November 1910): 572-578.

_____. "Gymnastic Costume for Women II." *American Physical Education Review*, Vol. 16: (November 1911): 521-524.

Gerber, Ellen W. *Innovators and Institutions in Physical Education*. Philadelphia: Lea & Febiger, 1971.

Godey's Lady's Book. "How to Begin." July, 1841.

Godey's Lady's Book. January, 1864.

Hazzard, Florence Woolsey. *Heart of Oak: The Story of Eliza Moser*. Unpublished. Insert 6.5. Bentley Historical Library, University of Michigan.

Kellerman, Annette. "Why and How Girls Should Swim," *The Ladies' Home Journal* August, 1910.

Lewis, Dio. *The New Gymnastics for Men, Women, and Children*. Philadelphia: Ticknor and Fields, 1864.

McCurdy, Persis Harlow. "The History of Physical Training at Mount Holyoke College," *American Physical Education Review*, Vol. 14:3 (March 1909).

Mr. McGee's Scrap Books (1880s). University Archives. University of California, Berkeley.

Mitford, Nancy. *Madame de Pompadour*. New York: E. P. Dutton, 1984.

Murray, Anne Wood. "The Bloomer Costume and Exercise Suits," Waffen-und Kostümkunde, München, Berlin: Duetscher Kunstverlag, 1982.

Second Annual Catalogue of the State Normal and Industrial School. Greensboro, North Carolina, 1893-94.

Third Annual Catalogue of the State Normal and Industrial School. Greensboro, North Carolina, 1895-95.

The University of Michigan. An Encyclopedic Survey. Vol. 4, Pt. 9. Ann Arbor: University of Michigan Press, 1958.

Warner, Patricia Campbell. "Public and Private: Men's Influence on American Women's Dress for Sport and Physical Education," *Dress 1988, The Journal of the Costume Society of America*, 14. (1988): 48-55.

_____. "Public and Private: Clothing the American Woman for Sport and Physical Education, 1860-1940." Diss. University of Minnesota, 1986.

Simplicity of Dress:
A Symbol of American Ideals

Patricia A. Cunningham

During the colonial period in America, and well into the early decades of the new republic, symbols associated with dress evolved which reflected both consistent and changing American ideals such as simplicity, liberty, independence, equality, federal union, opportunity, industry and plenty. Of all these ideals simplicity alone best expressed American virtues, and was often drawn on to suggest the other ideals as well. In both artistic expression and everyday life, individuals used clothing to visually communicate simplicity, a concept especially linked with republican ideals of liberty and equality. Since these republican ideals were associated with the classical world which was held in high esteem, artists often drew on Greek and Roman styles of dress to suggest these values. In everyday life, too, individuals could express simplicity by wearing contemporary clothing made in plain simple fabrics with no ornamentation. Indeed, from the colonial period to the present day, American ideals have been symbolized through the representation of clothing in a variety of art forms—sculpture, prints, paintings, coins, textiles and cartoons. More importantly, perhaps, Americans have worn clothing with symbolic meaning to aid in bringing about their political goals. In both art and life, then, it was simplicity of dress that often visually communicated the rhetoric of republican ideals.

The Evolution of the Symbol of America in Art
Many symbols used to represent America in art have been personifications in which the clothing of the figure is crucial to the identity of its character. For instance, the familiar Statue of Liberty is derived from the Roman Goddess of Liberty.[1] The meanings of the statue are in part connected to the simplicity of the draped clothing and the idea of liberty associated with the Roman republic. Of course, we know Liberty by her attributes and through the clothing she

wears. The use of classical mythological figures to represent America in art began in the eighteenth century, but the ideas associated with the Liberty goddess, and classical dress in general, have been passed down to us through history, art and literature. With the neoclassical revival in Europe in the eighteenth century it is not surprising that these ideas prevailed.

The desire of print makers, artists and crafts people to have a simple representation of the American people came about with the rising importance of the American colonies as a force affecting Britain, and the self-conscious realization of the colonists of their own distinctive nationality. According to E. McClung Fleming there were five stages in the development of an American allegorical figure in art (65). During the first stage, 1575 to 1765, "'America' symbolized in the arts was the entire western hemisphere conceived as one of 'the four continents'" (65). An Indian Queen with attributes of a Caribbean culture was the chosen emblem. During the second phase the term America also began to denote the thirteen colonies, personified by an Indian Princess depicted as the daughter of Britannia with attributes pertaining to the colonies. After independence in 1783, "America" in the third phase, signified the independent United States, which retained the qualities of an Indian Princess but with added symbols of American sovereignty. In the fourth stage the Indian Princess is metamorphosized into a Greek goddess. During the last stage, early nineteenth-century masculine figures of Brother Jonathan and Uncle Sam replaced female personifications (65-66).

The Colonial Era

Although male figures were used as symbols of America, especially native American figures, the more usual representation was of an Indian Princess who appears to be in her twenties or thirties. It is through her clothing that meaning is communicated. She wears:

a feathered headdress and a loosely fitting cape or skirt, and is armed with a bow and quiver of arrows. Except for the one distinguishing detail of the feathered headdress, however, the complexion, dress, ornament, weapons, and attributes of the Indian Princess vary considerably. Sometimes her skirt is made of feathers, sometimes of tobacco leaves, occasionally it is replaced by a long, flowing gown. The bow and arrow frequently are replaced by a tomahawk and scalping knife. The American flag, officially adopted by the Continental Congress in 1776, appears from time to time as an attribute of the Princess as does the shield with thirteen stars and stripes (Fleming, "American Image" 77).

Throughout the period the allegorical situations in which the Indian Princess appears focus on her mother-daughter relation to Britannia, overseas trade and most importantly her pursuit of liberty. As seen in political prints and engravings on commemorative objects, prints, sculpture, textiles and other art forms America is personified as an Indian Princess. She is the central figure in an allegory depicted with other positive symbols of liberty—the liberty tree, Goddess of Liberty and the liberty pole and cap[2] (Fleming, "American Image" 77).

The New Republic

Between 1783 and 1815, the era of the new nation, America was personified for hundreds of purposes—commemorative coins, banners, prints, textiles and architectural decoration. The symbol continued to be predominantly female, using either the Indian Princess or one of several goddesses. The neoclassic movement provided impetus for the transformation of the Indian Princess into a Greek goddess called the Plumed Goddess. Her clothing and attributes determined whether she was Indian or a classical deity. Hercules, Minerva, Liberty and finally a uniquely American deity, Columbia, were drawn on at various times. Again, in each case meaning is communicated through clothing and other attributes suggestive of liberty, freedom, independence, frugality and prosperity.

While Hercules appeared occasionally, this very masculine image was almost always depicted in the allegory as a friend of America. John Quincy Adams objected to Hercules because it had too much heathen mythology for his taste (Fleming, "Indian Princess" 54). Minerva, Roman goddess of wisdom, also appeared more frequently as a friend of the Indian Princess or the Plumed Goddess than as a representation of America. The Goddess of Liberty, on the other hand, was very frequently drawn on to represent America, and was strongly identified with the American cause for independence. She was often "Americanized" by draping her in the American flag, or by being guarded by the American eagle. She appeared in an engraving which included portraits of Washington and Jefferson, as a sculptural figure in the Capitol of the United States, and on coins and commemorative medals minted by the new republic (Fleming, "Indian Princess" 56).

The most popular of the classical deities was Columbia (Fig. 1), a unique and poetic personification taken from the name of Christopher Columbus. The name Columbia appeared frequently in literature and was popularized through the song "Columbia," a favorite with Washington's troops. She was usually depicted bareheaded, or helmeted, wearing a simple white dress surrounded

Fig. 1. The goddess Columbia as a seated figure. Samuel Harris, "Emblem of the United States of America," Boston, 1804. Courtesy, Winterthur Museum.

with attributes of freedom—the liberty pole and cap, American eagle and flag, an olive branch, or perhaps a banner that read "independence" (Fleming, "Indian Princess" 60-3).

Because of their strong associations with the idea of liberty, the goddesses Columbia and Liberty continued to be used as figures to represent the United States until the Civil War era. However, new masculine figures also known by their clothing, Brother Jonathan and Uncle Sam, were introduced in the early decades of the nineteenth century. The use of male personification to represent America reflected perhaps a need to associate America, or rather the United States, with ideas of "flexibility, vitality and robustness" that only a male figure could provide (Fleming, "American Image" 66), at least in the minds of the nineteenth-century public.

Considering the dominance of neoclassical thought in the late eighteenth century, it is not surprising that America was personified as a Greek or Roman deity. What appears to be more unusual, perhaps, is that in numerous allegorical representations prominent American patriots also were depicted in classical dress. For instance, a printed English textile commemorating the war for independence includes Benjamin Franklin dressed in the toga of a Roman senator holding a scroll (Fleming, "Indian Princess," 44-45). Indeed, in both painted and sculptural portraits, prominent Americans were clothed in classical draperies, often a toga or even the dress of a Roman general. The association with liberty and equality, or with any particular classical deity was not apparent.

Artists, especially sculptors, frequently drew on the imagery of the classical period. They did so not only to avoid depicting the fashions of the time, but to lend a feeling of timelessness and dignity to the portrait. Apparently the artists did not intend to connect the ideas of liberty and equality to dress for these portraits. It seems to have been merely an artistic device which also could denote the importance of an individual. For historical paintings it was common practice to depict heroes in Roman armor. The use of Roman armor for portraits had been in practice since antiquity. In the sixteenth century its acceptance rested on the belief that military service was the only true profession for a man of rank (Jenkins 41). Roman dress also had been popularized through costumes worn for court masques and theatrical productions (DeMarly 448-449). In several of Sir Joshua Reynolds' portraits eighteenth-century women are depicted in clothing which gives them an air of the antique and a feeling of simplicity which, for Reynolds, was the ideal style for a portrait. The simplicity of antique dress was greatly admired, and according to Reynolds it brought an air of negligence, ease and timelessness to a portrait (Reynolds 88-89).

Yet, when Thomas Jefferson asked the sculptor, Houdin, to portray George Washington for a monument to be placed in the Virginia State Capitol, Reynolds' precepts regarding the antique, especially for sculptural works, was not followed. Instead, Houdin "wanted to portray the great American as a farmer-citizen who had sheathed his sword and retired to the peace of Mt. Vernon" (Larkin 82). The idea was approved by Jefferson and by Washington himself who observed "'a little deviation in favour of the modern costume would be more expedient than a servile adherence to the garb of antiquity'" (Larkin 82). However, to meet orders of the Virginia legislature, Washington was depicted in military uniform holding a cane. His sword rests on the fasces at his side with the blade of a plough behind him. The sculpture is proof that "modern" costume could be as sculpturally expressive as a toga (Larkin 83).

So while the country "America" could be personified in the abstract as a classical deity, it became clear that for modern historical works American citizens should be dressed in appropriate and correct clothing for the period. Indeed, it was the American painter, Benjamin West who set the precedent by using modern dress for his "Death of General Wolfe" in 1771 (Mitchell 20-33). The effectiveness of simple everyday dress went beyond art and, indeed, became a rallying symbol for Americans in the revolutionary era.

Homespun: Symbol of American Independence

Adapting everyday dress for portraying an American was consistent with the colonists' politics of dress. For when they needed a symbol to express their ideals and sentiments, or to show their support for independence, it is clear they did not adopt the image of the Indian Princess or use symbols of liberty from antiquity. Their solution was more pragmatic; they stopped importing English goods and wore clothing of their own making called homespun. Wearing homespun was not only a defiant act, it suggested simplicity, frugality and self-reliance. Thus simple dress became a symbol of independence from England.

During the colonial era in America, if they could afford it, people generally wore styles fashionable in Europe. Since the colonies were English, the citizens initially did not consider themselves distinct; they were British citizens and dressed accordingly. At this time fashions in dress usually were determined by the elite and then filtered down to the middle and lower classes. Men and women had few clothes; class position could be determined by quantity, but more often by quality and cut of the clothing. People who worked at manual jobs dressed in distinctively simple clothing. Their clothes set them apart from the middle and upper classes who could afford expensive imported silk and woolen fabrics. Rural dress was generally simpler than clothing worn in urban centers where people were more likely to set the pace for fashion change.

It was not until England began to place strong economic sanctions against the colonists that a distinctively American form of dress emerged, a style which came to symbolize the struggle for independence. The colonists chose to wear their own "homespun" clothing instead of imported fabrics to symbolize this cause. It was distinctive because it had no lace or embroidery trim. It was very plain and hence symbolized their frugality. That it was of their own making reflected their independence and industry. Although homespun symbolized the quest for independence, the colonists' ability to produce their own cloth had begun much earlier. Indeed, Benjamin Franklin was not entirely wrong when he testified before Parliament in 1776 that he did not know of a single item imported into the colonies that they could not make themselves or do without (Clark 1:211-13).

Prior to 1640 the textile needs of the American colonists were easily met by the steady flow of ships from England bearing both emigrants and provisions. However, after 1640 a decline in the traffic to the colonies occurred and all commodities grew scarce. These straits "set our people on work to provide fish, clap boards, planks, etc., and to sow hemp and flax" (Hosmer 31). Since many of the settlers had come from districts of England where textile production flourished, it was natural for them to engage in similar endeavors in their new country. They were inspired by bounties such as that offered in 1640 by the Massachusetts General Court of "three pence on every shilling-worth of linen, woolen, and cotton cloth." Similar bounties were offered in Connecticut "'that we might in time have supply of Lynen Cloath amongst ourselves.'" Further, General Court "encouragement" for yarn production was a regulation passed in 1656 requiring "that everyone assessed as a whole spinner...spin for 30 weeks every year 3 pound per week of linen, cotton, or woolen...under penalty of 12 d̲. for every pound short" (Bishop 1:299-300).

The abundance of fabrics produced by the colonists included tammies and light worsted fabrics, as well as heavier cloth for men's wear. The fibers used were wool, flax, cotton and hemp. Linen fabrics for bed and table use, as well as for inner garments, were supplied from looms of the household industry. The fabrics were "more remarkable for service than for elegance," the coarser kind worn by apprentices and laborers, the finer worn by the middle classes. The wealthier classes generally wore garments made from imported fabrics— woolens from England, linen from Ireland and Scotland, even silks (Cappon 107; Bishop 1:330-31).

The general policy of the British government regarding the colonies was to increase the economic strength of the mother country, especially to render Britain independent of foreign supplies for naval stores. In light of this general policy, Britain became alarmed at the extent of trade carried on by the colonists, and in an effort to limit it passed the Navigation Acts in 1650, 1651, and later in 1661. While England's motive was to insure the colonies dependence, these early acts were not highly regarded by the colonists, and, in fact, were often ignored.

Still later the amount of textile manufacturing in the American provinces caught the attention of Britain. Not only were the colonists in the late seventeenth century producing woolen fabrics in competition with exports from the mother country, but France and Holland, England's two largest markets for textiles, began to produce their own fine woolen goods. To replace the lost continental market, the British government passed the Woolen Act in 1699 to discourage the continued growth of textiles, particularly woolen cloth, in the colonies and to ensure a market for English woolens. The act restricted the exportation of woolen products from the colony in which it had been produced. As a further discouragement to colonial textile production, England in 1700 lifted the export tax on British woolen, thereby reducing their cost in the colonies (Clark 1:9-10, 21; Bishop 1:325-27; Nettles 232-33).

Following the signing of the Treaty of Paris in 1763, the British government with George Grenville as minister began looking for means to reduce the war debt. Grenville was especially interested in establishing a plan whereby the colonies could help defray the cost of maintaining British troops as a protective force in America. The colonists had long ignored the Navigation Acts and Grenville's plan was to enforce these, as well as new duties, through a passage of a bill now called the Sugar Act. His plan would create a source of revenue to defray military expenses in the colonies, and through these new enforcement measures he hoped to gain more control over the colonies. In 1764 the measure was passed by Parliament along with an agreement to institute a Stamp Act the following year.

Feeling that these measures were far too stringent, the colonists desired a means to exert pressure on Britain to repeal the act. One measure they chose was to renew "the movement against extravagance in dress and lavishness of display at funerals [that] had begun early in the decade." The non-consumption of British goods was encouraged, support was asked for a non-importation policy, and local manufacturing encouraged. The first hint at a non-consumption policy was given in November, 1764, in a letter to Jasper Mauduit in England in which the writer, a merchant, asserted that "necessity would oblige them [the colonists] to do without such luxuries as cambric, lawn, calico, and other foreign imports...." In the previous August, "fifty merchants of Boston" set an example "by signing an agreement to discard laces and ruffles, to buy no English clothes but at a fixed price, and to forego the elaborate and expensive mourning of the times for the very simplest display" (Andrews 191; Tryon 105).

The colonists again promoted manufacturing because they learned early that "closely connected with political was economic independence." Many colonies acted on this plea. For instance, in New York "The Society for the Promotion of Arts, Agriculture and Economy" was formed to encourage the manufacture of linen, "it having been thought necessary...in the present deplorable state of our trade" (Bishop 1.369; Schlesinger 64). Such promotion had a wider purpose to serve than to further frugality or non-consumption, of course, for it was agreed from Massachusetts to Virginia that an increase in manufacturing would bring England to terms, and a more recent interpretation strongly suggests that the merchants believed that "the development of domestic industry [would be] an integral part of a program to achieve economic sovereignty to counter the restrictions imposed by membership in the British Empire." For this reason the merchants "were willing to encourage native industries, such as the production of linen and woolen cloth, that directly competed with their importations" (Andrews 197; Egnal and Ernst 20, 29).

Britain was soon to react to these industrial movements by the colonists. It was reported in England early in 1765 "that no less than fourteen new manufactorys had been lately established in North America..." which was computed by the British to be a loss annually of one half million sterling. Yet they passed the Townsend Act of 1767, and again the colonists chose to use the now successful economic boycott as a means of retaliation—the non-consumption and non-importation of British goods (Bishop 1.369).

In February of 1768 the General Court of Massachusetts approved a motion to establish manufacturing in the colony, as well as one to renew the non-importation agreements. Other colonies followed with similar resolutions. Soon there was an actual decrease in the exports from Great Britain to the colonies (the exception being the southern colonies). British Custom House returns reveal the following:

Exported from Great Britain to:	1768	1769
New England	430,807	223,696
New York	490,674	75,931
Pennsylvania	441,830	204,976
Maryland and Virginia	669,422	614,944
North and South Carolina	300,925	327,084
Georgia	56,562	58,369

The decreases were considerable in the northern colonies, but trade actually increased in the southern colonies where they were limited in their ability to supply themselves (Gipson 180; Labaree 22; Bishop 1.372-74). The effectiveness of the boycott was clearly felt in London and soon the Townsend Act, too, was repealed, with the exception of the duty on tea. This particular duty, of course, later became a symbol of resistance for the colonists.

Although the non-importation agreements proved to be an effective measure in bringing England to terms, the impact of the corresponding movements to promote non-consumption of "superfluities" and domestic manufacturing can be seen in the real efforts to increase the production of textiles. In Boston the town meeting on March 31, 1769, voted to subsidize a free spinning school to be run by William Molineux. By March of 1770 "at least 300 women and children had...been thoroughly instructed in the art of spinning.... They had then on hand about forty thousand "scanes[sic] of fine yarn, fit to make any kind of women's wear." So successful was Molineux that he was inspired to begin weaving the yarn into cloth as well, and erected, at much expense, "twisting-mills...looms, furnaces, hot and cold presses for finishing goods...[and] a dye house." This establishment is the earliest mention of an improved mechanism in cloth manufacture, for it employed some self-acting warping machinery, enabling two boys to keep fifty looms supplied with yarn (Schlesinger 121; Bishop 1.375-76).

The southern colonies also made an effort to produce textiles. The quantity of hemp had doubled in Charleston, and it was noted that "the inhabitants now manufacture most of their linens." Although the southern colonies did not cease their imports of British goods, they did make an effort to increase their home production. Indeed a weaving house was established at Mt. Vernon, the Washington plantation, where in 1767 and 1768 a total of 1,059 yards of cloth was produced for plantation use, and 499 yards for neighbors (Walton 128; Weedon 3.732).

The efforts of the colonists to increase their production of domestic manufacturing and establish factories was no doubt enhanced by the political maneuvers of Parliament to maintain its sovereignty over the colonies, and subsequent American reaction to them—the frugality, non-consumption, non-importation policies and eventually the revolution itself.

The effect of the war for independence was more positive and permanent than that of the non-importation agreements and pleas for increased manufacturing during the earlier reactions to British laws. Not only was there an urgency in meeting the material demands of the war years themselves, but the future was bright for manufacturing with prospects of free trade and economic sovereignty.

"In June 1776, each state was asked to furnish a suit of clothes, a blanket, a felt hat, two shirts, two pairs of hose, and two pairs of shoes for each soldier enlisted therein." The main dependence for clothing was apparently the region north of Maryland where domestic manufacturing had long been established. In general, however, each town was to provide clothing for each of their soldiers in the army (Clark 1:225).

Although it is usually stated that the efforts to establish factories failed, the kind of "factory" or textile business that did flourish during this period was that which augmented the production of textiles in the home. These were the fulling and carding mills, dye houses, and bleaching fields, as well as the itinerant weavers and the textile printers. These businesses were managed by craftspeople skilled in a particular stage of the operation. The extent of these small factories suggests that they were an important ingredient in the successful production of homespun, for each was a process that took special equipment, or was a particularly time consuming operation. Bleaching of linen, for instance, not only took a large open space, but it often took weeks to accomplish (Cox:19-20).

These specialists were no doubt integral parts of the system of homespun production, and their dependence on the home craftsperson for their business, as well as their pervasiveness throughout the colonial period, suggest that the production of homespun was the system that worked the best. The successful production of textiles by this system of home manufacturing must have contributed to the colonists' growing confidence and sense of self sufficiency which they needed before engaging in a battle with England.

The uniqueness of this homespun system is that it had virtually no labor cost because it employed the women and children in the household, it was seasonal (the weaving often was completed in the winter months), capital outlay was negligible, hence production could fluctuate without adverse effects, and the techniques involved were stable. (Cox 19-20, Tryon 105).

If it can be said that the Sons of Liberty were responsible for "enforcement" of the colonial "resolves" regarding non-importation, then perhaps one can find a corollary in the activities of the Daughters of Liberty. They displayed great enthusiasm and zeal throughout the period of the Stamp and Townsend Act crises, through the war years, and still later in the 1780s for promoting the non-consumption of British goods and encouraging domestic manufacturing. By their own example they exerted social pressure which convinced the colonists not only to produce more homespun, but to wear it as well.

The most effective "coercive" tool used by the Daughters of Liberty was the "spinning bee." Although not a new form of social gathering, "bees" became the rage from 1766 to 1771 in New England. The *Boston Chronicle*, April 7, 1766, noted that a gathering was held in Providence, Rhode Island, of "eighteen Daughters of Liberty assembled at the house of doctor Ephraim Bowen...where they...exhibited a fine example of industry by spinning from sunrise until dark, and displayed a spirit for saving their sinking country...." Similar gatherings were held in other parts of New England— Salisbury, Connecticut in 1767, Byfield, 1768, and Newbury 1768. Newspapers reported "bees" held throughout 1770 in the Massachusetts towns of Rowley, Ipswich, Beverly and Boston. During these gatherings there was usually a sermon preached by the local minister encouraging the young ladies to "cast aside the English goods for the product of their own hands" (Tryon 107-8; Clark 1.215). Further pleas of a poetic nature appeared in print:

> Young ladies in town and those that live round
> Let a friend at this season advise you.
> Since money's so scarce and times growing worse,
> Strange things may soon hap and surprise you.
> First then throw aside your high top knots of pride,
> Wear none but your own country linen.
> Of economy boast. Let your pride the most.
> To show cloaths of your own make and spinning.
> (*Massachusetts Gazette*, 2 November 1767).

Such stimulation in effect created a "fashion" for wearing homespun. In Massachusetts the clergy generally promised to wear cloth and shoes only from domestic manufacturers, and the senior classes at Harvard, Yale and the College of Rhode Island (Brown University) voted to take their degrees "dressed altogether in the manufactures of this country" (Andrews 195; Bagnall 56).

The social movement was, in fact, highly effective, for the wearing of homespun ceased to be a matter of particular record; "people were now clothed in their own garments as naturally as they were fed by their own Indian corn." The patriotism that had previously spread the curtailment of excessive mourning dress at funerals in the north spread to the south for "the people of Charles Town began to cloathe themselves in their own manufactures, reducing the 'enormous expense of funerals.'" Christopher Gadsden set an example for his wife's funeral in 1769. Only 3.10 was spent on manufactures from England (Weedon 3.789).

That wearing homespun became a symbol of the colonists' need to assert independence cannot be doubted. For even after the revolution, when there was a reaction to "excessive superfluities" in dress, when spinning bees were again the rage and the establishment of factories encouraged, homespun was worn by those who wished to display their patriotism, as well as assert their interest in economic independence from Great Britain. Portraits of Benjamin Franklin, John Adams, Thomas Jefferson and many other patriots wearing homespun clothing attest to their being caught up in the movement.

The use of sartorial symbols, in this case the manifestation of plainness in dress, became more than a symbol of liberty and frugality, or even an assertion of economic independence, for such dress continued to be seen as a reflection of unique American qualities. Most Americans "shared Washington's view that 'a plain genteel dress is more admired and obtains more credit than lace and embroidery in the eyes of the judicious and sensible.'" Simplicity came to distinguish the American from the European.

The New Republic

Dress at Court

By the time America became a new nation, linking the ideas of simplicity and frugality with concepts of liberty and republicanism was well imbued in the minds of American citizens. Indeed, as noted earlier, these ideas had been symbolized during the revolutionary era by the wearing of simple, plain, homespun clothing. The appearance in various art forms of classical deities to personify America also evoked ideas of simplicity and republicanism. It is no wonder, then, that dressing in the simple clothes of an American began to concern American diplomats. Indeed the social life and etiquette which called for elaborate dress at Court was an anathema to many patriotic diplomats.

In the early national period in America it was clear that Americans desired to assert their uniqueness and act on newly acquired principles of democracy.

The need to express this sentiment within the European diplomatic community, especially at Court occasions, became a major concern of American ministers abroad. The common theme that emerged through various presidential and State Department directives was that Americans should "dress their foreign representatives in a manner which would reflect American qualities of republicanism and simplicity" (Davis 164-65). Most American diplomats truly shared Washington's belief that a plain dress is more admired than lace and embroidery. Yet, very strict protocol for court occasions usually demanded elaborate dress, which for men in the early years of the republic meant velvet, gold embroidery, lace, powdered wigs, knee breeches and swords. The problems in developing appropriate dress for diplomatic Court occasions between 1789 through the Civil War era were addressed by Robert Ralph Davis, Jr. in "Diplomatic Plumage: American Court Dress in the Early National Period."

Davis observed that until 1790 matters involving court dress were left to the discretion of individual diplomats. The first directive came from Thomas Jefferson who advised consuls and vice consuls that they "are free to wear the uniform of their navy, if they chuse to do so." John Quincy Adams supported this concept but thought it also should be applied to diplomats because such dress was "more comfortable to republican simplicity, than the court dresses which they are now obliged to use.... The substitution of fine broadcloth instead of silks and velvets, and lace embroidery... would I presume be agreeable to every American." The essence of American costume, according to Adams, should be simplicity so it would not be confused with the "tribe of courtly butterflies in Europe" (169).

It was not until Madison's presidency in 1813 that ministers were given a directive regarding court dress. The prescribed uniform consisted of "blue cloth, lined with silk...standing collar and single breasted. The collar, cuffs, buttonholes and pocket flaps embroidered, either in gold or silver, and the buttons to correspond..." (Davis 169, n 22). A similar directive in 1817 added that plain buttons could be substituted for buttons with "an eagle flying, with a wreath in its mouth, grasping lightning in one of its talons." White cassimere breeches were to be worn with gold knee buckles, a three-cornered hat, not as large as the French, or as small as the English, also was prescribed. This was to be worn with a black cockade, with an eagle attached. This uniform was called the "small uniform." The "great uniform" was worn on gala occasions such as sovereign birthdays, princes' weddings and other extraordinary times. This was like the small uniform but with embroidery "round the skirts (of the coat) and

Fig. 2. Sir Amedee Forestier, "The Signing of the Treaty of Ghent, Christmas Eve 1814." Courtesy, National Museum of American Art, Smithsonian Institution.

down the breasts as well as at the cuffs and cape (collar)...." Moreover there "should be a white ostrich feather, or plummet, in the minister's hat, sewed around the brim" (Davis 170-71).

According to Davis these directives remained in place until the latter part of John Quincy Adams' presidency when future president and state representative, James Buchanan, protested that these uniforms "were not congenial to the simplicity and dignity of our institutions." Buchanan believed the uniforms were especially ridiculous for any minister who had never served in the military. Moreover, he noted that Americans do not even know that such a dress has been prescribed for their ministers abroad (Davis 170-71; Horton 106-15). As is apparent from the artist's portrayal in the "Signing of The Treaty of Ghent," Americans are easily distinguished by their plain dress. (Fig. 2)

While the Jacksonian era brought relief to advocates of republican simplicity, Davis noted that it was not until the administration of Franklin Pierce, with William L. Marcy as Secretary of State, that diplomatic costume etiquette was revolutionized. Indeed, in 1853 Marcy distributed a circular which stated that American ministers abroad would appear in court "in the simple dress of an American citizen" as originally asserted by Benjamin Franklin in the early years of the republic (172-73). While this highly publicized circular was greeted with approval at home, by diplomats themselves, and in some cases by the nations where they served, others were less enthusiastic. Parisians, in particular, criticized the new look and sarcastically dubbed the American charge d'affaires, Henry S. Sanford, the "Black Crow" (175-76).

As Davis observed, formalities of European court etiquette continued to hold a relatively high degree of importance during the nineteenth century. Several ministers did not comply to the directive for fear of offending the sensibilities of those they needed to conciliate. They adopted the optional dress of "a full dress diplomatic uniform" (176). Other diplomats like James Buchanan of Pennsylvania, a strong believer in republican simplicity, thought the directive would hamper his effectiveness as a minister. Nonetheless, although he was told he could not expect to be invited to court balls or dinners, he complied to the directive but, as he observed, he would now "be placed, socially, in Coventry" (177). Buchanan later reported that he never felt prouder "than when I stood amidst the brilliant circle of foreign ministers and other court dignitaries, in the simple dress of an American citizen" (178-79). It was, after all, important to look like an American. (Fig. 3)

Fig. 3.   Portrait of James Buchanan, George Peter Alexander Healy, 1859.   Courtesy, National Portrait Gallery, Smithsonian Institution.

Simplicity of Fashionable Dress

While wearing simple clothing at Court was an obvious means to communicate political beliefs, such clothing would go without notice on the streets of Paris or London. Indeed, in the late eighteenth century men's everyday clothing became increasingly sober and simple, taking its cue from country and sporting dress worn by the English aristocracy. French fashion for men which required velvet, silk, lace and embroidery was losing ground to a more sober style which was perceived to reflect patriotism, liberty, enterprise and manliness. Plainer dress for men spread from England to France in the 1770s and 1780s in a wave of Anglomania that at least to some degree implied appreciation of British political liberties (Steele 32-33). It certainly reflected American sentiment. And while *sans culottes* are the clothes most often associated with the French revolution, it was the ordinary suit and shoes without buckles that made a profound political statement when worn by the revolutionary official Roland for a meeting with the King's cabinet (Steele 46). It is apparent that Americans were not alone in using the simplicity of clothing to make a statement about political concerns.

Women's fashion also took on the air of simplicity. The 1770s and 1780s brought increasingly simpler styles of gowns to Paris which, like men's fashion, was based in part on English country clothing. A chemise style was worn in Paris by women of fashion before the French revolution. This look of simplicity, as mentioned previously, was in part influenced by portrait artists, like Sir Joshua Reynolds, who posed their subjects in classical draperies. What was worn in Paris, of course, influenced fashions worn in other parts of the world, for that stylish city was the center of European fashion. So when Parisians returned to the chemise style in 1789, Americans soon followed their fashion. The high-waisted "empire" style continued to be the mode through the first decade of the nineteenth century.

Conclusion

Simplicity of dress has long been used by artists to evoke ideas of timelessness and beauty. During the eighteenth century at the height of neoclassicism artists drew on images associated with classical ideology, one of which was the classically draped female figure. Artists used classical deities to personify America and project ideas of liberty, equality and republicanism. Symbolizing liberty and equality through dress was fundamental for both American and French patriots. In the American revolutionary era simplicity emerged in the wearing of homespun. During the French revolution *sans culottes* and the liberty cap, the *bonnet rouge,* were the most potent sartorial symbols of protest . However, plain black and simple clothes also prevailed as symbols of their cause. In both France and America the notion that everyone would wear simple clothing was meant to bring about the demise of social distinctions in dress and aid the movement toward true democracy. American diplomats in Europe pressed this issue by wearing their simple republican dress at Court.

Simplicity of dress was a reaction to ostentatious dress worn in pre-revolutionary times, and was an effective tool for patriots to communicate their sentiments. The classical dress of deities depicted in art, such as the Goddess of Liberty, carried the correct sentiment. However, when worn by citizens, classical dress had different meanings; it did not usually evoke ideas of liberty. Furthermore, because the simple chemise was worn by aristocrats before the French revolution, the return of this classically inspired style to Paris in 1789 did not symbolize a new democratic regime. The chemise instead reflected the reemergence of Paris as the center of women's fashion, and a return to class distinctions in dress (Steele 50-55). Nonetheless, in America equating the concept of liberty and equality with simplicity of dress remained in the public mind well beyond the Jacksonian era, when republicanism was at its height. Certainly these ideas can in part be responsible for the sober quality of men's business dress which has prevailed since the early nineteenth century.

Notes

[1]For further explication of the meaning of this monument, see Marvin Trachtenberg's *Statue of Liberty.* New York: Viking P, 1976.

[2]The liberty cap, or more correctly, the Phrygian bonnet- *pilleus liberatatis* -was bestowed upon slaves in Rome when they were granted their freedom (Trachtenberg 63).

Works Cited

Andrews, Charles M. "The Boston Merchants and the Non-Importation Movement." *Publications of the Colonial Society of Massachusetts*, 19 (1916-17).

Bagnall, William R. *The Textile Industries of the United States.* New York: Augustus M. Kelly, 1893.

Bishop, J. Leander. *A History of American Manufacturers from 1608 to 1860.* 2 vols. Philadelphia: Edward Young, 1868.

Boston Chronicle 7 April 1766.

Cappon, Lester J., ed. *Atlas of Early American History.* Princeton: Princeton University Press, 1976.

Clark, Victor S. *History of Manufacturers in the United States.* 2 vols. New York: Peter Smith, 1949.

Cox, Ruth Yvonne. "Textiles Used in Philadelphia 1760-1775." Master's Thesis. University of Delaware, 1960.

Davis, Robert Ralph, Jr. "Diplomatic Plumage: American Court Dress in the Early National Period." *American Quarterly* 20 (Summer 1968): 164-79.

DeMarly, Diana. "The Establishment of Roman Dress in Seventeenth-Century Portraiture." *Burlington Magazine* 117 (July 1975): 443-51.

Egnal, Marc and Ernst, Joseph A. "An Economic Interpretation of the American Revolution." *William and May Quarterly* 29 (January 1972): 3-32.

Fleming, McClung E. "The American Image as Indian Princess, 1765-1783." *Winterthur Portfolio* 2 (1965): 65-81.

_____. "From Indian Princess to Greek Goddess: The American Image, 1783-1815." *Winterthur Portfolio* 3 (1966): 37-66.

Gipson, Lawrence H. *The Coming of the Revolution.* New York: Harper & Row, 1954.

Hosmer, James K. ed. *Winthrop's Journal.* New York: C. Scribners, 1908.

Horton, R.G. *The Life and Public Services of James Buchanan.* New York: Derby and Jackson, 1856.

Larkin, Oliver W. *Art and Life in America.* New York: Holt, Rinehart and Winston, 1960.

Labaree, Benjamin W. *The Boston Tea Party.* New York: Oxford University Press, 1969.

Massachusetts Gazette 2 November 1767.

Mitchell, Charles. "Benjamin West's Death of General Wolfe and the Popular History Piece." *Journal of the Warburg and Courtauld Institutes* 7 (1944): 20-33.

Reynolds, Sir Joshua. *Discourses on Art.* Ed. Robert R. Wark. San Marino, CA: Huntington Library, 1959.

Ribeiro, Aileen. "Some Evidence of the Influences of the Dress of the Seventeenth Century on Costume in Eighteenth-Century Female Portraiture." *Burlington Magazine* 119 (December 1977): 834-40.

Schlesinger, Arthur M. *The Colonial Merchants and the American Revolution.* New York: F. Unger, 1957.

Steele, Valerie. *Paris Fashion: A Cultural History.* New York: Oxford University Press, 1988.

Trachtenberg, Marvin. *The Statue of Liberty.* New York: The Viking Press, 1976.

Tryon, Rolla Milton. *Household Manufacturers in the United States 1640-1860.* Chicago: University of Chicago Press, 1917.

Walton, Perry. *The Story of Textiles.* Boston: John S. Lawrence, 1912.

Weedon, William B. *Economic and Social History of New England 1620-1789.* 3 vols. New York: Hillary House, 1963.

"War"Drobe and World War I

Susan Voso Lab

The basis of American culture and many distinct American characteristics are firmly rooted in the nation's many experiences with conflict. An escape from tyranny brought a hearty breed of souls to a new land full of peril. Subsequent generations found themselves battling one form of conflict or another, from raids by native Americans to Revolutionary, Civil and World Wars. Any challenge to the values and concepts sacred to the spirit of a free America were met with unflinching resolve. When Germany sank American ships without warning in March 1917, President Wilson and the Congress did not hesitate to approve the declaration of war on April 6th (Greenwood and Murphy 19).

War is connected to many aspects of social life because it requires human interaction with the economic, social and political environment (Ferguson 2, 5). "Waging war usually involves mobilizing people, marshalling resources, and a host of other processes" (Ferguson 3). War does not occur without economic impact and resulting effects on such diverse things as foreign policy, monetary exchange rates, raw materials, trade, production, technology, and demographics (Ferguson 25,27; Sherry 435,439). Each change plays a role in altering culture and history (Sherry 435).

War related stress increases both public support for the government and the level of solidarity in society (Landau 487-489). Such was the case during World War I when Americans developed strong feelings of social solidarity and readiness for economic sacrifices (Landau 503). Indeed, the population of America during World War I showed an active willingness to contribute personally to the reduction of inflation caused by the war (Landau 505).

World War I influenced many American cultural practices and ideals, not the least of which involved American dress. Clothing and textiles were resources marshalled for war use. The economic impact of World War I affected not only the apparel trade and production processes, but also the design methodologies used in the creation of both textiles and clothing. The entire apparel industry had to retool for either war production or civilian needs. The social solidarity which formed as a result of the perceived threat to the nation can be measured in the significant way dress was viewed and altered to accommodate both war and social activities. The status of women, the apparel industry, and the nation changed during and because of World War I. This paper examines the impact of World War I on clothing and textiles in the United States. In many ways, the world's conflict altered for all time many of the ways clothing and textiles were produced and appreciated. This single form of material culture was altered to accommodate the needs of the burgeoning war machine with an almost unhesitating acceptance and support by the entire country.

Textile War Resources

When Marion Weller wrote "we are in a war that must be won through the complete cooperation of all the people and all the industries in the country" (401), she not only expressed the sentiments of social solidarity but did so in direct relation to the country's clothing situation. Amy Rolfe noted that as early as March 1918, the government commandeered material resources for soldiers' uniforms and blankets, leaving little for civilian use (Rolfe 125). By June 1918, the Commercial Economy Board of the National Council of Defense, a part of the Conservation Department under the War Industries Board, urged new clothing sacrifices for women (Gilman 478; Weller 401). The government created a Textiles Division in the Conservation Department with three sections: Wool, Cotton, and Silk (Weller 401). The Textiles Division focused on the need for clothing conservation in order to equip both the army and navy, and to clothe the general public (Weller 401). It was the Wool Section that had the most challenging task.

Wool

War use for good wool fibers, as Charlotte Gilman observed, included inner and outer military garments, blankets and millions of yards of worsted cloth (at a cost of $3 per yard in 1918) used for bagging or covering the propellant and explosive charges for big guns (Gilman 478; Rolfe 125-126). The War Industries Board determined that an army of five million soldiers would leave no wool for civilian needs (Weller 404). It was estimated that a soldier required thirteen times as much wool as a civilian (Weller 402). Wool consumption records for 1916 showed that each civilian required a little over eight pounds of wool per year compared with between 106 and 190 pounds of wool per year per soldier (roughly the wool from 20 sheep) (Weller 402).

In order to meet national wool demands, the United States had to rely heavily on its own raw material sources (Weller 402). Unfortunately, United States wool production was down by 25% (15 million sheep). Since 1903 (and even prior to the war), the United States grew only two-thirds of the wool used in its mills. Imports from Australia, New Zealand and Argentina were no longer available to the United States due to the Allies' war needs (Weller 401), and only wool from South America was imported following the war's onset (Rolfe 125).

Reasons for the decrease in the amount of wool available in the United States included a rise in land rental costs and demands for higher sheep herder wages. Larger tracts of government land, once available for grazing, were sold to individuals and broken into smaller areas requiring fences which were expensive to build and maintain. Sheep ranchers became discouraged because these expenses outweighed the benefits (Rolfe 125). By 1917, the number of sheep fell to less than 50 million and the U.S. needed three times that number to supply the wool demand (Weller 402). An estimated one-in-seven farms had sheep with barely enough wool to make one suit per person every four years (Weller 402).

On November 8, 1918, the Philadelphia Wool and Textile Association met to discuss the nation's wool problem and to devise relief measures (Rolfe 125; Weller 402). The Association organized a national "More Sheep- More Wool" campaign with help from the Pennsylvania State College of Agriculture and the United States Department of Agriculture in order to effect an immediate increase in American flocks. State extension workers produced and spread posters, bulletins and folders urging every farmer to raise a few sheep (Weller 402).

The "More Sheep" campaign helped bring about a number of changes. There was an increase of 125 million sheep in the United States. State lands were opened for grazing. Wool marketing techniques were studied and ways sought to create a paying industry. States passed and enforced legislation dealing with the restriction of dogs, which often ravaged the sheep population. These laws were important considering the fact that, in Ohio alone, dogs killed 25,000 out of 3 million sheep in 1917 (Weller 402-403).

The textile industry faced another important wool problem once the production of wool fibers was raised. Yarn was so hard to find even Red Cross knitting projects were difficult to complete (Rolfe 125). At first clothing manufacturers could only purchase a small amount of available wool fibers.

Although the majority of the labor intensive clothing industry was comprised of women (1880 accounts show 22,253 out of 25,200 clothing workers were women), men held various positions (Ziegert 6). When power machines were introduced in 1876, some positions were considered too hard for women. Men, therefore, took over positions like power cutters and spinners (Ziegert 6). When male spinners and other textile workers were drafted into military service the scarcity of labor again limited yarn production. The scarcity of labor, because of war duty, was so severe in France that mills had to close (Rolfe 126).

The scarcity of both United States wool resources and skilled spinners forced the price of wool cloth to increase beyond the means of many Americans. In an effort to alleviate the situation, the War Industries Board, through the Textile Division, requested all manufacturers and dealers to account for any wool held in their warehouses and inventories. The Board then stabilized raw wool and cotton goods prices (Rolfe 126; Weller 404-405). A combination of wool and cotton fibers were then woven for the apparel market with cotton placed either inside the wool yarn or on the cloth back. Thus, cotton extended the use of wool which produced an estimated raw wool savings of 25% (Rolfe 126).

Cotton

The United States produced more than half the world's cotton before World War I (Rolfe 126). Cotton was so abundant and cheap that American consumption at 35 pounds per person per year far surpassed Great Britains' consumption (at ten and five-eigths pounds per person) (Weller 401,405). Unfortunately, the military's need for cotton was great. The Red Cross needed unbleached muslin and gauze for bandages. The government transformed cotton fibers into Khaki uniforms and tents. The army used one bale of cotton each time it fired one large gun (Rolfe 126-127). The demand for cotton resources skyrocketed. Large quantities of cotton were needed for the war and substituted for scarce wool and linen fibers normally found in apparel and household fabrics. Increased demands for cotton, combined with increases in mill wages, drove the price of cotton to alarming heights (Weller 404).

Linen

Linen stock in stores and warehouses was all that America had left after the war started. Almost no flax was grown in the United States and shipments from abroad were negligible. The War destroyed flax grown in Belgium, an area near the German border, and even a section in Russia which was within the war zone. Great Britain was using its linen resources for airplane wings and other war purposes. (Without the linen resource, the U.S. instead used steel rolled to one hundredth of an inch thick on its airplanes.) The minute amount of linen that remained was out of reach of most civilians (Rolfe 127; Weller 405).

Silk

Silk, although in abundance from China and Japan, was in demand for both military and civilian needs. The government needed silk for balloon cases and recommended silk underwear for soldiers fighting in the trenches. Silk was thought to be gas resistant and less irritating to shrapnel wounds than cotton (Rolfe 127). Because of other shortages, it became a "patriotic duty to use silk in place of wool whenever possible" (Weller 405). The use of silk underwear and silk substitutions for wool by civilians aided the War Industries Board's efforts to conserve the use of material needed by the military.

Textile and Clothing Conservation

All available textile fibers were put to war use. This required citizens to do their bit by conserving individual textile use (Rolfe 127). The American people's ready-to-wear choices were controlled by textile and apparel manufacturers. Knowing the vital role played by mills and manufacturers in the conservation process, the Commercial Economy Board (CEB) made a series of general recommendations and specific style restrictions regarding cloth, apparel and shoes ("Clothing" 62; Weller 403). They recommended that clothing manufacturers (1) avoid excess variations of styles and use only the number of models actually required by trade, (2) avoid models with unnecessary adornments (revers, patch pockets, belts, cuffs and pleats), (3) use cloth with re-worked wool and cotton to substitute for part of the wool and reduce the average weight of fabrics, (4) design garments that require the least practical amount of fabric, (5) reduce the amount of fabric used for samples, and (6) design fewer fabrics with standard construction and colors only (no novelty fabrics) (Rolfe 128; Weller 403). The CEB further recommended that schools and colleges offering military training should reduce the wool content of student uniforms by 25% or more. The estimated result of the above recommendations, along with better apparel quality, color, style, and weave standards, would be a wool savings of 40% in men's and 25% in women's clothing (Weller 403).

Clothing conservation efforts abroad varied greatly from American methods. Great Britain fixed prices for standard civilian clothes at $13.00 for a

Table 1

Style Restrictions on Clothing and Shoes

Consumer	Apparel or Accessory Category	Conservation Requirements
Men	"Slack suits"	single breasted, chesterfield style no inside pockets one center back vent 30" length for size 36 (increase 1/2" size) 4 1/2" facings no unnecessary flaps, straps, pockets, or lengths
	Waistcoats (vests)	1" facings wool front fabric reduced lining back fabric increased
	Light Weight Overcoats	single breasted, chesterfield style 43" length for size 36
	Raincoats	48" maximum length 3 1/2" collar width
Women	Shoes	all spring 1919 shoes: not more than 8" high from ground laced overgarters 8" high 4 colors only - white, tan, black, med. brown leather linings discouraged fabric linings encouraged
Misses	Shoes and Overgarters	not more than 6 1/2" high from ground
Children	Shoes (sizes 8 1/2 to 11)	not more than 6" high from ground
Boys & Youths	Shoes	not more than 5 1/2" high from ground
Infants	Shoes (sizes 4 to 8)	not more than 5 1/2" from ground fabric baby shoes, no color restrictions patent leather in black only

man's suit, $12.77 for a boy's suit, and $15.33 for an overcoat (Weller 404). France put an additional tax on all suits costing more than $50, and Germany tried to limit the number of suits in a man's war-time wardrobe to two ("Clothing" 64). The United States did not restrict the number or cost of clothing or shoes but did require style restrictions (see Table 1). In particular, shoe manufacturers were asked not to produce any new styles or lasts, to use economical cutting patterns, and to reduce the number of women's new boot samples. Shoe manufacturers were also urged to cooperate with retailers and wholesalers to reduce return rates, to discourage buyers from purchasing unnecessary samples, and to encourage the sale of low cut shoe styles ("Clothing" 64). Style restrictions were extended even to the shoe carton which had to be all white or gray paper except for the front label and flange. No fly sheets, printed tops, buttons, trim, or string were permitted ("Clothing" 62).

Industry Conservation

American textile companies began to rethink yarn production and weaving processes so that other fibers could be substituted for virgin wool. Cotton and wool fibers were combined to form fabrics of flannel, voile, twill weave serge, plain weave and gabardine suiting, plaids, and tweeds. Cotton and silk were found in plain weave cloths as well as poplin, mull, crepe, and printed designs. Silk was incorporated with linen and woolen fibers to create plain, twill and Eolienne (like poplin but lighter) fabrics (Hickmans 363-366). Reworked or remanufactured wool, a product called Shoddy, was used as a substitute for virgin wool in both civilian and army fabrics. Army contracts allowed for a certain percentage of Shoddy (such as 35% for army blankets) (Weller 406). Evelyn Hickmans pointed out that good quality Shoddy had better wearing characteristics than poor quality virgin wool, although it was generally considered not as strong or as evenly dyed as virgin wool (Hickmans 362; Weller 406).

The use of Shoddy or reworked wool by the industry led to additional clothing conservation practices. Old suits, sweaters, and fabric scraps of wool were no longer sent to Europe to be reworked (Weller 406). State extension workers organized wool salvage work (Weller 406). Boston's Women's City Club established a clothing fact center in a War Hut on Boston Common which, as Alice Norton reported, exhibited information on wool substitutes and clothing conservation practices (Norton 325; Weller 407). Pattern companies advertized economical designs and remodeling of old garments. The Home Economics Division of the Bureau of Education urged economical remodeling projects in sewing classes. Women were asked to adopt more conservative styles for longer periods of time and encouraged to bring out stored textile items for home use or for relief organizations (Rolfe 128; Weller 407). Ethel Ronzone, for both patriotic and economic reasons, suggested the elimination of changes in fashion and the standardization of the entire wardrobe. Ronzone recommended garments with beauty dependent on simplicity of line, good proportions and adaptability to body needs, and which were harmonious with social attitudes by being hygienic, modest and economical (426-428).

A 1918 National Coat, Suit and Skirt Manufacturers Association Meeting assembly went on record accepting the conservation concept and offered adherence to strict simplicity in designs with sound tailoring, few interrupted lines, and restraint in ornamentation (Weller 407-408). Manufacturers, in evaluating their business practices and government contracts, estimated that enough wool to make 67,000 soldier's uniforms could be saved by eliminating the practice of sending out samples. Additionally, 31,250 more overcoats could be made by making 750,000 army overcoats six inches shorter (Weller 403).

Civilian Conservation

The American public, in a show of social solidarity, reacted in a supportive manner to the CEB's recommendations and restrictions. The New York Sun reported "the effect of the curtailment plan and the severe styles which are introduced will serve to influence everyone to purchase only such clothing as is necessary to meet ordinary needs" ("Clothing" 62). The purpose behind conservation for cloth was not just to save energy, labor and textile fibers, but to spend less for all lines of clothing, known as "Voluntary Dressing." By reducing personal expenses, the patriot could use their savings to service the country through the purchase of Liberty bonds (Gilman 478).

A few complaints about style restrictions did find public forum. An unsigned protest in the *Journal of Home Economics* referred to manufacturers making skirts so narrow, women could not take a long free step. The author suggested safer, moderately full skirts that were not too long, and sensible clothes, with simple lines that were attractive because of the quality of material and workmanship rather than ornamentation ("A Protest" 524-525). Charlotte Perkins Gilman took a more Victorian viewpoint in the matter of making skirts shorter. She stated: "it may be possible to make women's garments cheaper, but in the name of that ancient power known as Common Decency let us not try to make them [skirts] any scantier" (478).

Clothing care, mending and remodeling arts were revived in order to conserve textiles from old clothes (Rolfe 129). Betty Barlow felt that by wearing clothes longer materials were conserved and labor associated with apparel production was also saved. Barlow discussed clothing care with both men and children as active participants in that responsibility and also described cleaning, mending and remodeling techniques (35).

The importance of wise clothing selection, because of the war's inflationary effect, was the primary focus of Ida Van Auken's *Ladies Home Journal* article "How to Spend and Yet Save" (128). Van Auken stated: "A careful expenditure of the income allotted to clothes is one of the most important economic and household problems" because of the "present higher cost of apparel" (128). Van Auken offered wise and reliable information on initial purchases and conservation techniques for adult and children's apparel and accessories that were not only applicable in 1918 but could also be useful now. She suggested 1) choosing loose, straight styles with a limited number of pieces, 2) selecting material that could be used on both sides in colors that would not show soil, and 3) buying the best quality fabric you could afford. Garments with these characteristics could be more easily remodeled or remade into either adult or children's garments (Van Auken 128).

The mending, remodeling and reuse of apparel were not concepts practiced only within the confines of one's own family. "Gift clothes" or clothes handed down from one person to another was a long practiced tradition. New York City's Bayard Street was recognized as "the greatest second-hand-clothing business in the New or Old World" (Stevenson 24). Fifty percent of men's and ten percent of women's ready-made apparel found its way to the stores on Bayard Street. It is interesting to note that the reason given for the percentage difference was that the "gentler sex have a knack of remaking and remodelling their garments so many times that when at last it is considered that their days of usefulness have passed, they are then fit only for the bag of the rag-picker" (Stevenson 24). Every afternoon from two to four p.m. approximately three to four thousand old-clothes men, who had scoured every borough from New York to New Jersey and beyond, would come to deal with the second-hand-clothing shops. No matter how old, garments were purchased, repaired and offered for sale again.

There was some social sympathy offered toward those individuals whose apparel situation necessitated the use of second-hand clothing. An unsigned article in *The Atlantic Monthly* suggested that gift-clothes required heart-searching by both the recipient and the giver. The recipient should consider him/herself strong if he/she retained his/her own identity in another person's garment because "Clothes acquire so much personality from their first wearer" ("Old Clothes" 139-140). The person who could give someone his/her old clothes without wounding that person's self-respect was "fit to be the king of all philanthropists" ("Old Clothes" 141). A suggestion was offered that protected the feelings of both the recipient and the giver: "The best way to restore a pauper's self-respect is to present him with some old clothes to give to someone still poorer" ("Old Clothes" 141).

1 9 58

Apparel Design and Manufacturing

Educating the Industry

World War I also brought about great changes in the design and manufacture of apparel and textiles. Elizabeth King noted that, prior to the war, America was the greatest rival of France, and New York the rival of Paris, when it came to both prestige and accomplishment in the apparel industry (592). Importation of wearing apparel from Paris came only with great difficulty and personal danger after France fell under siege in World War I. The few Paris gowns that made the trip were treasured by manufacturing houses for copy purposes (King 592-593). Paris, as an apparel design center suffered greatly during the war. Milliners and dressmakers came to New York. In April 1918, a former dressmaker to several monarchs, Baroness Franciska Von Heddeman, lamented:

> Paris has grown old, indifferent to her former standards of fashion, a victim to the economic plague that has come upon her. The great French city of world coquetry has transferred the spirit of her gaiety to New York, and it is spreading over the whole of the United States. (404)

World War I provided American clothing manufacturers with an opportunity to reevaluate, not only their own potential as a world-wide design force, but also their ability to supply apparel to two sets of distinctly different and needy consumers~ the civilian and military populations. The garment industry watched cotton, silk, and wool apparel imports fall from $4,510,948 in 1915 to $2,245,288 in 1916 and to less than one million dollars in 1917 (King 593). Clothes manufacturers calculated the value of their products second to the steel business in the U.S. (King 592). One estimate of New York's cloak and suit trade was $150 million, and on Twenty-third Street alone the estimate was $12 million. The estimate for ready-made women's garments for the whole country was $2.5 billion per year, or an average expenditure of $50 per woman (King 592). The industry had a good chance, with available technology and a willing work force, to develop an international reputation.

The only limitations to the success of the industry were the need to change both the unsuccessful apparel design habits and the treadmill attitudes toward design to those of enlightenment and inspiration. American "designers" had previously become expert copyists of French dressmaking ideas, not full-fledged designers in their own right (King 597). European designers had known and handed down design development fundamentals for generations. Designers were protected by both national patronage and legislation. King described the situation as: "Over there [France] dressmaking is considered an art. In America it is regarded as machine-work" (597). King evaluated and compared both the attitudes and the techniques of American designers to their Parisian counterparts:

all the American designer needs is realization and education in the methods of Parisian inspiration. The inclination of the American designer is to be practical rather than artistic. He will not make a costume entirely for its beauty but works in terms of the market.... He eliminates in his working process that intermediate stage of hand-draping which has given the Parisian designer self-confidence and brilliance. (597)

According to Ethylwyn Miller, an energetic, intelligent and farsighted textile assistant in the Anthropology Department of the American Museum of Natural History in New York City, M.D.C. Crawford, became interested in the problems facing both American clothes designers and manufacturers during the war (207). Crawford knew that the fundamental principle behind the success of the Paris couturiers was persistent study and application of fine art and history to dressmaking (King 594). Crawford went about the formidable task of bringing designers and manufacturers together with museum scientists and artifacts for the purpose of raising the quality of American costume design (King 594-95).

Museum scientists joined Crawford in the process of educating apparel designers and industrial experts. They exposed manufacturers and artists to lectures and specimens of American primitive art and design. Examples of South and Central American Indian baskets, pottery and printing motifs were their sources of inspiration. Spinden, a museum scientist, explained that: "The fundamental designs of the American Indian are good today. All they need is expert separation into motifs and arrangements that are adaptable to present clothes" (King 595). Spinden urged the American designer "to think hard on the subject of the relation of design to construction" (King 595). The theme of design relating to function was emphasized through a lecture series given by industrial experts on the practical phases of art work, the influence of materials, and the processes of construction upon design (Miller 209). The Metropolitan Museum of Art also offered textile art lectures and on December 3, 1917 opened a new Textile Gallery to show that textiles were considered a vital part of the national art (Miller 210).

Crawford and his colleagues took an interdisciplinary approach to the problem of improving both the apparel manufacturing and design process Crawford found that young artists, unconditioned by past copying habits, produced the best designs. Young artists sold their textile and apparel designs to manufacturers for good sums. Manufacturers became interested in the new talent and, therefore, found permanent design positions for some of the artists (King 594-95).

A few individuals could not see the value in art and museum study and, for them, the "treadmill" label used to describe manufacturers who viewed designing as a 9-to-5, time controlled job would forever remain. The treadmill manufacturer was not satisfied with a design unless thousands of that one style were produced by their factory (King 597-98). As King observed in 1917:

> If we can only get some of the museum atmosphere, the inspiration of the Louvre, learn to get at the source of art for our color and form, learn to stop sweating and get a little mental ventilation, learn to look a little farther than the basting-thread cost per thousand garments, we shall build, and build well, on the good start already made. (598)

Only a few enlightened companies, however, allowed the designer time flexibility and diversification in their studies.

Educating the Public

The next hurdle to conquer was fear that the American consumer would not stand behind their home industry (King 594). Art and the American spirit became the overall theme in a series of distinctly different design competitions which became yearly events. Crawford and *Woman's Wear* promoted the first design contest for women's apparel held at the Art Alliance of America (Miller 207). A manufacturer sponsored a design contest called the Albert Blum Contest for Hand-Decorated Fabrics. A retailer, Wannamaker's Store, held a contest for school children from 4 to 15 years of age (Miller 208). In addition to the design contests, the Art Alliance held a textile master craftsman's exhibit at Carnegie Galleries in Pittsburgh which exhibited needlework from American homes that connected the owners to their international heritage. They also hosted "Heroland," a winter bazaar, which emphasized international textiles and needlework in their vendor exhibits (Miller 210).

Commercial organizations began emphasizing the spirit of American designs. At the December 1918 meeting of the Fashion Art League, an organization made up of American dressmakers, art topics were discussed, including "How Style Changed in Italian Painting." The Dress and Skirt Designers Association showed 49 model skirts that they advertized as "American designed, American manufactured, American made" (Miller 211). The study of art and the use of American designs and materials built confidence in the artistic and economic value built into American made clothing (Miller 211). Americans found that "Home Stock" was exceptionally well designed and made (King 593). Of all the types of clothing produced, American sports-clothes were considered the world's finest because "We have the sporting inspiration at its best" (King 598).

American retail buyers began to view the few Parisian models on the market as "weak in inspiration and freshness, and at higher prices" (King 596). The touch of French couturiers, under the strain of war, had "sadly dulled" (King 596). Indeed, Von Heddeman lamented "Paris will never reign supreme again, at least, for a long while, as the arbiter of fashion. New York has taken its place" (406). While Paris was losing its importance and status in the fashion world, American women were gaining the nation's recognition and respect regardless of the pervading patriarchal attitudes.

Women's Roles and Apparel

While World War I ushered in new and exciting directions in apparel and textile design, some Americans perceived the war as having negative effects on women's dress and, consequently, on how women would be viewed by society. Indeed, the average person's clothing reflected the limited resources and economic condition of the country (Rolfe 128). In an unsigned *Literary Digest* article, the author warned that if women adopted "sober garb" that it would threaten men's visual sexual stimulation and therefore endanger the proliferation of the race. Indeed, the visual sense was the predominant vehicle for sexual attraction and the visual appeal of women's dress was "falling to disuse" as a result of war requirements being placed on women and their garments ("The Frills" 19-20). The author explained:

The war is calling woman into its service; she has found her place in the munitions-factory, on the farm, in the subway, on street-cars and railways, and all these activities demand a simplification of dress. We see it in the farmerette's costume, in the uniform of the conductor, in the overalls of the woman munitions-worker ("The Frills" 20).

Walter Muirheid also expressed negative perceptions about women, their dress and their reaction to the end of the war. Muirheid believed that women had a history of reacting recklessly and in excess in regard to dress after every big war, for: "As surely as war ends and man-power is depleted, women, impelled by competition to seek mates by any means in their power, cast off reserve in dress at the sacrifice of modesty" (32). Muirheid's obvious low opinion of the moral character and intellectual abilities of women is but a small sample of the attitudes women had to endure.

Women's roles and responsibilities clearly increased during World War I. Gilman observed that women were meeting the challenges of war as well as men when she wrote, "The women of our country are fully as earnest in their war work as the men" (478). Labor statistics indicated that there were eight million women in productive industry, helping to alleviate war labor needs. War needs were estimated at four workers per soldier for ammunition and transportation requirements, and five workers per soldier for food, shelter and massive office work (478). Women were anxious to help the war effort and replaced men in many occupations formerly considered unsuitable or even improper (Greenwood and Murphy 19). "We have women in overalls, doing farmwork and machine work; we have women in uniforms doing all manner of military service, even in direct fighting" (Gilman 483). Women delivered ice and packages, drove trolly cars and taxis, all jobs previously held by men only (Frings 14). Participation in the work force required the design and construction of work clothes and undergarments to be functional, simple and healthy.

Fortunately, fashions as far back as 1914 showed a trend away from the constrained curves of the Victorian hourglass silhouette. Less constricted waists required only lightly boned or boneless corsets (Frings 14; Steele 71,229). When America entered the war, women were only too glad to donate the corset steel bones which had been used to fortify the now out-of-date Victorian curves. No tears of loss were shed by those whose war donations of corset steel totalled 28,000 tons of metal—enough steel to build two battleships. Schnurnberger's reference of "Loose Hips Build Ships" was certainly true (336). World War I afforded women the opportunity to rid themselves of constricting garments which provided both personal and patriotic relief.

The Commercial Economy Board's recommendations and style restrictions, combined with functional requirements for work clothing, initiated a tailored, more somber colored masculine look to women's apparel. Fashions with decorative details removed, shorter and wider skirts allowing easy movement, and simple, uncomplicated designs with a tubular silhouette reflected the new independence women were experiencing. In addition, World War I work experiences built self-confidence in women, allowed them to make more money, and consequently have more control over clothing purchase decisions (Steele 97). Women could be self-supporting and independent. Women in work clothes commanded new respect and social status (Frings 14).

Style restrictions were not limited only to women's clothing. During the war, restrictions pared down the length, flair and detail in men's suits and coats. Their liberty suits were worn with resolve and patriotic pride in support of their family members and friends in the trenches. A small but significant lasting change occurred in men's wear due to World War I. Prior to the war men wore separate, stiff collars which were buttoned to a neck band on their business shirts. Stiff separate collars, however, proved impractical in battle. War tested uniform shirts had soft attached collars that proved to be effective and practical. When young men returned from the war, they continued to wear shirts with attached collars (Martin 9).

World War Won and Inflation

When the supply of goods failed to meet the demand during the war, everyone felt the rise in expenditures and the frustrations of inflation. Pierre Mille reflecting on the war, inflation, and his own clothing problem noted: "At the beginning of the war...prices were still within the range of reason...the war continued. I went to my tailor—a minor tailor—who used to make me a suit for 140 francs. He asked 200" (279). While waiting for the war to end and for prices to fall, Mille explored his clothes closet and discovered forgotten treasures: clothes that could be made over and made wearable. After the war, with his last pair of trousers unrepairable, the tailor wanted 450 francs for an unlined suit! Similarly, the uppers on his last pair of shoes, after being resoled four times, were gone and new shoes would cost 80 francs. His solution for the clothing problem was to go to a theatre costumer who provided him with the perfect after work attire—a Persian robe and Hindu sandals—for a sidewalk job of selling shoe strings for 6 francs a pair (Mille 279-280).

The frustrations experienced by a creative and resourceful Frenchman over the cost and availability of clothing were not unique. In Great Britain, pre-to-post war prices increased 160% for boots, 170% for men's suits and overcoats, 220% for cotton underclothing material and hosiery, 240% for woolen underclothing and hosiery, 250% for woolen material for women's outer garments, and 290% for cotton material for women's outer garments ("Retail Prices" 554). The end of the war did not bring about a reversal in the inflationary cost of clothing.

Americans, full of spunk and spirit, did not accept the high cost of clothing as a fact of life. Clothing manufacturers and retailers were viewed as profiteers. By mid-April 1920, a nation-wide protest over inflated clothing costs caused the formation of denim "overalls clubs" (Fig. 1). The Literary Digest called America "A Nation in Overalls":

> Overalls are now correct for all occasions; ministers drest [sic] in them perform the marriage ceremony and deliver their sermons on Sunday; mayors parade in them; judges preside in them; Senators save the country in blue denims instead of the traditional frock-coat and gray trousers ("A Nation" 24).

Blue denim overalls were seen in New York on elephants in parades, on waiters and head-waiters in one of New York's best-known restaurants, and in state capitals. At Yale it was considered a "serious breach of social etiquette to wear a new suit" ("A Nation" 24-25). Dallas women asked their district attorney for permission to wear overalls along with men, while other women supported the cause by wearing gingham dresses ("A Nation" 24).

The National League of Overalls Clubs formed with individual clubs having distinct sets of rules. In Hartford, Connecticut, members agreed not to buy any unnecessary clothing during 1920. Birmingham, Alabama members only did business with other men in overalls. Sharon, Pennsylvania's members were dunked in the canal if they did not wear overalls at all times ("A Nation" 24). Numerous newspaper articles promoted the use and concept behind wearing "the blue badge of honor" or "Teddy-bear" overalls ("A Nation" 25). The Richmond, Virginia *News Dispatch* stated:

> They are of all clothes the most comforting and comfortable. They breed democracy. They encourage ease. Wearing coveralls, you have handy pockets for whatever you may wish to carry and you never have to worry about creases in your trousers. ("A Nation" 25)

The Newark, New Jersey *Evening News* concluded that overalls were:

> the symbol of honest work, service, and sacrific...Putting on overalls is putting on democracy. Every one who has ever worn them knows something of this. The man who wears them for the first time feels at once a new sense of freedom and of fellowship... He breathes deeper and his pride quickens. And he is proud of the discovery that, afterall, all men are much alike. ("A Nation" 26)

THE STANDARD OF REVOLT.
—Harding in the Brooklyn *Eagle*.
("A Nation," 1920, p. 24)

Fig. 1. A cartoon titled "The Standard of Revolt" from the *Brooklyn Eagle*.

Before long, New York City's *World* pointed out that leading department stores in Brooklyn and other cities had lowered their clothing prices since the overall movement. The overall movement proved to be more than just the whim of a few irrational reactionaries. Wide use of overalls sent a message from the people about clothing price fairness.

A sharper awareness in the American consumer began to bud. The war made it evident that consumers needed to select textiles and clothing with discrimination. The scarcity of textiles and the rising cost of living made the need for knowledge imperative for economy in both the home and industry (Norton 325). Clothing facts, that were provided during the war by Boston's Women's City Club, were provided in order to become a permanent part of the general flow of information.

Textile specialists needed to investigate more fully the price and value of textiles. In August 1920, Hickmans cited the need for manufacturers to correctly label textile goods as to their composition and value (359). Hickmans, who tested textile fabric content, pointed out that the public was paying prices for material far beyond their real value. Poor labeling disadvantaged the consumer who then paid a soaring price for goods that wore unsatisfactorily. Hickmans called for standardization and honesty in textile labeling

Summary

World War I was a catalyst that hastened change in fashion, the clothing industry, and the roles of women in America. War needs brought about shortages in three of four normally available textile materials used in everyday clothing, needs the industry had not dealt with in the past. A new era of frugality necessitated new methods of clothing construction, new combinations of textile fibers, remodeling and reworking of older clothes, and a greater tolerance for everyday fashion. The world conflict also prompted a shift in the center for fashion design and production from the European continent to the United States. Yet another major influence on fashion was the movement of women out of stereotypical roles into responsible workforce positions. Artists and industrial experts realized together that, indeed, form follows function and for women to function efficiently in the labor force necessitated changes in the form and expectations of female attire. Tightly corsetted women's apparel was replaced by less restrictive clothing which allowed comfort, safety and ease of movement in the workplace. As independent consumers, women and their "voting rights" at the cash register and elsewhere were gaining attention. The end of the war did not portend a reversal to the new position of power and confidence surging forth in the clothing and textile marketplace. Rather, the inflationary times following the war guaranteed that the improvements and changes started during the war in American fashions would continue to flourish for many years to come.

World War I challenged the resourcefulness of the nation's people and called for sacrifices which were met willingly and with understanding. Certainly, victory was also earned by farmers, who added sheep raising to their responsibilities; by scientists and museum personnel, who added Saturday lectures and demonstrations to their schedules; by manufacturers, who reexamined their production and design priorities; and by women, who kept the war machine supplied, manufacturers' quotas filled and the nation's transportation and delivery systems moving. Women from the era, like Marion Weller, Amy Rolfe, Charlotte Perkins Gilman, Elizabeth King, Betty Barlow, Ethel Ronzone, Ethelwyn Miller and Ida Van Auken rose to the challenge and willingly offered their knowledge, time, and energies to the nation and it's peoples war needs. Regardless of the well ensconced patriarchal attitudes of family, friends, business, industry and government, energetic and responsible women, using both brawn and brain, proved themselves a vital partner in the nation's affairs. When men donned overalls, women sought the same right, and why not? Blue denim symbolized honest work, democracy and sacrifice~ all characteristics women had shown the nation they earned during World War I.

Works Cited

"A Nation in Overalls." *The Literary Digest* 59 (1920): 24-26.

"A Protest." *Journal of Home Economics* X (1918): 524-525.

Barlow, Betty. "Making Clothes Wear Twice as Long." *Ladies Home Journal* 35 (1918): 140.

"Clothing and Shoes to be Restricted in Order to Effect Savings." *The Literary Digest* 57 (1918): 62-64.

Ferguson, R. Brian. "Introduction: Studying War." *Warfare, Culture and Environment.* Ed. R. Brian Ferguson. Orlando: Academic Press.

Frings, Gini S. *Fashion: From Concept to Consumer.* Englewood Cliffs, NJ: Prentice-Hall, 1991.

Gilman, Charlotte Perkins. "Concerning Clothes." *Independent* 94 (1918): 478,483.

Greenwood, Kathryn Moore and Mary Fox Murphy. *Fashion Innovation and Marketing.* New York: Macmillan, 1978.

Hickmans, Evelyn M. "The Price and Value of Textiles." *Journal of Home Economics* *XII* (1920): 359-366.

King, Elizabeth Miner. "War, Women and American Clothes: Dress, The Money-Maker." *Scribners' Magazine* 62 (1917): 592-598.

Landau, Simha F. "The Effect of Objective Social Stress Factors on Subjective

Perceptions of Well-Being and Social Solidarity: The Isreali Case." *Human Relations* 42 (1989): 487-508.

Martin, Richard. "Swords into Ploughshares, Bivouac to Mall: The Pacification of Military Clothing." *Textile and Text* 13 (1991): 8-14.

Mille, Pierre. "Outwitting the Tailor: A Leaf from the Diary of a Needy Parisian." *The Living Age* 302 (1919): 278-280.

Miller, Ethylwyn. "Americanism: The Spirit of Costume Design." *Journal of Home Economics* X (1918): 207-211.

Muirheid, Walter G. "Fashion Follies Follow War." *The Mentor* 9 (1921): 32-33.

Norton, Alice P. "A Clothing Information Bureau." *Journal of Home Economics* XII (1920): 325-326.

"Old Clothes Sensations." *The Atlantic Monthly* 66 (1915): 139-41.

"Retail Prices of Clothing in Great Britain, 1914 to 1921." *Monthly Labor Review* 13 (1921): 554-555.

Rolfe, Amy L. "For the Homemaker: What We Shall Wear This Year and Next." *Journal of Home Economics* X (1918): 125-129.

Ronzone, Ethel. "Standardized Dress." *Journal of Home Economics* X (1918): 426-428.

Schnurnberger, Lynn. *Let There Be Clothes*. New York: Workman Publishing, 1991.

Sherry, Michael S. "War and Weapons: The New Cultural History." *Diplomatic History* 14 (1990): 433-446.

Steele, Valerie. *Fashion and Eroticism*. New York: Oxford UP, 1985.

Stevenson, Frederick Boyd. "At the Second-hand-clothes Mart: In Bayard Streed, New York, One Buys and Sells Without Fear and Without Reproach." *Harper's Weekly* 55 (1911): 24.

"The Frill's Farewell." *The Literary Digest* 58 (1918): 19-20.

Van Auken, Ida Cleve. "How to Spend and Yet Save." *The Ladies Home Journal* Nov. (1918): 128.

Von Heddeman, Baroness Franciska. "The Extravagance of Women's War-Clothes." *Forum* 59 (1918):403-410.

Weller, Marion. "The Clothing Situation." *Journal of Home Economics* X (1918): 401-408.

Ziegert, Beate. "American Clothing: Identity in Mass Culture, 1840-1990." *Human Ecology Forum* 19 (1991): 2-34.

Contributors

Patricia Cunningham is a Professor in the Department of Applied Human Ecology at Bowling Green State University where she teaches such courses as Dress in American Culture, American Material Culture, Twentieth-Century Fashion and Introduction to Women's Studies. She has been a frequent contributor to *Dress, The Journal of the Costume Society of America* and serves on the National Board of that Society. Her current research focuses on women's clothing reform.

Beverly Gordon is Associate Professor in the Department of Environment, Textiles & Design and Women's Studies at the University of Wisconsin-Madison. She also serves as Research Director of the Helen Allen Textile Collection at that University.

Susan Voso Lab is an Associate Professor in the Department of Applied Human Ecology at Bowling Green State University. She teaches Historic Costume, Collections Management, and Advance Design courses and works with the collections at the University and Wood County Historical Society.

Carolyn R. Shine is a graduate of Bryn Mawr College, was Curator of Costume and Textiles at the Cincinnati Art Museum until 1985. Since she retired she has been engaged in research into American vernacular clothing of the eighteenth century.

Barbara M. Starke is Associate Professor in the Art Department of the College of Fine Arts, has been a member of the faculty at Howard University since 1973. Her research interests include African Textiles and Designs in Contemporary American Dress, African-American 19th Century Slave Clothing, Guatemalan textiles, Mexican Otomi Indian Apparel and Molas of the Cuna Indians of the San Blas Islands of Panama.

Patricia Campbell Warner is an Associate Professor, teaches Costume

220

History and related women's issues courses at the University of Massachusetts-Amherst. Her interest in gym suits, ongoing and purely historic, stems from work on sports clothing for women.

Linda Welters is Associate Professor and Chairperson of the Textiles, Fashion Merchandising and Design Department at the University of Rhode Island. She is active in the Costume Society of America, serving as national board member since 1985, regional board member from 1985-90, and Region I President from 1988-90. Her research interests are varied, including folk costume, archaeological textiles, quilts, and material culture of New England.

Patricia Williams is Assistant Professor of Fashion/Interior Design and curator of the Historic Costume Collection at the University of Wisconsin-Stevens Point. Her work in European folk costume has been furthered by faculty development grants in 1991 and 1992 and has led to her current research on Slavic ceremonial and ritual cloths.

Laurel Wilson is Associate Professor in the Department of Textile and Apparel Management at the University of Missouri at Columbia. She has published in *Dress* and *Clothing and Textile Research Journal.* Her interest in cowboys can be attributed to her Montana ranch background.